The Orthodox Church
A to Z

A Practical Handbook
of
Beliefs, Liturgy, Sacraments, Customs,
Theology, History and Prayers
for
Orthodox Christians

by
Fr. George W. Grube

2nd Printing, 2012

*"Every good gift and every perfect gift is from above
and comes down from the Father of Lights,
with Whom there is no variation or shadow of turning."*
– Epistle of St. James 1:17

Light & Life Publishing Company
Minneapolis, Minnesota

Light & Life Publishing Company
P.O. Box 26421
Minneapolis, MN 55426-0421

ISBN No. 978-1-880971-74-1

DEDICATION

TO MY PARENTS - GEORGE and ELLEN

and to the victims of hate (9-11-01)

May they rest in the Peace of the Lord.

O Lord, grant me to greet the coming day in peace. Help me in all things to rely upon Thy Holy Will. In every hour of the day, reveal Thy Will to me. Bless my dealings with all who surround me. Teach me to treat all that comes to me throughout the day with peace of soul and with firm conviction that Thy Will governs all. In all my deeds and words, guide my thoughts and feelings. In unforeseen events, let me not forget that all are sent by Thee. Teach me to act firmly and wisely, without embittering and embarrassing others. Give me the strength to bear the fatigue of the coming day with all that it shall bring. Direct my will. Teach me to pray. Pray Thou Thyself in me. Amen.

– As used by Metr. Philaret of
Moscow

* * * * * * * * * * * * * * *

Stand at the crossroads, and look, and ask for the ancient paths, where the good way lies; and walk in it, and find rest for your souls (Jer. 6:16).

ACKNOWLEDGEMENTS

Principles For a Pious Life by Bishop Averky, published by St. Tikhon of Zadonsk Society.

Holy Scripture taken from the King James version of the Bible, Thomas Nelson, Inc. Used by permission. All rights reserved.

Meditation of St. John Chrysostom used with the kind permission of the V. Rev. Basil Stroyen, "Orthodox Herald."

Lay Ministry in the Church from a publication of the "Ukrainian Orthodox League" UOC of the USA.

On the Duty of the Flock Towards the Pastor taken from Journey to Heaven published by Holy Trinity Monastery. Originally written by St. Tikhon of Zadonsk.

Great Miracles Given by God–Miracle of the Tomb from *Differences Between Orthodoxy and Roman Catholicism* by Irene Economides.

To the Orthodox bishops, priests, and laypeople who helped with the review and correction of the original manuscript, and for their valuable contributions to this final version, I am deeply indebted.

INTRODUCTION

This handbook, **"The Orthodox Church A to Z"** contains prayers and pertinent facts about the theology, history, practice and beliefs of the Orthodox Catholic Church.

It is not an exhaustive presentation of the Tradition of the Church, nor does it pretend to be. It is a summary of some of the most important **teachings** of Orthodoxy, along with the Church's **structure, history** and various **customs** which true believers hold dear, making them love her and cherish her as a true "gift from above" (James 1:17).

I have tried to give a balanced presentation of general information about the Church. While the basic teachings of the Faith remain unaltered for Orthodox Christians, there is some difference in local usage, i.e., the listing of saints, customs as regards festive celebrations, and language. I have tried to be as accurate as possible in this regard. A number of clergy of the Church have reviewed the text to maintain its integrity. However, there may be slight variations when it comes to local practice which in no way detracts from the essence of the Faith, or its genuine importance to believers.

I present this handbook to you as a legitimate offering of the marvelous Gift of the Church, which Almighty God, in His goodness has given us for our salvation.

The Author

TABLE OF CONTENTS

1. WHAT WE BELIEVE

2. LIVING AS ORTHODOX CHRISTIANS

3. PRAYER TRANSFORMS OUR LIVES

Prayer - A Spiritual Bond

4. GIFTS OF THE HOLY SPIRIT

The Practice of Virtues as Duties of Orthodox Christians

5. FASTING: A Noble Discipline

6. WORSHIP: Returning the Gift

7. THE HOLY MYSTERIES: Gifts of Salvation

8. THE BIBLE AND ORTHODOXY: The Gift of His Word

9. THE CHURCH TEACHES MORALITY: Teaching the Gift

10. THE SETTING FOR WORSHIP: Returning the Gift

11. GOD'S KINGDOM ON EARTH: The Church

12. SAINTS: Special Friends of God

13. TIME IN THE KINGDOM: The Calendar of the Church

APPENDICES

1. WHAT WE BELIEVE

"You are a chosen generation, a royal priesthood, a holy nation, His own special people, that you may proclaim the praises of Him Who called you out of darkness into His marvelous light."

1 Peter 2:9

SOURCES OF ORTHODOX DOCTRINE

THE ORTHODOX SYMBOL OF BELIEF: THE CREED

The Orthodox Christian's statement of belief, which was composed at the Councils of Nicaea in 325 A. D. and Constantinople 1 in 381 A.D. is called the Nicene – Constantinopolitan Creed. It places the very essence of what we profess as Orthodox Christians into our hands so that we may not stray from the Truth of the Faith.

OUR SYMBOL OF FAITH: THE NICENE CREED

I believe in One God the Father Almighty, Maker of heaven and earth, and of all things visible and invisible. And in One Lord Jesus Christ, the Only-begotten Son of God, begotten of the Father before all ages; Light of Light, true God of true God, begotten not made, of one essence with the Father; by Whom all things were made.

Who for us men, and for our salvation, came down from heaven and was incarnate of the Holy Spirit and the Virgin Mary, and became man.

He was crucified for us under Pontius Pilate, and suffered and was buried. He arose again on the third day according to the Scriptures; and ascended into heaven, and sits at the right hand of the Father; and He shall come again with glory to judge the living and the dead, Whose Kingdom shall have no end.

And in the Holy Spirit, the Lord, the Giver of Life, Who proceeds from the Father, Who with the Father and the Son together is worshipped and glorified; Who spoke by the prophets.

I believe in One, Holy, Catholic and Apostolic Church, I confess one baptism for the remission of sins.

I look for the resurrection of the dead and the life of the world to come. Amen.

WHY THE CREED IS IMPORTANT TO ORTHODOX CHRISTIANS

If someone were to ask you what you believe, could you answer intelligently and with God's own proof? Of course. The Nicene Creed of the Church concisely expresses our beliefs with the authority of God's word – Holy Scripture.

The Nicene Creed was composed by the Fathers of the Church in the fourth century. The purpose was to establish for all time a complete, yet readily understandable statement of what the Orthodox Christian Faith is all about. By having such a statement of belief we are also able to recognize false teaching and protect ourselves from pursuing error.

We recite the Nicene Creed at every Divine Liturgy. Each statement, based on Holy Scripture, is a brief, yet by no means exhaustive, compilation of what the Church teaches, and what we must believe as Orthodox Christians.

> *"I do not cease to give thanks for you, making mention of you in my prayers: that the God of Our Lord, Jesus Christ, the Father of Glory, may give to you the spirit of wisdom and revelation in the knowledge of Him, the eyes of your understanding being enlightened that you may know what is the hope of His calling, what are the riches of the glory of His inheritance in the saints."*
>
> *Ephesians 1:16-18*

WHAT DO WE LEARN IN THE CREED?

We learn that there are twelve major articles or statements of belief and that they can be further divided into three major areas:

1. We learn about the Holy Trinity, God as Father, as Son, and as Holy Spirit.

2. We learn of the life to come for all faithful Orthodox Christians.

3. We learn about the Church and its earthly mission.

"God is nearer to us than any man at any time. He is nearer to me than my raiment, nearer than the air or light, nearer than my wife, father, mother, daughter, son or friend. I live in Him, soul and body, I breathe in Him, think in Him, feel, consider, intend, speak in Him, or undertake work in Him. For in Him we live, move and have our being."

St. John of Kronstadt

WHAT DOES THE CREED TELL US ABOUT GOD?

We learn that **God is One**, not many gods but One God, the Father Almighty.

We learn that **God is Spirit.** He has no body and He is immaterial. Human eyes can never see God but the heart and mind can discern His works in the world.

We learn that **God is eternal.** He is without beginning or end. All creation started with God and will end in Him. God is not limited by space, time, or human language.

We learn that **God is unchanging,** that He is Immutable in deed and judgment. God can never change or be held hostage by human whim or design.

We learn that **God is Omnipresent**, that He is in all places at all times and is not confined by earthly things. He sees and knows our every thought and deed. Wherever we are – there too, is God.

We learn that **God is All-knowing**. He is Omniscient. God knows the past, the present and future, and He is incapable of being deceived by anyone, at any time.

We learn that **God is Almighty,** and that He is the **Master of the Universe.** God cannot be held captive by any person, place, or thing. Nothing can ever stand in His way.

We learn that **God is All-perfect and good.** He has no defects, lacks nothing and all that He does comes from perfect love and goodness. God is love itself, and can have no partnership with the evil that man commits, human evil that mocks His Divine perfection.

We learn that God's love and goodness give rise to His **mercy and infinite patience** with all mankind. God is just and good in every way, which is His Divine perfection.

WHAT IS THE PURPOSE OF THE CHRISTIAN LIFE?

> *"Christ loved the Church and gave His life for her, that He might sanctify and cleanse her with the washing of water by the word."*
> *Ephesians 5:25-26*

The true purpose of life may be found in the **quality of our relationships.**

Our relationship with God –

We are called to live as Christians, ever-conscious that we are loved by God. We live in His presence at all times, and He listens to our prayers.

Our relationships with people –

We must remember that each of us is a Child of God and therefore we should treat each other with this thought in mind. Christ calls us to love one another as He loves us.

We are further called to become "gods by grace" (Deification) and to work together with Almighty God to bring forth His Kingdom on earth.

Our relationship with God's creation –

We are expected to approach all of God's creation with respect and dignity.

Our relationship with God's earth –

It is our responsibility to care for God's gifts of the earth and environment, protecting them for present and future use.

Scriptural references: St. Matthew 11:4-5, 6:33, St. Mark 8:36, St. Luke 19:10, St. John 8:12.

WHAT ORTHODOX CHRISTIANS BELIEVE ABOUT ALMIGHTY GOD

Orthodox Christianity is grounded in the belief that God is the Eternal Being who exists beyond our space and time. God is the Lord of All and He has revealed Himself to us through Jesus Christ's birth, life, death and resurrection. Even though we can understand God's energies (or how He acts in the world) His essence, or inner nature, is a Divine Mystery, due to our limited intellect and language.

While we know God in His energies, i.e. in what He does for His people, we can never know in this life, His essence or exactly who, or what, He is.

Orthodox Christians believe:

• All that exists depends upon Almighty God.

• We, as mortal human beings, rely on Him for every good thing which comes our way.

• Through His sustaining energy God makes Himself known throughout creation and therefore is the very source and substance of life itself.

• Our language is not equipped to describe all that God is. He has told us in Holy Scripture, "Neither are your ways my ways" (Isaiah 55: 8), and when we speak of His love we are confined by the limitations of human thought and speech.

TO SUMMARIZE WHAT WE BELIEVE ABOUT GOD:

1. He is the source of all life.

2. He shows His love for us in creation.

3. He wants to offer His life to us and calls us into union with Him by imparting all that He has to share.

4. God is existence itself and each moment of our lives depends on God offering to share Himself with those beings He created.

5. God revealed Himself completely through Jesus Christ, His Only-begotten Son. Jesus Christ imparts to us the fullness, and perfection, of God's own life.

6. Christ, as God, lived in this world and gave us the Commandments of Salvation. Christ brought us the will of the Father and told us what His Father desires each of us to become. God lives with us today in the Holy Spirit.

Jesus Christ is Lord

> *"For by Him all things were created that are in heaven and that are on earth, visible and invisible, whether Thrones or Dominions or Principalities or Powers. All things were created through Him and for Him."*
> *Colossians 1:16*

THE CREED OF THE CHURCH AS SUPPORTED IN HOLY SCRIPTURE:
Our Statement of Belief

The Creed of the Church composed by the Church Councils of Nicaea (A.D. 325) and Constantinople 1 (381 A.D.), is the basic statement of what we believe as Orthodox Catholic Christians. The Fathers of the councils wished to create a precise, complete, and simple statement of the Christian Faith so that believers would recognize any opinions which contradicted the Orthodox teachings of the Church. False teaching was found in many places, even within the clergy and hierarchy of the Faith itself, therefore the formulated Creed protected believers from accepting something which was patently false, or heretical.

To protect the Creed's validity, the early Fathers knew that what was taught must be supported by Holy Scripture. The following Scriptural references show where statements of the Creed may be found in the Holy Bible, as lived in the Tradition of the Church.

I believe in one God, the Father Almighty . . . Gen. 17:1-8; Deut. 6:4; Matthew 6:9

Maker of heaven and earth . . . . Gen. 1:1-31;Job 38:1-30

And of all things visible and invisible . . . . Col.1: 15-16; John 1:3

And in one Lord Jesus Christ . . . . John 20:28; Acts 16:31; John 3:16

The Only-begotten Son of God . . . . Psalm 2:7; Matthew 3:17; John 1:1

Begotten of the Father before all ages . . . . John 1:1-2; 8:58; Col. 1:16; Phil 2:6

Light of Light . . . . John 1:1-9

True God of true God . . . . John 16:27-28; John 1:1-2

Begotten, not made . . . . John 1:1-2; 16:28

Of one Essence with the Father . . . . John 14:10-11; 17:22-23

By Whom all things were made . . . . John 1:3 -10; Col. 1:16

Who for us men and our salvation . . . . Luke 2:30; John 3:16;
1 John 4:14; 1 Tim 2:5-6

Came down from heaven . . . . John 3:13,31; John 6: 12-38

And was incarnate of the Holy Spirit . . . . Luke 1:35

And the Virgin Mary . . . . Isaiah 7:14; Luke 1:35-46

And became man . . . . John 1:14; Phil 2:6-8; Heb. 2:14-17

He was crucified for us under Pontius Pilate . . . . Matthew 27:24-31

And suffered and was buried . . . . Mark 15:16-46

He arose again on the third day according to the Scriptures . . . . . . 1 Cor. 15:3-4;
Luke 24:1-12; Matthew 12:38-40;
Matthew 28:1-8; Mark 16:16-19

And ascended into heaven . . . . Luke 24:50-53; Mark 16:16-19

And sits at the right hand of the Father . . . . Rom. 8:34; Eph. 1:20

And shall come again with glory . . . . Psalm 72:9-19; Isaiah 40:5

To judge the living and the dead . . . . Rev 20:11-15; Acts 10:42

Whose Kingdom shall have no end . . . . . Psalm 145:13; John 3:16; John 6:40-47

And in the Holy Spirit, the Lord . . . . Gen. 1:2; Matthew 3:16; Acts 2:1-4

The Giver of Life . . . . John 15:26; John 14:16-17; Rom. 8:2; Gal 6:8

Who proceeds from the Father . . . . John 15:26

Who with the Father and the Son together is worshipped and glorified . . . .
Luke 10:22; Matthew 3:17; John 4:24

Who spoke by the prophets . . . . Acts 2:17-18; 2 Peter 1:21

I believe in One, Holy, Catholic, and Apostolic Church . . . . 1 Cor. 12:12-13;
Eph. 2:19-22; 4:11-16;
2 Thess. 2:15; 1 Tim 3:1-15

I confess one baptism for the remission of sins . . . . Matt 3:16; John 3:5;
Acts 2:38; 8:36-40; Eph. 4:5

I look for the resurrection of the dead . . . . 1 Cor. 15:12-58

And the life of the world to come . . . . . . Rom. 8:17-25; Phil 3:20-21; 2 Peter 3:13

Amen.

GOD; FATHER, SON AND HOLY SPIRIT IN THE WORLD
Salvation and the Second Coming

THE ATTRIBUTES OF ALMIGHTY GOD
The power and virtues which make God who He truly is:

Almighty – Omnipotent, His power is infinite – Gen. 17:1, Ps. 91:1, Rev. 19:6
"I am the Almighty God, walk before me and be blameless" … *"He who dwells in the shadow of the Most High, shall abide under the shadow of the Almighty"* … *"Alleluia! For the Lord God Omnipotent reigns."*

Eternal – without beginning or end – Deuteronomy 33:27, Titus 1:2
"The eternal God is your refuge..." "In the hope of eternal life, which God, who cannot lie, promised before time began."

Omniscient – All- knowing – 1 Samuel 2:3, Job 21:22
"For the Lord is a God of knowledge; and by Him actions are weighed."

Omnipresent – everywhere present – Psalm 46:1
"God is our refuge and strength, a very present help in trouble."

All – Merciful – Ephesians 2:4, Luke 1:50
"God, who is rich in mercy, because of His great love with which He loved us."
"And His great mercy is on those who fear Him."

All – Just – Isaiah 30:18, Malachi 2:17, Acts 3:14
"For the Lord is a God of justice, blessed are all those who wait for Him."
"Where is the God of justice?"

Immutable – never changing – Malachi 3:6
"For I am the Lord, I do not change."

All-Wise – Job 9:4, 1 Timothy 1:17
"God is wise in heart and mighty in strength."

All-Holy – Revelation 4:8, 1 Peter 1:15, Isaiah 41:14
"He who called you is holy, you also be holy in all your conduct."

All-Good – Exodus 33:19, Psalm 16:2, Psalm 52:1, Romans 2:4
"The goodness of God endures continually."

All-Faithful and True – Psalm 143:1, Psalm 89:1, Psalm 89:9
"O God, in your faithfulness answer me and in your righteousness do not enter into judgment with your servant."

Who Is God?

"There is no God except God the Father, nor was there ever in times past, nor will there ever be in the future. God is the beginning of all things, and has no beginning. God possesses all things, but is possessed by none. God's Son, Jesus Christ has been with the Father before the beginning; through Christ all things were created, both material and spiritual. Christ became human, and conquered death, and was taken back into heaven to the Father. The Father has given the Son power over all things in heaven and on earth and under the earth, that every tongue should confess that Jesus Christ is Lord. God has poured the Spirit upon us so that our spirits are overflowing. Through God's Spirit we receive the promise of eternal life. And in the Spirit we are taught to trust and obey the Father, and with Christ, become God's sons and daughters."

"The Confession of Faith of St. Patrick of Ireland"

WHAT DO WE KNOW ABOUT JESUS CHRIST?

"Jesus is the power of God and the wisdom of God."
1 Corinthians 1:24

The Creed tells us the following about Jesus Christ, Our Lord and Savior.

1. He is the Son of God, Only-begotten, of the same essence, co-eternal with the Father, begotten, not made.

2. He came to us for our salvation.

3. Christ was born of the Holy Spirit and the Virgin Mary and became man.

4. Christ was crucified for the forgiveness of our sins.

5. Christ arose from the dead on the third day according to the Holy Scriptures.

6. He ascended into heaven and sits at the right hand of the Father.

7. He shall come again to judge the living and the dead.

> *"Therefore you are no longer strangers and foreigners, but fellow citizens with the saints and members of the household of God, having been built on the foundation of the apostles and prophets, Jesus Christ Himself being the chief cornerstone, in whom the whole building, being fitted together, grows into a holy temple in the Lord, in whom you are also being built together for a dwelling place of God in the Spirit."*
> *Ephesians 2:19-22*

HOW DOES CHRIST SAVE US? (*Atonement*)

We can find the answer to this question in the fourth article of the Creed. "He was crucified for us under Pontius Pilate, suffered and was buried, He arose on the third day."

Christ's whole life was a redemption especially when He voluntarily accepted suffering and death for us so that we might be saved. When we should have been on the Cross, Christ took our place. The Savior atoned for all humans and made us one again with Almighty God. Thus, we were made whole through Christ's suffering, death, and resurrection. He gave us full-life once more, a privilege that was lost because the sin of the Adam and Eve carried the stings of death throughout all creation.

This "Ancestral Curse," imparted to the human family by disobedience to Almighty God, is called by some "Original Sin," and is passed on to succeeding generations of mankind. Thus, atonement was necessary because man's communion with Almighty God had been fractured by the transgressions of our first parents.

We were separated from God through sin. Yet, in His infinite goodness and love, God opened a pathway whereby we might once more gain our salvation. Christ paid the price for us, as a brother would lay down his life for his friend, and we were united again with the Father.

Christ, however, did not save us from an angry or vengeful God, or to satisfy His Father's sense of justice. From the Orthodox viewpoint, salvation is more than Christ simply having paid some penalty to satisfy the Father's wounded "honor." Salvation is the will of the Father, that we return to Him so He can love us with an everlasting love.

Regardless, this idea of a hateful, spiteful God is just what contemporary Evangelical and Pentecostal Christians are teaching today, deluding thousands of good people into believing salvation is a payback to a petty, spiteful God and His imagined "hurts."

Orthodox Christians believe that we are **redeemed to a loving, compassionate God by Christ, rather than being released from an angry, vengeful God.** Redemption, to an Orthodox Christian means that Christ restored the fallen human nature of mankind, making right, once again, our debilitating bondage to sin. To introduce a wounded, or hateful God into the picture is to demean His great and lasting love for us.

The Church, therefore, continues the work of Christ's loving redemption and we are transformed into "fellow-citizens with the saints" by our membership in the Orthodox Church.

Scriptural references: St. John 12-47, St. Luke 19-10

> "If Christ has not been raised, our preaching is empty and your faith is also empty." (1 Cor. 15:14)

AN ORTHODOX VIEW OF SALVATION

> "Christ is the head of the body, the Church." Col. 1:18

SALVATION to Orthodox Christians involves the following:

1. **Accept** the redeeming work that Christ accomplished on our behalf. Christ died for our sins so we must respond to this greatest of gifts whole heartedly and with the utmost gratitude.

2. **Show** our gratitude, accept this gift, and retain it, by living a life of devotion in faith to our Savior, Jesus Christ.

3. **Receive** this gift of redemption, which made Christ mount the Cross for our sake, to give His life for us. This gift of life should excite and move us to live in total devotion to the Savior, keeping us from moral degradation and iniquity.

4. **Understand** that Christ paid the price for our sins. We should remind ourselves that we were sentenced to alienation from Almighty God, yet Christ took our place upon the Cross to regain the gift of eternal life for us.

5. **Know** that Christ gave everything for us, His spotless life, His blood. As stated in 2 Peter 1:3-4, "All that pertain to life and godliness has been given to us."

6. **Believe** that God offers this redemption to all men and women. However, we must understand that it is impossible to appropriate the work of Christ's redemption unless we respond in faith to God's reaching – out and offer ing salvation to us! "Without me you can do nothing," says the Lord in St. John 15: 5.

7. **Realize** that everyone is offered the gift of redemption. Yet, we are not forced or coerced by Almighty God to accept it. We are free to refuse the gift. That is why some are saved with ardent faith, while others reject the gift and condemn themselves to eternal separation from a loving Father.

8. **Understand** that sinful mankind needs Divine enlightenment, and help, to accept the redemption offered us. This is what is meant by Divine grace, which rests within Christ's Church and is transmitted through the Holy Mysteries or Sacraments.

9. **Believe** that Christ is in the Church and His grace abides in her. That is why the Church became necessary for salvation and outside the Church there is no remission of sins, no redemption, no justification (being made right with God), and no hope for eternal life.

10. **Live** in faith that we are called to Divine enlightenment which, as St. Nicodemos the Hagiorite, tells us is the equivalent of "Theosis," or union with God. Since Christ became man so that man might become God-like by grace, the Mysteries of the Church serve to deify us and to unite us with Christ Himself.

Scriptural references: St. John 3, Rom. 5:1-5, 2 Corinthians 3:18, 4:16, 5:17, 1 Peter 2:4-10, Ephesians 2:8-9, Philippians 2:12-13, James 2:14-26.

"Christ loved the Church and gave Himself up for her...that He might present the Church to Himself in splendor, without spot or wrinkle or any such thing, that she might be holy and without blemish."

Ephesians 5:25-27

"(At the Second Coming the good and the evil will be raised from the dead and judged by Christ)...those who have done good to a resurrection of life, and those who have done evil, to a resurrection of judgment."

John 5:29

THE SECOND COMING OF OUR LORD

When we recite the Creed of the Church we proclaim that Jesus Christ, "will come again in glory to judge the living and the dead." At the Second Coming, Our Lord will fulfill the Scriptures and will raise the dead to be judged according to their deeds. The righteous will be with God forever, since they loved Him while in their earthly bodies, and those who rejected Him will proceed to an existence without His loving presence.

We will all be judged by our capacity to love, since we are commanded in this life to accept and spread God's infinite mercy and compassion to others. God is love itself. It is His very essence. If we want to live in intimate union with God, then we must communicate this Divine life by loving Him above all things and sharing the fruits of this love with all people. We will be judged, therefore, on how faithful we were to this command of Our Lord, "Love one another as I have loved you" (John 13:34). The blessed who lived in God's love will be granted eternal fulfillment and joy, while the wicked will suffer the pain of being in the presence of Divine love which they cannot accept. This is the immense pain of hell as St. Cyprian of Carthage, in his treatise on the Second Coming, describes so well.

"The Second Coming" by St. Cyprian of Carthage

"Oh what a day that will be when the Lord presents us with the reward of faith and devotion. What will be that glory, and how great will be the joy of being admitted to the sight of God! To be so honored as to receive the joy of eternal life and salvation in the presence of Christ the Lord, your God. To greet Abraham, Isaac, and Jacob, and all the patriarchs, apostles, prophets and martyrs...in the delight of the immortality that will be given! To receive there what eye has not seen nor ear heard, what has not entered into the heart of man."

Scriptural references: Titus 2:12-14, St. Matthew 24: 3-8, 36-50, St. Luke 21:7-36, 2 Peter 3:8-10.

"Believe me that I am in the Father and the Father is in me, or else believe me for the sake of the works themselves."

John 14:11-12

THE TRINITY

Orthodox Christians believe that there are three "persons" (i.e. hypostases) – Father, Son and Holy Spirit – in ONE GOD. They are separate and distinct persons yet:

1. Each is God

2. Each is equally perfect, knowing all things, having all power and existing eternally. The three persons of the Trinity are fully united, existing in All-perfect love. Think of love encompassing everything, and you describe the life of the Trinity. The Father is the source of all things, who, because of perfect love, sent us His Son Jesus Christ to live and die for us. Christ became man while remaining God and through His life, death and resurrection, an act of perfect love, He offers us the possibility of eternal salvation.

God, as Holy Spirit, keeps us in His love. The Holy Spirit is the Sanctifier and Comforter who inspires us to remain in God's All-embracing, eternal care. We know this because the Church has always taught that each of us is infinitely precious in the sight of Almighty God , and the Spirit leads us to this infinite, intimate and eternal love.

Scriptural references: Ephesians 2:18-22, and 2 Corinthians 13:14

HOW DOES THE HOLY SPIRIT WORK AMONG US TODAY?

The Holy Spirit brings to perfect completion the work of salvation through Jesus Christ. The Spirit, according to the Creed, proceeds from the Father, was promised by the Son, and comes to us to open our eyes and minds, in order to receive salvation. It has been said that Christ is the door to the Father and the Holy Spirit is the key which opens this door.

> *"There is one Spirit, who is God and who is revealed to man through the Son. He is the image of the Son, the 'Perfect of the Perfect'; He is Life – the cause of the living, the 'Holy Fountain'; He is sanctity; the dispenser of sanctification in whom is revealed God the Father, who is above all and in all; and God the Son who is through all."*
>
> St. Gregory Thaumaturge

THOSE WHO HAVE BEEN DEIFIED BELONG TO THE LORD

> *"You are like stones for a temple of the Father, prepared for the edifice of God, hoisted to the heights by the crane of Jesus Christ, which is the Cross, using for a rope the Holy Spirit. Your faith is what pulls you up, and love is the road which leads you to God."*
>
> St. Ignatius of Antioch

"But you are not in the flesh but in the Spirit, if indeed this Spirit of God dwells in you. Now if anyone does not have the Spirit of Christ, he is not His."

Romans 8:9

THE LAST THINGS – ORTHODOX CHRISTIANS AND DEATH

WHAT HAPPENS WHEN WE DIE?

Our bodies must die and at death the soul is separated from the body. Immediately after death the soul is subjected to a particular judgment. Those who lived a righteous life will be rewarded and those who have practiced evil will be separated from the righteous. At the Second Coming of Christ, those who died will be reunited with their bodies so together they may share either eternal happiness, or unending alienation from God's All-embracing love.

"For God so loved the world that He gave His only-begotten Son, that whoever believes in Him should not perish but have everlasting life."

John 3:16

CAN ANYONE ESCAPE ETERNAL PUNISHMENT?

After death each soul pays for its evil deeds and those who are not condemned to alienation from God's care await the General Resurrection in the Intermediate State. This state is not Purgatory, (additional suffering) a false teaching found only in the Roman Church. Authentic Orthodox teaching says souls awaiting the General Resurrection can be helped by the prayers of the Church on earth. Therefore the Orthodox Church sets aside various days and occasions when the living may offer devout prayers for the comfort and repose of the souls of those who have gone on before us, to be with the Lord. However, we must remember that the official teaching of the Church is that there is no salvation beyond the grave.

The Intermediate State is a place where we experience a foretaste of heaven, the fullness of which will be known to us at the Second Coming of Christ.

"The souls of Christians go to an invisible place designated by God for them, and remain there until the Final Resurrection. Afterwards, receiving bodies and rising perfectly again (with their perfect bodies), just as Our Lord rose, they too will come to the sight of God."

St. Irenaeus

HEAVEN

To the Orthodox Christian, heaven is a real place and the ultimate destination of all the righteous. Heaven is promised by Almighty God to all who love Him. It is not just space or some region "up there," it is the abode of God! Orthodox teaching says that heaven is not reserved to a chosen few. Rather, and this is paramount, heaven awaits all those who devoutly serve the Lord, and that eternal life with God is the chief end of mankind! Christ conquered death by His resurrection. He would not have had to redeem us if heaven did not exist. Surely, it would be a cruel and heartless hoax to promise everlasting life and glory to those who love and serve God, if such an existence were not possible.

Scriptural references: St. Mark 12:25, St. Luke 10:20, St. Luke 15:17-25.

HELL

Holy Scripture mentions hell in several places, St. Matthew 25:30, 41, St. Mark 8:34-38, Rom. 6:20-23:2, Thessalonians 1:9 and Philippians 3:17-21. Hell is the "outer darkness" where those who refuse the Kingdom offered by God proceed by their own choice.

Christ taught that hell was a real place, and that we choose our eternal habitation by choices during our earthly life. But we know that God will not force our free will in accepting His love. Obviously then, there will be some who choose to oppose God out of pride, vanity and unbelief, and who signify by their lives that they are opposed to God's offer of eternal love in His sublime presence.

We must remember that each soul undergoes a particular judgment at the time of death and will experience the General Judgment/Resurrection on the last day, at the end of time.

> *"Those who do not love God will be chastised with the scourge of love. How cruel and bitter this torment will be the sorrow which takes hold of the heart, which has sinned against love, is more piercing than any other pain."*
>
> St. Isaac the Syrian

WHAT HAPPENS TO OUR SOUL WHEN WE DIE?

The teaching of the Orthodox Church about the state of the soul after death is found in the writings of the Fathers.

> *Condemnation of all teachings that the soul can wander after death:*
> *"Nor, indeed, is it possible for a soul, once separated from its body, to*

wander here anymore. For, the souls of the righteous are in the hands of God... and the souls, also of sinners, are straightaway led away hence – and it cannot be that a soul, when it has gone out of the body can wander here."

St. John Chrysostom

"The Holy Apostles have commanded us... to let the third day of the departed be celebrated with psalms and lessons and prayers, on account of Him who arose within the space of three days: and let the ninth day be celebrated in remembrance of the living, and of the departed: and the fortieth day according to the ancient pattern: for so did the people lament Moses and the anniversary day in memory of him. And let alms be given to the poor out of the (reposed one's) goods as a memorial of him."

(The Instructions of the Holy Twelve Apostles)

"The Kolyva (ed. wheat and honey) is offered because man is also a seed and like a fruit from the earth and like seeds sown in the earth he will be raised up again by God's might. The third day service is celebrated for the reason that the reposed received his being from the Trinity, and having passed to a state of goodness and being changed he shall (at the resurrection) appear in his original state, or one superior. The ninth day is celebrated that his spirit, being immaterial and naturally similar to the angels – whose rank is nine in number – will proclaim and praise God in the Trinity. We remember the reposed in memorials so they may be united with the holy spirits of the saints. The Tessaracost (fortieth day) is celebrated because of the Savior's ascension which came to pass so many days after His resurrection."

St. Symeon of Thessaloniki

"He who believes in the Son has everlasting life; and he who does not believe in the Son shall not see life, but the wrath of God abides on him."

St. John 3:36

"Most assuredly, I say to you, he who hears my word and believes in Him who sent me has everlasting life, and shall not come into judgment, but has passed from death into life."

St. John 5:24

Scriptural references: St. John 5:25, 1 Corinthians 15:12-19, Ephesians 2: 1-10, Revelation 20:12-15, 21:1-8.

ON THE SUBJECT OF BODILY DEATH

To a woman whose husband has just died:

> *"If he has only sailed to a tranquil haven and set out to his true King, then one should not grieve but rejoice! For that death is not death, but a voyaging forth, and a translation from the worst to the better, from earth to heaven, from men to angels."*
>
> St. John Chrysostom

HOLY UNCTION FOR THE SICK

There is no service in Orthodoxy, comparable to the Roman Catholic "Last Rites." Holy Unction includes the Mystery (Sacrament) of Confession, anointing with oil, and prayers for healing. It is not strictly for those in danger of repose since the Scriptures mention nothing of impending death. This is a healing service for the health and well-being of the afflicted believer.

Holy Unction is used primarily for those who are ill and who feel the need for the support and prayers of fellow Christians in the Church. It is a call to Almighty God to grant His healing power to those who are afflicted or suffering. It is a Mystery (Sacrament) of the Orthodox Church based on James 5:13-15. (See: Section on the Mysteries (Sacraments) of the Church).

INTERCESSION FOR THE DEAD

We pray for Christians who have passed away because the Church – the Body of Christ – is ONE and we should never deny any member of the Church the help of intercessory prayer. Since those who have died are members of the Church Triumphant we have the obligation to continually remember our reposed brothers and sisters in prayer.

Praying for the reposed and asking the Church on earth, and in heaven, to assist us with our struggles, helps us meet the demands of a Christian life while preserving the unity between the Pilgrim Church on earth and the Church Triumphant in heaven.

THE FUNERAL SERVICE

As faithful of the Orthodox Church we are all members of the Body of Christ. When a member of the Church reposes in the Lord, it is a death which affects us all. The Orthodox funeral service emphasizes the fact of death and the reality of the Lord's Resurrection, namely, that each of us must someday die but that we shall, if faithful, rise again in the glory of our Savior, Jesus Christ.

We mourn for the deceased, yet we comfort one another in the joyful knowledge that only one phase of life has ended, while a new and more glorious one has begun in heaven. The love that God has for each of us is more powerful than the sting of death, and we are reminded of St. Paul's words: "Death has been swallowed up in victory. Where, O grave, is your victory? Where, O death is your sting? The sting of death is sin, and the power of sin is the Law. But thanks be to God, who gives us the victory through Jesus Christ, Our Lord" (1 Corinthians 15:54-57).

The Funeral Service of the Church consists of prayers for the soul of the departed, memorial commemorations, and the continuous reading of psalms. Subsequently, the body is taken to the church for a service on the day of burial, after which a memorial service is offered at the graveside of the deceased.

Christ Conquers Death and Gives Life

"Therefore my Father loves me, because I lay down my life that I may take it again. No one takes it from me, but I lay it down of myself. I have the power to lay it down, and I have the power to take it again. This command I have received from my Father."

St. John 10:17,18

"I am He who lives, and was dead, and behold, I am alive forevermore. Amen. And I have the keys of Hades and of death."

Revelation 1:18

IF GOD IS ALL-GOOD WHY DOESN'T HE END EVIL AND SUFFERING?

Because God is All-Goodness, He offers His gifts of love and creation to all mankind, along with the free will to distinguish right from wrong. Therefore, we are free to resist or give into the temptations of the world. In resisting evil and doing good, mankind shows its faith in God and loyalty to His word. In this way men and women work out their salvation "with fear and trembling" as St. Paul says in Philippians 2:12. Salvation is a gift of God's grace. It can never be earned, yet it involves a daily renunciation of Satan and commitment to Christ and His commandments.

THE ANTICHRIST

The term "Antichrist" means "in the stead of Christ." As His chief adversary, Antichrist will appear as "Christ," claiming to be the returned Messiah. The New Testament mentions "Antichrist" in the First and Second Epistles of St. John. In the Book of Revelation the Antichrist seems to be equated with some form of animal or beast; however, the Fathers of the Church teach very clearly that the Antichrist will someday come as a man of peace and love, acclaimed by all mankind, misleading even the elect and claiming to lead the whole Church. His hidden purpose, however, will be total depravity and corruption, or "evil personified."

The coming of the Antichrist will be a sign of a complete spiritual and moral catastrophe which will only be resolved at the Second Coming of Jesus Christ.

SATAN

"Satan" is a fallen angel, according to the Fathers, and has a personal presence. He is followed by other fallen spirits, or demons, who do his bidding.

Satan, to Orthodox Christians, is the total embodiment of evil and moral degradation. The name itself comes from an ancient Hebrew which denotes "adversary," or one who opposes Almighty God and His goodness. To be in opposition to God, the Supreme Good, should be interpreted to mean someone who is the epitome of evil, and who seeks the ruin of souls, rather than their sanctification and redemption.

From St. Gregory of Rome 7th century:

> *"Perhaps each of you will say to himself: I have believed. I shall be saved. He speaks what is true if to faith he joins good works. That is indeed true faith which does not deny in work what it professes in word. For Paul says of certain false faithful: 'They profess they know God, but in their works they deny Him' (Titus 1:16). St. John also says: 'He who says that he knows God, and does not keep His commandments, is a liar, and the truth is not in him'" (1 John 2:4).*

2. LIVING AS ORTHODOX CHRISTIANS

"PRINCIPLES FOR A PIOUS LIFE" by Bishop Averky

"Always force yourself to get up early and at a fixed time. Without particular reason do not sleep for more than seven hours. As soon as you awake, raise yourself, thinking of Our Crucified Lord Jesus Christ, who died on the Cross for our salvation. Immediately rise, and do not permit yourself to lie awake in bed for a long time.

While dressing, remember that you are in the presence of Our Lord and your Guardian Angel. Keep in mind the fall of Adam, who because of his sin was deprived of his attire for innocence. Pray to the Lord to give you the grace to be arrayed in Him.

Then promptly begin your morning prayers. Kneeling, pray reverently, attentively, and with deep humility, as one would before the sight of the Almighty. Pray for faith, hope and love; pray for blessings for the coming day. Pray for the endurance of all burdens, hardships, miseries, disturbances, misfortunes, sorrows, maladies of the soul and body, out of love for Jesus Christ. Take the firm resolution to do everything from His Fatherly hand with a special determination to do some particular good, or to avoid some particular evil. Every morning, consecrate for at least a quarter of an hour, a short meditation about the inconceivable mystery of the Incarnation of God's Son and about the dreadful Second Arrival, about Hades and Paradise.

Think: perhaps this day may be the last day of my life, and do everything as you would do getting ready to stand before God's judgment now. Thank the Lord God for having kept you during the past night from the awful judgment of the Lord. Also, thank God that you have time for grace and mercy, for penitence to acquire heaven. Every morning think that only now you begin to be, and wish to be a real Christian, with the previous time passed uselessly.

After prayer and meditation, if you have time, read some spiritual book, or the Holy Scriptures for the day. Read until your heart is warmed. Having thought enough on one place in your reading, go further and pay attention to what God is telling your heart.

After that, occupy yourself with your work so that it may be to the glory of God. Remember, that God sees you everywhere, sees all your actions, all your occupations, all your feelings, intentions and desires and will generously reward you for your good deeds. Never begin your work without a prayer to God because that which we do or say without prayer afterwards proves to be a sinful or harmful action and accuses us through deeds in a way unknown to us. Our Lord Himself said, "Without my help you can do nothing!" In your work always be kindly and entrust the success of your deeds to God's blessing. Fulfill all that is hard for you as a penance for your sins in the spirit of obedience and humility. During your work say short prayers, especially prayers to Jesus, and think of Christ who ate His bread in the sweat of His face, working hard with Joseph. If your work is going on successfully, according to the designs of your heart, praise the Lord God; if unsuccessful remember that God let it be and God does everything well.

At dinner think that the heavenly Father opens His hands to satiate you; never forget to pray before dinner; share your meals with the poor. After dinner think of yourself as one of those whom Jesus fed miraculously among five thousand. Thank Him with all your heart and pray that He will never deprive you of the heavenly food of His word and His All-pure Flesh and Blood.

What you do not wish for yourself, do not do it to others, and what you wish for yourself from others, do it first to them. If somebody comes to visit you, raise your heart to the Lord, praying to Him to give you a kind, gentle and collected spirit. Be friendly, modest, discrete, prudent, blind and mute, according to the circumstances. Do not say anything inconsiderately, remembering that time is short and that men will have to give an accounting for every useless word. Give your conversations a certain purpose and try to conduct them to soul salvation. Do more listening than speaking; in much speaking you cannot be safe from committing some sin. Pray to God for the favor to speak and be silent at the right time. Do not be curious about news, that will distract your spirit. If your words will be of use to someone, acknowledge in them the favor of God. When you are alone, try to find out whether you are getting worse than before. Have you committed sins you have not committed before?

Having sinned, pray to God for forgiveness, humbly with contrition, trusting His kindness, and hasten to repent before your father confessor, because every unrepented sin is a sin to death. If you will not be repentant about the sin you committed you will fall in it soon again.

Try to do good to everybody. Do what good you can, and where you can, without thinking whether it will be appreciated or not, or whether people will be thankful to you, or not. Do not rejoice when you do something good for someone, but when you endure, without revenge, some insults from a person to whom you were beneficent. If someone will not obey the first word, do not force him through controversy-use yourself the good he has lost, because your gentleness will do you much good. But when the harm extends to many people, do not tolerate it. Do not strive after your own profit but after that of many people. The general welfare is more important than personal welfare.

During supper time think of the Last Mystical Supper of Jesus Christ, praying to Him to admit you to His heavenly supper.

Before going to bed examine your conscience and pray for knowing your sins. Think of them, pray for forgiveness, promise amendment, determining clearly and precisely in what things, and in what manner, you firmly propose to improve yourself. Then entrust yourself to God as if you had to appear before Him that very night, and trust yourself to the Mother of God, your Guardian Angel, and to the saint by whose name you are called. Present your bed as your coffin, and your blanket as your shroud. Crossing yourself and kissing the Cross you bear, sleep under the protection of the Pastor of Israel, "Who will neither slumber nor sleep." If you cannot sleep and are awake at night remember the words, "And at midnight there was a cry made; behold the bridegroom comes!" Or think of that last night when Jesus prayed to His Father 'till bloody sweat covered His body' pray for those who are seriously sick at night and in death agony, for the suffering and the dead. Pray to the Lord that you are not covered with eternal darkness. At midnight, get up from your bed and pray as much as your strength will allow you.

During your illness, first of all, trust in God. Many times think of the passions and death of Jesus Christ, to strengthen your spirit in your hard suffering. Unceasingly repeat the prayers you know, pray to the Lord God to forgive your sins and to give you patience to endure your illness. In every way abstain from irritation and grumbling that are so common during illnesses. The Lord

Jesus Christ suffered the most impressive illnesses and pains for the sake of our salvation, and what have we done, or endured, for our salvation?

If you wish to lead a peaceful life, give your whole self to God. You will never find peace of soul until you devote yourself to Almighty God, loving Him alone. Always, and in everything, remember the Lord God and His great love for us sinners. In everything, try to carry out God's will and to please God alone. Do everything for God's sake. Do not care for the respect and love of the people of our time, but try to please the Lord God and see that your conscience does not accuse you of your sins. Watch yourself attentively, your feelings, thoughts and every movement of your heart, your passions; consider nothing to be of small importance when the salvation of your soul is concerned. When thinking of God, increase your prayers for God to remember you when you forget Him. Let Jesus Christ be your teacher in everything. Looking at Him with the eye of your mind, ask yourself more often; what would Jesus Christ do or say in this case? Be gentle, be quiet, mild, silent and patient, according to Christ's example. He will not charge you with a Cross that is heavier than you can bear; He Himself will help you to carry your Cross.

Do not think that you can acquire some virtue without any sorrow or pain of soul. Pray to God for grace to fulfill His Holy Commandments the best way possible, though they may seem to you very hard to maintain. Having carried out some of God's Commandments, expect some temptation because love of Christ is tested by the mastery of obstacles. Even for a short time do not remain idle but always be at work in some occupation, since an idle person is not worthy of the name of man. Retire, as Jesus did, setting yourself away from the presence of people, and pray to your heavenly Father. During times of weariness of the soul, and indifference to prayer, do not leave the deeds of piety. Our Lord, Jesus Christ, prayed three times when His soul was exceedingly sorrowful even unto death. Do everything in the name of the Lord Jesus, and thus every one of your works will be a deed of piety.

Avoid even the smallest sins because one who does not avoid them will constantly fall into greater and heavier sins. If you wish to be undisturbed by evil thoughts, humbly accept humiliations of the soul and physical afflictions, not only at some time, but at every time, in any place and in any form. Expel from your heart every thought that keeps you away from our Lord, especially unclean thoughts of the flesh. Do it as quickly as you would throw off a spark of fire from your clothes. If such a thought comes, pray fervently "O Lord, have mercy. O Lord, do not leave me. Deliver me from temptation!" Or use similar prayers. But do not be troubled by such temptations for the One who gave you the chance to fight, will give you the strength to conquer. Be quiet in spirit. Trust in God! If God is for you, how can anything be against you? Pray to God that He would take away from you anything that maintains your selfishness even though it would be very bitter for you to lose it. Long to live and die for the Lord alone, and to be entirely for Him.

Having food and clothes, be content with them. Like Jesus Who was impoverished for our sake! Never quarrel or do anything against your superiors or neighbors without necessity or obligation. Be simple and sincere in your heart, accept with love all instructions, admonitions and convictions from other people, though you may indeed be intelligent. Do not be one who hates, do not be envious or excessively strict in words and deeds.

As often as possible go to church, to the Divine Services: especially try to be present at Holy Liturgy. Consecrate Sundays and feast days to good deeds. In church, remember always that you are in the presence of God, His angels and all the saints. Devote the remainder of the day, after Liturgy, to spiritual reading and deeds of piety and love. Consecrate your nameday and your birthday to good deeds. Every month of every year make a strict examination of conscience. As often as possible confess and receive Holy Communion. Always come into the Mysteries with real hunger and thirst of soul, with contrition of heart, devotion and humility; with belief, hope and love. As often as possible think of the Passion of Our Lord, Jesus Christ, imploring Him to cover your sins with His merits and accept you into His Kingdom. Always keep the name of Jesus on your lips in your mind and in your heart. As often as possible, think of the great love given to you by Our Lord, praised and worshipped in the Trinity, so that you yourself will love Him with all your heart, with all your soul, and with all your strength. During that time you will lead a peaceful life on earth and a blessed one in heaven, forever and ever.

May the grace of Our Lord Jesus Christ be with you forever. Amen."

From Homily 69: St. Isaac of Syria:

"Those who have truly decided to serve the Lord God should practice the remembrance of God and uninterrupted prayer to Jesus Christ, mentally saying: "Lord Jesus Christ, Son of God, by the prayers of the Mother of God, have mercy on me a sinner," or one may have recourse directly to the Most Holy Mother of God, praying the angelic greeting: "Rejoice, Virgin Theotokos, full of grace, the Lord is with thee. Blessed art thou among women, and blessed is the fruit of thy womb: for thou has borne the Savior of our souls."

By such exercises in preserving oneself from dispersion and keeping peace of conscience, one may draw near to God and be united to Him. Without prayer, we cannot draw near to God."

"The sons of God are distinguished from others by the fact that they live in afflictions, while the world prides itself on luxury and ease."

St. Isaac the Syrian

GOD INVITES US TO COME TO HIM

"But without faith it is impossible to please Him, for he who comes to God must believe in Him, and that He rewards those who diligently seek Him."

Hebrews 11:6

"On the last day, that great day of the feast, Jesus stood and cried out, If anyone thirsts, let him come to me and drink."

St. John 7:37

"For whoever is ashamed of me and my words in this adulterous and sinful generation, of him the Son of Man also will be ashamed, when He comes in the glory of His Father."

St. Mark 8:38

3. PRAYER TRANSFORMS OUR LIVES

PRAYER: A SPIRITUAL BOND

"Make it a habit not to begin any work without prayer."

Monk Zosimus

TYPES OF PRAYER

Thanksgiving when we thank God for His manifold gifts.

Confession when we admit our sins before God and man while asking for forgiveness.

Intercession when we pray for the needs of others.

"There is no limit to increase in prayer. If it ceases to grow, it means that life has ended."

St. Theophan the Recluse

Petition when we bring our own needs before God and ask for His help.

Meditation when we listen to God in silence after prayer, or reading His word. We should pray alone, or read Holy Scripture and then wait for God's quiet voice to speak to us.

Adoration when we throw ourselves upon God's great love and mercy. This is motivated by our own love for God and His continual goodness.

AN ORTHODOX RULE OF PRAYER

"At our departure from our Rule of Prayer the Lord departs from our soul."

St. Nilus of Sora

Every Orthodox Christian should construct and maintain a Rule of Prayer which is utilized each day.

One's Rule of Prayer should be recited at the same time each day.

One's Rule of Prayer should not be excessive in length. It should suit a person's schedule and be able to be said in difficult times, when traveling, or in deep distress.

St. Paul said that we should "pray constantly." We should continually think of God, keep Him in our thoughts and converse with Him in prayer many times during the day. This is more beneficial than a prolonged period of prayer just once each day.

One's Rule of Prayer should be personal and intimate. Construct your Rule so that it is comfortable and works for you alone.

Spontaneous prayer is paramount. We should never let our prayers and thoughts of God be interrupted by mundane matters. Our thoughts, uplifted to God, must never be replaced by secular things.

We should have one particular place for prayer. Either an Icon Corner, or a place in our room where we can pray formally without interruption.

We should use formal prayers of the Orthodox Church interspersed with our own petitions and personal prayers, with which we feel especially comfortable.

Scriptural references: Colossians 4:2, Rom. 12:12, Acts 1:14.

MEDITATIONS of St John Chrysostom

St. John Chrysostom who died in 407, wrote a prayer which contained 24 petitions, or "Meditations," one for each hour of the day. Most of us could not keep this schedule but we would be spiritually strengthened by using one meditation a day for 24 days, then praying the cycle once again, each month.

1. O Lord, deprive me not of Thy heavenly blessings.

2. O Lord, deliver me from eternal torments.

3. O Lord, if I have sinned in mind or thought, in word or deed, forgive me.

4. O Lord, deliver me from every ignorance and carelessness, from littleness of soul and stony hardness of heart.

5. O Lord, deliver me from every temptation.

6. O Lord, enlighten my heart which evil desire has darkened.

7. O Lord, I, being human, have sinned: do Thou, being God, in loving-kindness forgive me, for Thou knowest the weakness of my soul.

8. O Lord, send down Thy grace to help me, that I may glorify Thy Holy Name.

9. O Lord, Jesus Christ, enroll me, Thy servant, in the Book of Life, and grant me a blessed end.

10. O Lord, my God, even if I have done nothing good in Thy sight, yet grant me, according to your grace, to make a beginning of good.

11. O Lord, sprinkle on my heart the dew of Thy grace.

12. O Lord of heaven and earth, remember me, Thy sinful servant, cold of heart and impure, in Thy Kingdom.

13. O Lord, receive me in repentance.

14. O Lord, leave me not.

15. O Lord, lead me not into temptation.

16. O Lord, grant me good thoughts.

17. O Lord, grant me tears, a remembrance of death, and a sense of peace.

18. O Lord, grant me mindfulness to confess my sins.

19. O Lord, grant me humility, charity and obedience.

20. O Lord, grant me endurance, magnanimity and gentleness.

21. O Lord, plant in me the root of all blessings, the fear of God.

22. O Lord, vouchsafe that I may love Thee with all my heart and soul and in all things obey Thy will.

23. O Lord, shield me from evil people, devils and passions, and all other unlawful things.

24. O Lord, who knows Thy creation and what Thou willed for it: may Thy will also be fulfilled in me a sinner: for Thou are blessed for evermore. Amen.

St. John Chrysostom

THE ORTHODOX PRAYER ROPE

An Orthodox Prayer Rope resembles the Western rosary, although it is much more ancient, and has a separate history of development. The Prayer Rope usually has 100 knots, divided into four equal parts separated by four beads. On each knot the Jesus Prayer is recited. (See below)

There is also a monastic Prayer Rope with 1,000 knots and another 50-knot rope for laypeople.

THE JESUS PRAYER

"Lord, Jesus Christ, Son of God, have mercy on me a sinner."

MATINS (ORTHROS) AND VESPERS

These two ancient services of the Church are times set-aside for morning and evening prayer. Vespers is celebrated at the setting of the Sun and is a time of thanksgiving for the gifts God has bestowed on us during the day. It is also an opportunity to closely examine the ways in which we have failed to live a Christian life. At this time we confess our sins, both voluntary and involuntary, asking the mercy of a forgiving God. It is always beneficial for one's spiritual life to take stock of our failures so that we will avoid them in the future. Vespers and Matins afford us a time to review and renew our lives in silence and contemplation.

Orthros (Matins) which should begin before dawn, and conclude at the rising of the sun, allows us to be ready for God's gift of a new day. We should use this time of daily prayer to concentrate our minds and hearts to God and therefore not begin our work with purely worldly or profane matters. To lift ourselves to God and offer our first thoughts to Him is a noble and glorious work much neglected in today's hectic and material world.

Note: In actual practice the Christian day begins at " the setting of the sun;" however, Vespers is traditionally said in the late afternoon. Other calculations of the Christian day may also be found, each of them equally ancient.

"Prayer is communion with life. Departure from it brings invisible death to the soul."

St. Ignatius Brianchaninov

OTHER SERVICES OF THE ORTHODOX CHURCH WHICH SANCTIFY THE DAY

Compline is a service of forgiveness. It is composed of prayers during which we ask for God's forgiveness for the sins of the day and His protection through the coming night.

The Midnight Office is usually celebrated only in monasteries. It is read at midnight in commemoration of Christ's agony in the Garden of Gethsemane. The service brings to mind that we should always be prepared to face death which will come, for some, like a thief in the night.

The First Hour depicts the first three hours of the day, for example from 6am to 9am. The First Hour makes the day holy with prayer and supplication.

(An "hour" is equivalent to the military watch which is mentioned in Holy Scripture. A "watch" is equivalent to three clock hours.)

The Third Hour extends from 9am to noon and commemorates the descent of the Holy Spirit upon the first Christian believers.

The Sixth Hour covers the period from noon until 3pm and brings to mind the period of time which Christ spent on the Life-giving Cross.

The Ninth Hour which extends from 3pm to 6pm, reminds us of the death of Jesus Christ upon the Cross and the loving care with which the disciples removed His sacred body for burial.

THE LENTEN PRAYER OF ST. EPHRAIM THE SYRIAN

"O Lord and master of my life, take from me the spirit of idleness, despondency, ambition, or vain talking. *(Make a prostration)*

But rather bestow on me Thy servant, a spirit of purity, humility, patience, and love. *(Make a prostration)*

O Lord and King, grant me to see my own sins, and not to judge my brother, for blessed art Thou unto ages of ages. Amen. *(Make a prostration)*

O God, cleanse me a sinner.
(Say this 12 times each time making the Sign of the Cross while bowing one's head.)

O Lord and master of my life, take from me the spirit of idleness, despondency, ambition and vain talking. Rather bestow on me, Thy servant, a spirit of purity, humility, patience and love.

O Lord and King, grant me to see my own sins, and not to judge my brother, for blessed are Thou unto ages of ages. Amen." *(Cross yourself and make a prostration)*

ARTOKLASIA (LITIYA) THE BLESSING OF THE LOAVES

This service may be held at the end of Vespers, Matins (Orthros) or even the Divine Liturgy. During this service five small loaves of bread are offered by the faithful as a sign of their personal devotion to the Lord. It is used on anniversaries, name days, or times of great need. The term Artoklasia means to "break bread" and is symbolic of the loaves Jesus Christ used to feed the 5000. It is also a remembrance of the Agape or "love meals" shared by the early Christians. The loaves also signify that Christ is indeed, the "bread of life", and that the Church, spread throughout the ages as wheat, was gathered by Christ into one body. The blessed bread of the Artoklasia, if taken with faith, is used as an aid to personal holiness and for the help or benefit of those who are ill. During this service oil, wine and wheat are also blessed and the broken bread is distributed to the faithful at its completion. The ceremony is also known as the Litiya.

Scriptural reference: Isaiah 58:7-9, Matthew 14:14-21

AKATHIST HYMN

This is a lengthy liturgical poem which begins with a hymn to the Mother of God. Composed centuries ago it is commonly used in Orthodox parishes today on the evening of the first four Fridays of the Great Fast. The term "Akathist" means the service is done "standing." It is a time to lift one's heart and soul to Almighty God and to contemplate the mysteries of the Faith relating to Christ and His Holy Mother. It is a masterpiece of Orthodox hymnology.

PARAKLISIS - THE SERVICE OF SUPPLICATION

This is a service of supplication offered at times of sickness, temptation or discouragement. The prayers of this service beg Almighty God for guidance, strength and healing from affliction. Many of the prayers are intercessions to Christ, the Theotokos and the saints. Just as we can turn to each other for prayer during our life on earth, the Church goes to Our Lord, His Mother (who was so close to Him on earth), and the holy saints – to ask for prayers in heaven. The service is found in "Lesser and Greater" forms. The Lesser Service of Supplication is most commonly used on the first fourteen days of the Dormition Fast, (the days before the Feast of The Dormition of the Mother of God) on August 15th.

DAILY PRAYERS

> *"Remember that not a single word is lost during prayer if you say it from your heart. God hears each word and weighs it in a balance Sometimes, it seems to us that our words only strike the air in vain, and sound as a voice of one crying in the wilderness, No, no it is not so! … The Lord responds to every desire of the heart, expressed in words or unexpressed."*
>
> *St. John of Kronstadt – "My Life in Christ"*

MORNING PRAYERS

In the name of the Father, and of the Son, and of the Holy Spirit. Amen.

Glory to Thee, O God, glory to Thee.

To the Holy Spirit

Heavenly King, Comforter, Spirit of Truth, Who is everywhere present and fills all things, Treasury of Blessings, and Giver of Life, come and abide in us, cleanse us of all impurity, and save our souls, O Good One.

To the Holy Trinity

Holy God, Holy Mighty, Holy Immortal, have mercy on us. (*Three times*)

Glory to the Father, and to the Son, and to the Holy Spirit, now and ever, unto ages of ages. Amen.

All Holy Trinity have mercy on us. Lord, wash away our sins. Master, pardon our iniquities. Holy One, visit and heal our infirmities for Thy name's sake.

Lord have mercy, Lord have mercy, Lord have mercy.

Glory to the Father, and to the Son, and to the Holy Spirit, now and ever, unto ages of ages. Amen.

To God Our Father

Our Father, Who art in heaven, hallowed be Thy name. Thy Kingdom come, Thy will be done, on earth as it is in heaven. Give us this day our daily bread, and forgive us our debts, as we forgive our debtors, and lead us not into temptation, but deliver us from evil.

For Thine is the Kingdom, the power and the glory, of the Father, and of the Son, and the Holy Spirit, now and ever, unto ages of ages. Amen.

To Jesus Christ

O come let us worship God Our King. O come let us worship and fall down before Christ, Our King and God. O come, let us worship and fall down before Christ, Our King and God.

To the "Theotokos" – Mother of God

It is truly meet to bless thee, O Theotokos, ever-blessed and pure, the Mother of Our God. More honorable than the Cherubim and more glorious beyond compare than the Seraphim, without corruption thou gave birth to God the Word, true Theotokos, we magnify thee.

O Virgin Theotokos, rejoice: O Mary full of grace, the Lord is with thee. Blessed art thou among women, and blessed is the fruit of thy womb, for thou has borne the Savior of our souls.

To Our Patron Saint

Pray to God for me, O Saint _____ who is well pleasing to God, for I fervently entreat thee, sure helper and intercessor for my soul. Amen.

Thanksgiving for the Morning

Having risen from sleep, we fall down before Thee, O Good One, and we cry to Thee, O Mighty One, the angelic hymn: Holy, Holy, Holy art Thou, O God, have mercy on us.

Glory to the Father and to the Son, and to the Holy Spirit. Now and ever, unto ages of ages. Amen.

Thou has raised me up from bed and sleep, O Lord: enlighten my mind and heart, and open my lips that I may hymn Thee, O Holy Trinity. Holy, Holy, Holy art Thou, O God, have mercy on us.

Now and ever unto ages of ages. Amen.

Suddenly, the Judge will come, and the deeds of each will be revealed; but at midnight let us cry with fear: Holy, Holy, Holy art Thou, O God; through the prayers of the Theotokos, have mercy on us.

Lord have mercy, Lord have mercy, Lord have mercy.

Glory to the Father, and to the Son, and to the Holy Spirit. Now and ever, unto ages of ages. Amen.

A Prayer to the Holy Trinity

Arising from sleep I thank Thee, All Holy Trinity, because of the abundance of Thy goodness and long-suffering, Thou was not angry with me, slothful and sinful as I am, neither has Thou destroyed me in my transgressions, but in Thy compassion raised me up, as I lay in despair, that at dawn I might sing the glories of Thy majesty. Do now enlighten the eyes of my understanding, open my mouth to receive Thy words, teach me Thy Commandments, help me to do Thy will, confessing Thee from my heart, singing and praising Thine All-holy name, of the Father, and of the Son, and of the Holy Spirit, now and ever, unto ages of ages. Amen.

The Creed – A Symbol of Our Faith

I believe in One God the Father Almighty, Maker of heaven and earth, and of all things visible and invisible. And in One Lord Jesus Christ, the Only-begotten, Son of God, begotten of the Father before all ages, Light of Light, true God of true God, begotten, not made, of one essence with the Father, by Whom all things were made.

Who for us men, and for our salvation, came down from heaven and was incarnate of the Holy Spirit and the Virgin Mary, and became man.

He was crucified for us under Pontius Pilate, and suffered and was buried. He arose again on the third day according to the Scriptures: and ascended into heaven, and sits at the right hand of the Father: and shall come again with glory to judge the living and the dead, Whose Kingdom shall have no end.

And in the Holy Spirit, the Lord, the Giver of Life, Who proceeds from the Father, Who with the Father and the Son together is worshiped and glorified, Who spoke by the prophets. I believe in One, Holy, Catholic and Apostolic Church, I confess one baptism for the remission of sins.

I look for the resurrection of the dead and the life of the world to come. Amen.

A Short Prayer for Anytime

May God be gracious unto us, bless us, and cause His face to shine upon us, and have mercy on us.

This is the day which the Lord has made, Let us rejoice and be glad in it. Amen.

> *"Prayer does not consist merely in standing and bowing your body or in reading written prayers…it is possible to pray at all times, in all places, with the mind and spirit. You can lift up your mind and heart to God*

while walking, sitting, working, in a crowd and in solitude. His door is always open, unlike man's. We can always say to Him in our hearts: Lord, Lord, have mercy."

St. Tikhon of Zadonsk

EVENING PRAYERS

In the name of the Father, and of the Son, and of the Holy Spirit. Amen.

Glory to Thee, O God, glory to Thee.

To the Holy Spirit

Heavenly King, Comforter, Spirit of Truth, Who is everywhere present and fills all things, Treasury of Blessings and Giver of Life, come and abide in us, cleanse us of all impurity, and save our souls, O Good One.

To the Holy Trinity

Holy God, Holy Mighty, Holy Immortal, have mercy on us. (Three times)

Glory to the Father, and to the Son, and to the Holy Spirit, now and ever, unto ages of ages. Amen.

Most Holy Trinity, have mercy on us. Lord, wash away our sins. Master, pardon our iniquities. Holy One, visit and heal our infirmities for Thy name's sake.

Lord have mercy, Lord have mercy, Lord have mercy.

Glory to the Father and to the Son and to the Holy Spirit, now and ever, unto ages of ages. Amen.

Troparia of Thanksgiving

Now that the day has come to a close, I thank Thee O Lord, and I ask that the evening with the night may be sinless, grant this to me, O Good One, and save me.

Glory to the Father, and to the Son, and to the Holy Spirit.

Now that the day has passed, I glorify Thee, O Master, and I ask that the evening with the night may be without offense, grant this to me, O Good One, and save me.

Both now and ever, unto ages of ages. Amen.

Now that the day has run its course, I praise Thee, All-Holy One, and I ask that the evening with the night may be undisturbed: grant this to me, O Good One, and save me.

Lord, have mercy. (*Twelve times*)

To God Our Father

Our Father, Who art in Heaven, hallowed be Thy name. Thy Kingdom come, Thy will be done, on earth as it is in heaven. Give us this day our daily bread, and forgive us our debts, as we forgive our debtors. And lead us not into temptation, but deliver us from evil.

For Thine is the Kingdom, the power, and the glory, of the Father, and of the Son, and the Holy Spirit, now and ever, unto ages of ages. Amen.

To Jesus Christ

O come, let us worship God Our King. O come, let us worship and fall down before Christ, Our King and God. O come, let us worship and fall down before Christ, Our King and God.

The Fathers: On Prayer

"Let my soul take refuge from the pressing turmoil of worldly thought behind the shadow of Thy wings. Let my heart, this sea of restless waves, find peace in Thee, O God."

"The more a religious person works at prayer, the more helpful he is."

"Do what you can, and then pray that God will give you the power to do what you cannot."

St. Augustine (354-430)

"All goods are hidden in prayer; intimate, penetrating prayer, which obtains everything, and transforms life."

St. Benedict of Nursia +547

"The Lord has become everything for you, and you must become everything for the Lord."

St. John of Kronstadt (1829-1908)

"A Christian is an Alleluia from head to foot."

St. Augustine (354-430)

"Prayer is the test of everything. If prayer is right, everything is right."

Bishop Theophan the Recluse (1815-94)

To the Theotokos

It is truly meet to bless thee, O Theotokos, ever-blessed and pure, the Mother of Our God. More honorable than the Cherubim, and more glorious beyond compare than the Seraphim, without corruption thou gave birth to God the Word, true Theotokos, we magnify thee.

O Virgin Theotokos, rejoice; O Mary full of grace, the Lord is with thee. Blessed art thou among women, and blessed is the fruit of thy womb, for thou has borne the Savior of our souls.

To Our Patron Saint

Pray to God for me, O Saint _____ who is well pleasing to God, for I fervently entreat thee, sure helper and intercessor for my soul. Amen.

Evening Prayers of Repentence

Have mercy on us, O Lord, have mercy on us. At a loss for any plea, we sinners offer Thee, Our Master, this supplication, have mercy on us.

Glory to the Father, the Son, and the Holy Spirit.

Lord, have mercy on us, we place our trust in Thee. Be not angry with us, remember not our sins; but regard us in Thy tender compassion, and deliver us from our enemies. For Thou art Our God, we are Thy people, we are the work of Thy hands, and we call upon Thy name.

Now and ever, unto ages of ages. Amen.

Open the door of thy loving kindness, O Blessed Theotokos, that we who put our hope in thee may not perish. Through thee, may we be delivered from adversities, for thou art the true intercessor of the Christian people.

Lord have mercy, Lord have mercy, Lord have mercy.

Glory to the Father and to the Son, and to the Holy Spirit, now and ever unto ages of ages. Amen.

(Recite the Creed here. *See: Morning Prayers.*)

Guard me, O Lord, by the power of Thy Holy and Life-giving Cross, and keep me from all evil.

Into Thy hands, O Lord Jesus Christ, my God, I commend my spirit and body.

Bless me, save me, and grant me eternal life. Amen.

In the name of the Father, and of the Son and of the Holy Spirit. Amen.

PRAYER WITH MEALS

Recite the "Our Father" (*Lord's Prayer*)

Lord have mercy, Lord have mercy, Lord have mercy.

Then recite: Prayer Before Breakfast, or Prayer After Breakfast, or Prayer Before Noon Meal, etc. (*See below*)

Prayer Before Breakfast

All Holy Trinity, have mercy on us. Lord, wash away our sins. Master, pardon our iniquities. Holy One, visit and heal our infirmities for Thy name's sake.

Glory to the Father, and to the Son, and to the Holy Spirit, now and ever, unto ages of ages. Amen.

Lord have mercy, Lord have mercy, Lord have mercy.

Christ Our True God, bless the food and drink of Thy servants. Thou art holy always, now and ever, unto ages of ages. Amen.

Prayer After Breakfast

It is truly meet to bless thee, O Theotokos, ever-blessed and pure, the Mother of Our God. More honorable than the Cherubim, and more glorious beyond compare than the Seraphim, without corruption thou gave birth to God the Word, true Theotokos, we magnify thee.

Prayer Before the Noon Meal

Recite the "Our Father" (*Lord's Prayer*)

Lord have mercy, Lord have mercy, Lord have mercy.

Christ our true God, bless the food and drink of Thy servants. Thou art holy, always, now and ever unto ages of ages. Amen.

Prayer After the Noon Meal

Glory to the Father, and to the Son, and to the Holy Spirit, now and ever, unto ages of ages. Amen.

Lord have mercy, Lord have mercy, Lord have mercy.

We thank Thee, O Christ Our God, that Thou has satisfied us with Thy earthly gifts. Deprive us not of Thy heavenly Kingdom, but as Thou came among Thy disciples, O Savior and gave them peace, come to us and save us. Amen.

Prayer Before the Evening Meal

The poor shall eat and be satisfied, and those who seek the Lord shall praise Him, their hearts shall live forever.

Glory be to the Father, and to the Son, and to the Holy Spirit, now and ever unto ages of ages. Amen.

Lord have mercy, Lord have mercy, Lord have mercy.

Christ Our True God bless the food and drink of Thy servants, for Thou art holy, always, now and ever, unto ages of ages. Amen.

Prayer After the Evening Meal

Glory to the Father, and to the Son, and to the Holy Spirit, now and ever, unto ages of ages. Amen.

Lord have mercy, Lord have mercy, Lord have mercy.

God is with us by His grace and love for mankind, always, now and ever, unto ages of ages. Amen.

Thoughts on Prayer

"He who really prays is a theologian, and he who is a theologian really prays."

Evagrius of Pontus (346-399)

"Prayer rises to heaven, and immediately God's mercy descends upon the earth."

St. Augustine +430

"Give rest to the weary, visit the sick, support the poor, for this also is prayer."

Aphahat

"What is pure prayer? Prayer which is brief in words but abundant in actions. For if your actions do not exceed your petitions, then your prayers are mere words."

"Sayings of the Desert Fathers"

"We celebrate the day of one's death because those who seem to die do not die. But we, do not celebrate the day of one's earthly birth because those who die are living eternally."

Origen

TRISAGION PRAYERS FOR THE DECEASED

Blessed is Our God always, now and ever, unto ages of ages. Amen.

Holy God, Holy Mighty, Holy Immortal, have mercy on us. (Three times)

Glory to the Father, and to the Son, and to the Holy Spirit, now and ever, unto ages of ages. Amen.

All Holy Trinity, have mercy on us. Lord, wash away our sins. Master, pardon our iniquities. Holy One, visit and heal our iniquities for Thy name's sake.

Lord have mercy, Lord have mercy, Lord have mercy.

Glory to the Father...

Recite the Our Father...

For Thine is the Kingdom, the power and the glory, of the Father, the Son, and Holy Spirit. Amen.

With the spirits of the righteous made perfect, give rest to the soul(s) of Thy servant(s)_____, O Savior, and preserve it (them) in a life of blessedness which is with Thee, O Thou who loves mankind.

In the place of Thy rest, O Lord, where all Thy saints repose, give rest to the soul(s) of Thy servant(s), for Thou only loves mankind.

Glory to the Father, and to the Son, and to the Holy Spirit.

Thou art Our God, Who descended into hell, and loosed the bonds of those who were there. Thyself, O Lord, give rest to the soul(s) of Thy servants.

Both now and ever, and unto ages of ages. Amen.

O Virgin Theotokos, alone pure, and immaculate, who gave birth to God, intercede for the salvation of the soul(s) of thy servants.

Have mercy on us, O Lord, according to Thy great mercy, we pray to Thee, hear us and have mercy.

Lord have mercy, Lord have mercy, Lord have mercy.

Again and again, we pray for the repose of the soul(s) of Thy servant(s) departed this life, and that Thou will pardon (his, her, their) every transgression, whether voluntary or involuntary.

Lord have mercy, Lord have mercy, Lord have mercy.

We pray that the Lord God will establish (his, her, their) soul(s) where the just repose, the mercies of God, the Kingdom of Heaven, and the forgiveness of (his, her, their) sins, let us ask of Christ, Our Immortal King and Our God.

Grant this O Lord.

O God of spirits and all flesh, Who has trampled down death and made powerless the Devil, and given life to the world, do Thou Thyself O Lord, give rest to the soul(s) of Thy departed servant(s) _____ in a place of brightness, a place of verdure, a place of repose, where all sickness, sorrow and sighing have fled away. Pardon every sin which (he, she, they) have committed, whether by word, or deed, or thought. For Thou art a good and gracious God who loves mankind, for there is no man who lives and does not sin, for Thou only are without sin, and Thy righteousness is to all eternity, and Thy word is truth.

For Thou art the resurrection, the life, and the repose of Thy departed servant(s) O God, and unto Thee do we ascribe glory, to the Father, and to the Son, and to the Holy Spirit, Amen.

Glory to Thee, O Christ Our God, and our hope, glory to Thee.

Glory to the Father, and to the Son, and to the Holy Spirit, now and ever, unto ages of ages. Amen.

Lord have mercy, Lord have mercy, Lord have mercy. Amen.

An Historical Note About Orthodoxy #1

The Orthodox Church maintains the teachings of the apostles. She stands fast to "pass on the traditions which they taught whether by word or by deed" (2 Thessalonians 2:15). We are also told to "withdraw from every brother who walks disorderly and not after the Tradition which he received from us" (Ibid. 3:6).

The Orthodox Church is the "pillar and ground of truth" (1 Timothy 3:15). Therefore we must honor and protect her teachings since they are from the very mind of the Lord. In the early Church there arose disputes as to the correct teachings to be observed. Leaders of the Faith gathered to discuss what was correct teaching, and what was not. In this way the Apostolic Faith, has been preserved and is taught to this day by the Orthodox Church, even though it has been buffeted by many who would pervert the truth to advance some novel idea or theology, in a quest for worldly power and secular control over men's minds.

For the first thousand years of the Faith, the entire Church (East and West), except for those who willingly severed themselves from the Truth, lived by the teachings of Holy Scripture, the Fathers, and Holy Tradition. It was not until the 11th century that a definitive break occurred. This is when the Western Patriarch at Rome, (the pope), decided to proclaim teachings which were incompatible with the ancient doctrines and Tradition of the Church. These actions, "de-facto" separated the Roman Church from the pristine beauty and practice of the earliest believers.

SACRED THOUGHTS FROM ST. ISAAC OF SYRIA (7TH CENTURY)

• What salt is for any food, humility is for every virtue. To acquire it, a man must always think of himself with contrition, self-belittlement and painful self-judgment. But if we acquire it, humility will make us sons of God.

• Let us love silence until the world is made to die in our hearts. Let us always remember death, and in this thought draw near to God in our heart – and the pleasures of this world will have our scorn.

• Walk before God in simplicity, and not in subtleties of the mind. Simplicity brings faith; but subtle and intricate speculations bring conceit, and conceit brings withdrawal from God.

• As a man whose head is underwater inhales pure water so a man whose thoughts are plunged into the cares of this world cannot absorb the sensations of that new world.

• It is a spiritual gift from God for a man to perceive his own sins.

• Ease and idleness are the destruction of the soul and they can injure her more than the demons.

• The purposes of the advent of the Savior, when He gave us His Life-giving Commandments as purifying remedies in our passionate state, was to cleanse the soul from the damage done by the first transgression and bring it back to its original state. What medicines are for a sick body, the Commandments are for the passionate soul.

- A life of spiritual endeavor is the mother of sanctity; from it is born the first experience of perception of the mysteries of Christ – which is called the first step of spiritual knowledge.

- To bear a grudge and pray, means to sow seed on the sea and expect a harvest.

- A small but persistent discipline is a great force, for a soft drop falling persistently, hollows out hard rock.

- The key to Divine Gifts is given to the heart by love for neighbor, and in proportion to the heart's freedom from the bonds of the flesh, the door of knowledge begins to open before it.

- Dispassion does not mean that the man feels no passions, but that he does not accept any of them.

- This life has been given to you for repentance, do not waste it in vain pursuits.

Other texts by St. Isaac can be found in "Early Fathers from the Philokalia" (Faber and Faber; 1954); "The Ascetical Homilies of St. Isaac the Syrian" (Holy Transfiguration Monastery; 1984); and "On Ascetical Life" from S. V. S. Press 1990.

PRAYER BEFORE READING THE HOLY SCRIPTURES

Illumine our hearts, O Master who loves mankind, with the pure light of Thy Divine knowledge. Open the eyes of our mind to the understanding of Thy Gospel teachings. Implant also in us the fear of Thy blessed Commandments, that trampling down all carnal desires, we may enter upon a spiritual manner of living, both thinking and doing such things as are well-pleasing unto Thee. For Thou art the illumination of our souls and bodies, O Christ our God, and unto Thee do we send up glory, together with Thy Father, who is from everlasting, and Thine All-holy, Good and Life-creating Spirit, now and ever, unto ages of ages.

What is Prayer?

> "O Father, light up the small duties of this day's life. May they shine with the beauty of Thy countenance. May we believe that glory can dwell in the most common task of every day."
>
> St. Augustine (354-430)

"Prayer is turning the mind and thoughts toward God. To pray means to stand before God with the mind, mentally to gaze unswervingly at Him, and to converse with Him in reverent fear and hope."

St. Dmitri of Rostov (1651-1709)

"In the Lord's Prayer we have a summary of the entire Gospel."

Tertullian

"We shall rest and we shall see;
We shall see and we shall love;
We shall love and we shall pray;
In the end which is no end."

St. Augustine (354-430)

PRAYERS AND PSALMS TO BE SAID BY ORTHODOX CHRISTIANS

The Jesus Prayer

"Lord Jesus Christ, Son of God, have mercy on me a sinner."

The Angelic Salutation

O Virgin Theotokos rejoice: O Mary, full of grace, the Lord is with thee. Blessed art thou among women, and blessed is the fruit of thy womb, for thou has borne the Savior of our souls.

Prayer to the Trinity

The Father is my hope, the Son is my refuge, the Holy Spirit is my protector. O Holy Trinity, glory to Thee.

The Lord's Prayer – The Our Father

Our Father, Who art in heaven, hallowed be Thy name. Thy Kingdom come, Thy will be done, on earth, as it is in heaven. Give us this day our daily bread, and forgive us our debts, as we forgive our debtors. And lead us not into temptation, but deliver us from evil.

For Thine is the Kingdom, the power, and the glory, of the Father, and of the Son, and the Holy Spirit, now and ever, unto ages of ages. Amen.

Glory to the Father, and to the Son, and to the Holy Spirit, now and ever unto ages of ages.

Amen.

A Prayer to Your Patron Saint

Pray to God for me, O Saint _____, who is well-hpleasing to God, for I fervently entreat thee, sure helper and intercessor for my soul. Amen.

Psalm 23 – The Lord is My Shepherd

The Lord is my shepherd; I shall not want.
He makes me to lie down in green pastures.
He leads me beside the still waters.
He restores my soul.
He leads me in the paths of righteousness for His name's sake.

Yea, though I walked through the valley of the shadow of death,
I will fear no evil, for Thou art with me.
Thy rod and Thy staff, they comfort me.

Thou prepares a table before me in the presence of my enemies;
Thou anoints my head with oil , my cup runs over.
Surely goodness and mercy shall follow me all the days of my life:
    and I will dwell in the house of the Lord forever.

Psalm 121 – The Lord is My Keeper

I will lift up mine eyes unto the hills, from whence comes my help?
My help comes from the Lord, Who made Heaven and Earth.

He will not suffer thy foot to be moved.
He that keeps thee will not slumber.
Behold, He that keeps Israel shall neither slumber nor sleep.

The Lord is thy keeper.
The Lord is thy shade upon thy right hand.
The sun shall not smite thee by day, nor the moon by night.

The Lord shall preserve thee from all evil.
He shall preserve thy soul.
The Lord shall preserve thy going out, and thy coming in,
    from this time forth, and even for evermore.

Psalm 141 - A Prayer for Preservation from Evil

Lord I cry unto Thee
   make haste unto me.
Give ear unto my voice, when I cry unto Thee.
Let my prayer be set forth before Thee as incense,
   and the lifting up of my hands as the evening sacrifice.

Set a watch, O Lord, before my mouth, keep watch over the door of my lips.
Incline not my heart to any evil thing, with men that work iniquity.
And let me not eat of their delicacies.

Let the righteous smite me,
   it shall be a kindness,
   and let him reprove me.
It shall be an excellent oil, let not my head refuse it.
For yet my prayer shall also be against the deeds of the wicked.
When their judges are overthrown in stony places,
   they shall hear my words; for they are sweet.
Our bones are scattered at the grave's mouth
   as when one plows and breaks up the earth.

But my eyes are unto Thee, O God the Lord.
In Thee is my trust; leave not my soul destitute.
Keep me from the snares which they have laid for me,
   and the traps of the workers of iniquity.
Let the wicked fall into their own nets, while I escape safely.

Psalm 142 - A Prayer for Help in Trouble

I cried unto the Lord with my voice;
With my voice unto the Lord did I make my supplication.
To Thee did I pour out my complaint,
Before Him I showed my trouble.
When my spirit was overwhelmed within me, then Thou knew my path.

In the way wherein I walked,
They have made a snare for me.
I looked on my right hand but there was no man that would know me;
Refuge failed me , no man cared for my soul.

I cried unto Thee, O Lord;
I said, "Thou art my refuge and my
   portion in the land of the living."
Attend unto my cry,
   for I am brought very low.

Deliver me from my persecutors, for they are
    stronger than I.
Bring my soul out of prison, that I may praise Thy name.
The righteous shall compass me about,
    for Thou shall deal bountifully with me.

You Cannot Hide from God

*"Can anyone hide himself in secret places, so I shall not see him?" says
the Lord, "Do I not fill heaven and earth?"*

Jeremiah 23:24

*"There is no creature hidden from His sight, but all things are naked
and open to the eyes of Him to whom we must give account."*

Hebrews 4:13

*"For nothing is secret that will not be revealed, nor anything hidden that
will not be known and come to light."*

St. Luke 8:17

PENITENTIAL PSALM 50 (51)

Psalm 50/51 is one of repentance for God's mercy. Of all the 150 psalms this
one is used more than any other. Sometimes it is found in our Morning and
Late-night Prayers and is repeated in every Divine Liturgy as the priest, or the
deacon, censes the church before the Great Entrance. Traditionally the psalm
is noted as King David's prayer of repentance for his sin with Bathsheba
(2 Samuel 12:1-15).

Have mercy upon me O God according to Thy loving kindness;
    according to the multitude of Thy tender mercies.
Blot out my transgressions.
Wash me thoroughly from mine iniquity and cleanse me from my sin.

For I acknowledge my transgressions, and my sin is ever before me.
Against Thee, only, have I sinned.
And done this evil in Thy sight;
That Thou might be justified when Thou speaks, and be clear when Thou
    judges.
Behold I was shaped in iniquity, and in sin did my mother conceive me.

Behold, Thou desires truth in the inward parts,
    and in the hidden part Thou shall make me to know wisdom.
Purge me with hyssop, and I shall be clean.
Wash me and I shall be whiter than snow.

Make me to hear joy and gladness,
    that the bones which Thou has broken may rejoice.
Hide Thy face from my sins, and blot out all my iniquities.

Create in me a clean heart, O God; and renew a right spirit within me.
Cast me not away from my presence, and take not Thy Holy Spirit from me.
Restore unto me the joy of Thy salvation,
    and uphold me with Thy free spirit.

Then will I teach transgressors Thy ways;
    and sinners shall be converted unto Thee.
Deliver me from the guilt of bloodshed, O God,
Thou God of my salvation;
    and my tongue shall sing aloud of Thy righteousness.

O Lord, open Thou my lips;
    and my mouth shall show forth Thy praise.
For Thou desires not sacrifice, else would I give it.
Thou delights not in burnt offering.
The sacrifices of God are a broken spirit,
    a broken and contrite heart, O God, Thou will not despise.

Do good in my good pleasure unto Zion;
    build Thou the walls of Jerusalem.
Then Thou shall be pleased with the sacrifices of righteousness,
    with burnt offering and whole burnt offering.
Then shall they offer bullocks upon Thine altar.

THE PENITENTIAL PSALMS

Psalm

6   A Prayer of Faith in Times of Distress

32   The Joy of Forgiveness

38   Prayer in Time of Chastening

51   A Prayer of Repentance

102   The Lord's Eternal Love

130   Waiting For the Redemption of The Lord

4. GIFTS OF THE HOLY SPIRIT

THE PRACTICE OF VIRTUES AS
DUTIES OF ORTHODOX CHRISTIANS

THE GIFTS OF THE HOLY SPIRIT

1. Wisdom   helps us value things in the Kingdom of God.
2. Understanding   helps us know the truths of our Faith.
3. Counsel   helps us choose the right path to God.
4. Fortitude   helps us overcome obstacles to our Faith.
5. Knowledge   helps us choose the right paths in life.
6. Piety   gives us eagerness to serve God in this life.
7. Fear of the Lord   helps us acknowledging God's power, giving Him
                        respect and worship.

Scriptural references: Isaiah 11: 2-3, I Corinthians 12:3-10

The Holy Spirit works within each one of us, usually in a quiet, confident way rather than with wild, noisy bursts of emotion, or the disturbed rantings of counterfeit religion.

We cannot see the Spirit work – nor can we always feel His Almighty power. However, we must remember the words of Christ who promised to send the Paraclete, the "Comforter", to guide us to our heavenly home:

> *"When the Spirit of truth comes, He will guide you into all the truth."*
> *John 16:13*

THE SEVEN CAPITAL VIRTUES
The opposite of the "Seven Grievous Sins"

1. Humility   accepting our sinfulness and our need for
                 forgiveness.
2. Liberality   willingness to share our good fortunes with others.
3. Chastity   desiring the moral good in all things pertaining
                 to sex.
4. Mildness   self-control over our emotions, understanding
                 weaknesses of others.
5. Temperance   self-control in eating and drinking.
6. Happiness   desiring the good fortune of others and ourselves.
7. Diligence   faithfully fulfilling our duties to God, to family
                 and society.

From the writings of St. Clement of Alexandria (150-216)

"Righteous conduct is twofold: that which is done for love and that which is done through fear. For indeed it is said, 'The fear of the Lord is pure, remaining for ever and ever.' Those who, because of fear, turn to faith and righteousness, remain forever. Fear does, in fact, motivate to abstaining from evil; but love, building up to free action, exhorts to the doing of good."

THE SEVEN GRIEVOUS SINS

1. Pride   a lack of humility or recognition of one's sins.
2. Greed   an excessive love of money, worldly goods or fame.
3. Lust   impure and unworthy desire for sexual activity.
4. Anger   lack of self-control over emotions.
5. Gluttony intemperance in eating or drinking.
6. Envy   jealousy or sadness at another's good fortune.
7. Sloth   excessive laziness which prevents us from doing what is expected of us in our duties to God, and others.

Scriptural reference: St. Mark 7:21-23

THE FRUITS OF THE HOLY SPIRIT

Orthodoxy believes that once the work of Christ's redemption was complete, our continued sanctification is accomplished by the work of the Holy Spirit. St. Athanasius recognized this fact when he said, "The Word-Christ-took flesh that we might receive the Holy Spirit."

At Pentecost, 50 days after Pascha, this Spirit came upon the early believers and the work of God's great love for us was continued. Every Orthodox Christian, therefore, is called upon to "acquire the Holy Spirit." Subsequently, when we perform good works in the name of Christ we will obtain the fruits of the Spirit, who will then guide us to the Truth.

Scriptural references: Acts 2:1-4, Acts 20:16, Galatians 5:22-23

This is why the faithful Orthodox Christian, in daily Morning Prayers, implores the Holy Spirit to enter his or her life, and work His Divine love in their hearts:

"Heavenly King, Comforter, Spirit of Truth, Who is everywhere present and fills all things, Treasury of Blessings and Giver of Life, come and abide in us , cleanse us from all impurity, and save our souls, O Good One."

These Fruits of the Holy Spirit, whereby we know we are squarely on the path of righteousness, and fulfilling our role as faithful Orthodox believers, include:

1. Love	7. Long Suffering
2. Joy	8. Mildness
3. Peace	9. Fidelity
4. Patience	10. Modesty
5. Kindness	11. Self-control
6. Goodness	12. Chastity

Scriptural references: Galatians: 5:22, Rom. 8:23-26, Galatians 5:17-21.

THE THEOLOGICAL VIRTUES
The virtues that have God as their object.

FAITH   – belief in God's infallible teaching
HOPE   – confidence in Divine assistance
CHARITY   – love of God and others

> *"Faith, hope and love (charity) abide... and the greatest of these is love."*
> *1 Corinthians 13:13*

THE FOUR CARDINAL VIRTUES

PRUDENCE   to use discretion in all things; careful management of one's life
JUSTICE   moral rightness; honesty ; fairness; equity; use of law in relation to others
TEMPERANCE   moderation and self-restraint in all matters
FORTITUDE   strength of mind which allows one to endure troubles with courage

THE THREE DANGERS TO THE SOUL

The World
The Flesh
The Devil

THE CORPORAL WORKS OF MERCY
Those works that pertain to helping our brothers and sisters in need.

1. Feed the hungry.
2. Give drink to those who thirst.
3. Clothe the naked.
4. Ransom captives or those who have an addiction and are slaves to dangerous conduct.
5. Shelter the homeless.
6. Visit the sick and dying.
7. Bury the dead.

Orthodox Christians are called upon to practice merciful acts for those less fortunate and in need. Holy Scripture commands this of all who claim to be followers of Christ.

> "Whoever does not love a brother (or sister) in need whom he has seen, cannot love God whom he has not seen."
>
> 1 John 4:20

> "Whoever says he loves God and yet hates his brother is a liar."
>
> 1 John 4:20

> "You are to love (and assist) your neighbor as yourself."
>
> St. Matthew 19:19

THE SPIRITUAL WORKS OF MERCY COMMANDED BY THE CHURCH

1. Admonish and teach the sinner.
2. Instruct the ignorant.
3. Counsel the doubtful.
4. Comfort those who are sorrowful.
5. Bear wrongs patiently.
6. Forgive all injuries.
7. Pray always for the living and the dead.

THE CHIEF AIDS TO RECOGNIZING OUR SIN AND CONFESSING OUR SORROW FOR THESE OFFENSES

> "If we confess our sins, He who is faithful and just will forgive us our sins and cleanse us from all unrighteousness."
>
> 1 John 1:9

We recognize our sins and atone for them through:
1. Prayer.
2. Fasting.
3. Performing Spiritual and Corporal Acts of Mercy.

SETTING YOUR PRIORITIES

> "Set your mind on things above, not on things on the earth."
>
> Colossians 3:2

> "Do not love the world or the things in the world. If anyone loves the world, the love of the Father is not in him. For all that is in this world – the lust of the flesh, the lust of the eyes, and the pride of life – is not of the Father but is of the world."
>
> 1 John 2:15-16

"There is hope of mercy in time and eternity; but there is confession in time only, and not in eternity. There is no confession of sins in any time except in this present life. By his own will, each man is permitted and has, throughout life, the freedom to choose confession. But when we die, we lose life, and along with it, the right to exercise our will."

St. Hilary of Poitiers

ORTHODOX CHURCH LAWS
Duties of Orthodox Christians

1. Pray to Almighty God; attend Divine Liturgy on Sundays and all appointed feasts of the Church.

2. Keep the Fast periods as prescribed by the Church.

3. Make your confession and receive Holy Communion often.

4. Pray to Almighty God for our spiritual and temporal rulers and every estate of mankind.

5. Observe the Fasts, Marriage regulations, and other laws of the Church as stipulated in Orthodox Tradition.

6. Contribute and support special projects of the Church for the upkeep of the poor and less fortunate.

7. Refrain from celebrating Marriage at forbidden times.

(Make sure you are free to marry the person to whom you have committed yourself.)

8. Show proper respect to the clergy of the Church.

WHAT ARE THE DUTIES OF ORTHODOX CHRISTIANS TOWARDS THEMSELVES ?

1. Preserve our honor and respect among others.

2. Be good stewards of those things which God has given us.

3. Practice humility and charity at all times.

4. Remember that our bodies are the Temple of the Holy Spirit. Keep them healthy and free from anything which could bring them destruction.

5. Attend Divine Liturgy on Sundays and feast days, observe the Fasts of the Church, practice charity and almsgiving.

6. Read Holy Scripture regularly.

7. Keep the Commandments of Almighty God.

8. Practice the commands of Christ as found in the Beatitudes (St. Matthew, Chapter 5).

GUIDES FOR THE CONTEMPORARY ORTHODOX CHRISTIAN

1. Know that God exists, and that Christ, His Son is the center and being of our lives. Believe that union with Christ is the goal of all human destiny.

2. Keep the commitment to the promises made for you at Baptism, with regular attendance at Divine Services and the pious reception of the Holy Mysteries.

3. Develop a life of true prayer and union with God.
   (*See: Baptismal Promises*)

4. Live the words of the Creed and the Commandments in advancing your life, while forming an Orthodox Christian system of values.

5. Recognize the presence of Christ in the Church, listen to its legitimate leaders and cooperate with all the members of the Church who strive to do His will.

6. Develop a deep and abiding concern for the unfortunate around you, those who are also God's creation, whether they be destitute, ill, lonely, homeless or hated for their goodness. Keep their needs constantly in your prayers and offer the precious gift of your time, talents, and resources for their welfare.

7. Live each day as if it were your last. Before each action ask if this would be pleasing to Jesus Christ. Pray without ceasing to discover God's will for your life.

8. Respect yourself and others as a child of God, also those who have positions of authority and responsibility. Pray that they will fulfill their roles with dignity and devotion.

9. Read Holy Scripture and good Orthodox literature to increase knowledge of your Faith. Take every opportunity to learn what the Church teaches. God gave us His Church to sanctify us, teach us, and keep us in His love. Honor the Church and keep her laws.

"By this you know the Spirit of God; every spirit that confesses Jesus Christ has come in the flesh – is of God."

1 John 4:2

"Whoever confesses that Jesus is the Son of God, God abides in him, and he in God."

1 John 4:15

5. FASTING: A NOBLE DISCIPLINE
Fasting

Fasting is an integral part of living an authentic Orthodox Christian life.

As human beings we are composed of body and soul. We discipline our souls by prayer, sober living and the Holy Mysteries. Our bodies are controlled and disciplined by fasting from both food and iniquities.

In Isaiah 58:6-7, the Scriptures tell us:

"Is this not the Fast I choose: to loose the bonds of injustice, to undo the thongs of the yoke, to let the oppressed go free, and to break every yoke?

Is it not to share your bread with the hungry, and that you bring the homeless into your house; or when you see the naked to cover them, and not to hide yourself from your own kin?"

Fasting from food, performing virtuous works, and avoiding iniquities are positive actions. They are not meant as self-punishment or to placate a vengeful God, but to maintain a life of self-control and authentic spiritual growth.

Fasting is a virtue and Orthodox Christians should know the rules of the Church regarding the Fasts as a basis of a healthy spiritual life.

PERIODS OF FASTING

The Great Fast or **Lent**, begins seven weeks before Pascha, including Holy Week.

The Fast of the Apostles begins on Monday, eight days after the Feast of Pentecost, and ends on June 28th, the eve of the Feast of Ss. Peter and Paul. Its length varies depending on the Feast of Pentecost.

The Dormition Fast lasts for fourteen days from August 1-14.
The Dormition is "The Falling Asleep of the Theotokos."

The Nativity Fast lasts forty days from November 15th to December 24th.

A good Orthodox calendar will denote the exact days of the yearly Fasts. In addition to the yearly Fasts, there is a weekly fast on Wednesday and Friday except for the time between the Nativity and Epiphany (Baptism of Christ) .

Other fast-free periods fall during Bright Week – (the seven days after Pascha), during the week following the Feast of Pentecost, and the week following the Sunday of the Publican and Pharisee – which begins four weeks before the Great Fast.

The Eve of the Nativity of Christ, along with the Exaltation of the Cross on Sept. 14th, the Beheading of St. John the Baptist on Aug. 29th, and the Eve of the Epiphany on Jan. 6. These are strict fast days.

The week following Meat Fare Sunday – two Sundays before the Great Fast – calls for abstinence from flesh-meat but no other fasting is required. In fact, any other fasting during a fast – free period is discouraged.

Through fasting we imitate those in Paradise before the "Fall of Adam and Eve," thus raising ourselves to an image of spiritual renewal and perfection.

The **general Rules of Fasting** in Orthodoxy are as follows:

• On a fast day we do not eat any animal products. This includes any part of a mammal or fowl, fish and by-products of these animals (milk, cheese, eggs).

• Wine is allowed on specific fast days. A good Church calendar will list these days.

• There are fast days when fish is allowed along with wine and oil.

• Shellfish are allowed on all fast days. (Turtle and frog legs are included in this context).

Scriptural references: 1 Corinthians 7:5, St. Matthew 17:21, Joel 2:12.

Non-dairy substitutes are often employed on fast days along with vegetable oils which do not violate the spirit of the Fast.

There are more specific fasting rules which are published by most jurisdictions, or in parish bulletins. Remember, however, that when we fast we must avoid a spirit of judgment or a feeling of superiority over those who do not fast. Our good example of fasting should serve as just that, an example for other Orthodox Christians to follow more closely the Tradition of the Church.

On Fasting

"Any time is the right time for works of charity, but these days of Lent provide a special encouragement. Those who want to be present at the Lord's Passover in holiness of mind and body should seek above all to win this grace, for charity contains all other virtues and covers a multitude of sins...

As we prepare to celebrate the greatest of all mysteries, by which the blood of Jesus did away with our sins, let us first of all make ready the sacrificial offering of works of mercy...

In this way we shall give to those who have sinned against us what God in His goodness has already given to us. Let us now extend to the poor and those afflicted in different ways a more open-handed generosity, so that God may be thanked through many voices and the relief of the needy supported by our fasting. No act of devotion on the part of the faithful gives God more pleasure than that which is lavished on the poor.

St. Leo, Pope of Rome +461

An Historical Note About Orthodoxy # 2

Orthodoxy maintains the purity of the Faith, not only by her teachings but also by the way in which we worship Almighty God. It is a commonly known fact that we understand what a Faith teaches by the way it worships. Jesus Christ Himself taught this to the woman at the well. "But the hour comes, and now is, when true worshipers shall worship the Father in spirit and in truth" (John 4:24). So our Faith is reflected in our liturgy and we know that there was a basic pattern of worship from the first days. The life of the early believers was lived in the liturgy of the Church. In their prayers the early Christian communities unfolded the truths of the Gospel for which they were willing to sacrifice their very lives.

There are also moments in life that are made holy by the worship of the Church. Holy Baptism and Chrismation ("being sealed with the Holy Spirit") were there from the beginning, as was the Eucharist , which imparts the very Body and Blood of Our Lord, who promised to feed us on our earthly journey through life. Confession of sin, healing, marriage and provisions for the official ministry of the Church are also integral parts of her worship. Therefore, the Church proclaimed and practiced what she taught, through worship, from the very first days of her existence.

Repentance for Sin

"I tell you, no; but unless you repent you will all likewise perish."

Acts 17:30

Then Peter said to them, "Repent, and let every one of you be baptized in the name of Jesus Christ for the remission of sins; and you shall receive the gift of the Holy Spirit. Repent, therefore and be converted, that your sins may be blotted out, so that times of refreshing may come from the presence of the Lord."

Acts 2: 38; 3:19

"How can a man ask for himself what he refuses to give to another? If he expects to receive any mercy in heaven, he should have mercy on earth... Human mercy has compassion on the miseries of the poor. Divine mercy grants forgiveness of sins...Remember, it was Christ who said, "I was hungry and you gave me nothing to eat." When the poor are starving, Christ hungers. Do not neglect to improve the unhappy conditions of the poor if you wish to ensure that your own sins be forgiven you...Show mercy, then, while you are on earth, and mercy will be shown you in heaven."

St. Caesarius , Bishop of Arles +542

TITHING – RETURNING THE GIFTS OF GOD

God provides us with the gifts of life and the means of existence (St. Matthew 6:24-34). He expects us to use His gifts wisely and with compassion.

The tithe is a voluntary offering of ten percent of one's income to God, to whom it belongs in the first place. This is a practice found in Holy Scripture whereby God's People return a portion of what He gives them as an act of obedience and true worship.

Tithing is Scriptural. In the Bible we see that Abraham gave Melchisedek, a priest of the Most High God, a full tenth of all he had (Genesis 14:18-20). But later in Genesis, Jacob had a vision from God. He saw ascending and descending angels on a ladder. As a thanksgiving for all that God did for him, Jacob set up an altar of stone and made a vow that he would return ten percent of what he had to honor God Almighty (Genesis 28:22).

Later on, Malachi, God's prophet (around the year 400 B.C.), tells the corrupt people of his time that they are robbing God of the honor due Him by offering only the worst of their flocks for the people's needs. Since even the priests were corrupt, and most everyone in Israel was unfaithful, Malachi warns them that they are, in fact, stealing what is God's. The people continued in their blasphemy and God responds by telling them, "Will a man rob God?

Yet, you have robbed me. And you say, Wherein have we robbed you? (I say) in tithes and offerings. You are cursed with a curse; for you have robbed me, even this whole nation" (Malachi 3:8-9).

Tithing then, is tied to worship and related to communion with God, who promises that those who share with Him and others will be blessed abundantly; "I will open the windows of heaven, and pour out to you a blessing, that there shall not be room enough to receive it" (Malachi 3:10-11).

Christ taught us that this practice of the Old Testament should not be neglected. Along with the major commands of practicing justice, mercy and faithfulness, Our Lord tells the Pharisees, in St. Matthew 23:23, never to forget the duty to return to God the things which rightfully belong to Him. Jesus never abrogated the duty to tithe goods. We are called to imitate Christ if, however, this proves impossible we can give a share of our time to continue the work of the Church.

Orthodox Christians should be generous in support of their particular parish or diocese. If they aren't able to tithe then they should do what they can to help Christ's Church. If financial giving causes great hardship then a tithe of time and special talents to your parish is always in order. To do less is to cheat God and show a callous disregard of His loving generosity and goodness.

6. WORSHIP - RETURNING THE GIFT

SOME GUIDELINES FOR ORTHODOX WORSHIP

Here are some traditional practices – in summary form – for those who wish to maintain an honest and devout spiritual life in the Orthodox Church.

Attend Divine Liturgy each Sunday and on feast days. Fast – with nothing to eat – from midnight before the Liturgy, when you are receiving the Holy Eucharist.

After entering the church building, reverence the icons and light a candle, then offer your prayer. Return to your place and await the start of the services. In many parishes pews are the norm, although there are still places where seating is unavailable. Here, standing is the normal posture with men on the right hand side and women on the left. Other parishes no longer follow this custom and families gather together, with no separation according to gender.

Women should have their heads covered and all in attendance should, out of respect for Christ, the King of Kings, be dressed in proper clothing, not in attire reserved for recreation or servile work. Unclean clothing is totally out of place in church, one's best should be reserved for the Lord.

Children should attend services with their family, even from an early age. The service should be quiet, dignified, conducted in subdued light with great piety.

A parish "community meal" usually follows Divine Liturgy-and all should try to attend. Even if the meal is as modest as a "coffee hour" the faithful should make an effort to be there and not rush to their car immediately after services.

PROPER CHURCH MANNERS FOR ORTHODOX CHRISTIANS

1. Arrive at the church fifteen minutes before the start of the Divine Liturgy.
2. If unavoidably late enter the church at a quiet moment.
3. Take part in the service with responses and appropriate gestures.
4. Sing the hymns, bow your head and make the Sign of the Cross at appropriate times during the Divine Liturgy.
5. Practice good manners in consideration of others. If you have disturbed worship for any one person, your manners have been poor.
6. Never miss the Divine Liturgy on Sunday or feasts, except for serious reasons.
7. Never smoke outside (or inside) the church building, nor gossip. Avoid spending your time in the church's recreation area, or undercroft, during the services to gossip or "socialize." Remember, you are in church to worship Almighty God, not to visit with friends or catch up on the latest news.

After entering an Orthodox Church there are several basic things one should remember in order to show respect to Almighty God, and the place where He dwells, along with appropriate manners, and consideration for other worshipers.

Enter the church and make the Sign of the Cross - three times, bowing from the waist each time – while saying:

> "Thou has created me, O Lord, have mercy."
> "O God, be merciful to me, a sinner."
> "Countless times have I sinned O Lord, forgive me."

Having reverenced the icons return to your place and follow the services with due respect listening intently to the prayers and the chants.

Prostrations and bows should not be made indiscriminately, (as seems to be a growing, yet erroneous, custom) but at the proper times such as:

At the Trisagion, "Holy God"…

At "O come, Let us worship"…

At the Three-fold Alleluia, make the Sign of the Cross three times with bows.

At "Vouchsafe O Lord" make the Sign of the Cross with bows.

At the beginning of the Great Doxology, "Glory to God in the highest…"

After the words of the priest, "Glory to Thee O Christ our hope."

After each exclamation of the priest and at the words "More honorable than the Cherubim…", one makes the Sign of the Cross with a bow.

Orthodox Christians usually do not kneel, but when the priest or deacon exclaims "Again and again, on bended knee" one bows with face to the ground.

Whenever people are blessed with the Gospel Book, the Holy Cross, an icon or chalice, they make the Sign of the Cross, bowing the head.

When blessed with candles, or the hands of the priest, or when censed, we do not make the Sign of the Cross, but simply bow the head.

During the week of Holy Pascha, when the priest censes with Cross in hand, we make the Sign of the Cross and answer the proclamation, "Christ is risen from the dead!" with "Truly, He is risen!"

When receiving a blessing from a bishop we kiss his right hand without making the Sign of the Cross. Do not kiss the left hand of the clergy (this is a pre- Christian custom), but the right hand with which the blessing was given.

> *"Let no one, conscious of his sinfulness, withdraw from our common celebration, nor let anyone be kept away from our public prayer by the burden of his guilt. Sinner he may be indeed, but he must not despair of the heart, especially on this day which is so highly privileged. For if a thief could receive the grace of paradise, how could a Christian be refused forgiveness?"*
>
> *Maximus of Turin, 5th century*

QUESTIONS ORTHODOX CHRISTIANS SHOULD ASK THEMSELVES
… at regular intervals:

1. Do I continually learn about my Faith, its teachings and Tradition?

2. Do I attempt to keep the Church's regulations in regard to fasting, worship and performing charitable works?

3. Do I examine my conscience at regular intervals during the week, not just before approaching the Mystery of Confession and Penance?

4. Do I attend Divine Liturgy, festal liturgies , or other services of the Church on a regular basis?

5. Do I offer my talents to Almighty God by singing in church, by serving in the sanctuary, in Christian education, visiting the sick or performing other works of mercy?

6. Do I keep myself from individuals and organizations which present a danger to my beliefs?

7. Do I stay away from people, occasions or places which would compromise me and lead me into sin?

8. Do I attempt to bring peace to my parish rather than dissension? Do I stand with my priest and support his policies to benefit the parish?

9. Am I an example of Orthodoxy which brings credit to the Church or do I bring discredit to the Faith by actions which divide the parish? Do I use the excuse that I am trying to "save" the parish from "those who were not born here," simply to advance my own selfishness?

HOW SHOULD WE OBSERVE THE GREAT FAST ?

"Behold the Bridegroom comes in the middle of the night, and blessed is the servant whom He shall find watching."

Matthew 25:6-13

PRACTICAL SUGGESTIONS FOR OBSERVING THE FAST

1. Limit the amount of time you spend watching television, listening to audio equipment or the radio. Use media such as the Internet sparingly except for spiritual reading or religious-oriented programming. This is no time for mere recreation, or mindless entertainment.

2. Do not recreate continually unless there is a firm reason for your activity. Keep useless talking to a minimum. Conduct only necessary business, and works of Christian charity.

3. Examine your life in every realm: family, work, society, politics, economics, values, and desires in relation to the life and teachings of Jesus Christ.

4. Question yourself as to how you exhibit love, truth, honesty, humility, peace, forgiveness, justice, mercy, hungering and thirsting for God, wisdom, and knowledge.

5. In the name of Our Lord, forgive all who have offended you in some way,

and ask forgiveness of others. If it will not be an embarrassment to others, misinterpreted as pompousness or a show of insincere piety, make this act of asking forgiveness as concrete as possible. Visit, make a phone call, write a letter, or perform some act to ask pardon for your sin or offer your own forgiveness to others, whom you may have wronged or offended.

6. Donate money to others – to the Church, to some poor family, some social or educational work of which you know. Be sure not to tell anyone what you have done. Ask nothing in return and do not advertise your goodness in any way.

7. Maintain the Fast as much as possible. Try to avoid all flesh meat. This should be the absolute minimum requirement of the Fast and an example of practicing self-control. In trying to observe the Fast as prescribed by the Church, use no meat, fish, eggs, or dairy products – no oil or wine except on Saturday and Sunday and a few special feasts. By fasting, you are showing your willingness to prioritize your life and illustrate that things of the spirit (self-control, moderation and prayer) which are paramount in the life of an Orthodox Christian. The Fast may be lessened, or changed for yourself, if you have a blessing from your spiritual father or confessor. With this blessing you may mitigate the Fast due to work, medical problems, or other situations. But even then, avoid extremes and tell no one the details of your Lenten pilgrimage.

   After establishing a fast from certain foods, attack the most difficult and subtle dangers to your salvation – those sins of flesh and spirit which hinder your growth and Christian attitude – sins such as hatred, selfish ness, lust, pride , extravagance, jealousy and a mean spirit. Again, do not advertise what you're doing and above all do not judge others who may not seem to be fasting. It may be possible that their personal struggle is, in reality, much more difficult than your own.

8. Observe prayer time at home, school, or work, at least once each day, preferably at the same time. Observe a short Rule of Prayer, but keep it faithfully every day of the Fast. If you are able to pray more often, and at greater length, so much the better.

9. Study the Holy Scriptures in a regular way each day by observing the Church calendar of readings. Set your mind to complete one of the Holy Gospels each week and the following books of the New Testament: The First Letter of St. John, Paul's Letter to the Romans, (chapters 12 through 16) , 1 Corinthians (any section) and the short Epistles near the end of the New Testament; 1, 2 Timothy; Titus; Hebrews; 1, 2 Peter; 1, 2, 3 of St. John; and Jude.

10. Observe the Commandments and practice the Gospel of Jesus Christ in your every word, thought or action.

Mercy and Charity During the Great Fast

"The earth bears crops for your benefit, not for its own: but when you give to the poor, you are bearing fruit which you will gather in for yourself, since the reward for good deeds goes to those who perform them. Give to a hungry man, and what you give becomes yours, indeed it returns to you with interest. As a sower profits from the seed which falls to the ground, you profit greatly, in the world to come, from the bread that you place before a hungry man. You are going to leave your money behind you here whether you wish to or not. On the other hand, you will take with you to the Lord, the honor that you have won through good works."

St. Basil of Caesarea

"It is folly to abstain all day long from food, but then fail to abstain from sin and selfishness."

St. John Chrysostom

"The Fast of Lent has no advantage to us unless it brings about our spiritual renewal. It is necessary while fasting to change our whole life and practice virtue.

Turning away from all wickedness means keeping our tongue in check, restraining our anger, avoiding all gossip, lying and swearing. To abstain from these things-herein is the true value of the Fast."

St. John Chrysostom

"It is possible for one who fasts not to be rewarded for his fasting. How? When, indeed, we abstain from foods, but do not abstain from inequities: when we do not eat meat, but gnaw to pieces the homes of the poor, when we do not become drunkards with wine, but become drunkards with evil pleasures; when we abstain all the day, but all the night we spend in profane entertainment. Then what is the benefit of abstention from foods, when on the one hand you deprive your body of a selected food, but on the other, offer yourself unlawful pleasure?"

St. John Chrysostom

"I acknowledge my transgressions," says David. "If I admit my fault, then Thou will pardon it." Let us never assume that if we live good lives we will be without sin; our lives should be praised only when we continue to beg for pardon. But men are hopeless creatures, and the less they concentrate on their own sins, the more interested they become in the sins of others. They seek to criticize, not to correct. Unable to excuse themselves, they are ready to accuse others."

St. Augustine

COMMEMORATION LISTS

The Church has always encouraged the commemoration of the departed in our prayers. It is vitally important to the life of the Church to remember the dead, since earthly believers are but a part of the Christian Community. We must always remember that those who have reposed are also members – so we must include the departed in the services of the Church at every appropriate opportunity. During the Great Fast take time to update and offer commemorations for the reposed on a regular basis.

It is known that those who have gone on before us to be with the Lord, have appeared to the living to request their prayers and to remind them of the importance of these earthly commemorations. Remembrances are appropriate throughout the Church Year, but especially during the periods of fasting and earnest prayer.

Most churches have commemoration lists at the candlestand, and some even have small booklets with places for listing both the living and the dead. These names are commemorated by the priest at the Proskomedia, or Service of Preparation, before the Divine Liturgy.

Some rules for preparing the commemoration lists :

1. Separate the names into the departed and living.
2. Proper baptismal names should be used, not nicknames.
3. Make sure the names are legible and that there are not numerous slips of paper which are easily misplaced. One list is sufficient, on one sheet of paper.
4. We commemorate Orthodox faithful at the Divine Liturgy. Separate lists for non-Orthodox may be commemorated with appropriate prayers.
5. Lists should be kept up-dated , with recently departed so noted.
6. Clergy and monastics should be given their proper title, i.e. bishop, priest, deacon, hieromonk, monk, nun, etc.
7. Make sure the custom of the parish is followed in providing the lists to the priest. They are either given at the candlestand or to an usher, who will see that the priest receives them in time for the proper commemorations to be made.

Fasting During Great Lent

"With the return of that season marked out in a special way by the mystery of redemption, and of the days that lead up to the Paschal Feast, we are summoned more urgently to prepare ourselves by a purification of spirit...Initially all men are made new by the rebirth of Baptism. Yet there is still a daily renewal required to repair the shortcomings of our

mortal nature. All must therefore strive to ensure that on the day of redemption no one may be found in the sins of his former life.

Dear friends, what the Christian should be doing at all times should be done now (during the Great Fast) with great care and devotion, so that the Fast enjoined by the apostles may be fulfilled, not simply by abstinence from food, but above all by the renunciation of sin."

Pope St. Leo of Rome

The Promises of Christ

"I will see you again and your heart will rejoice; and your joy no one will take from you."

St. John 16:22

"These things I have spoken to you, that my joy may remain in you, and that your joy may be full."

St. John 15:11

"Because there are two periods of time-the one that is now, beset with the trials and troubles of life, and the other yet to come, a life of everlasting serenity and joy – we are given two liturgical seasons, one before Pascha and the other after. The season before Pascha signifies the troubles in which we live here and now.

What we commemorate before Pascha is what we experience in this life; what we celebrate after Pascha points to something we do not yet possess. This is why we keep the first season with fasting and prayer...Both these periods are represented and demonstrated for us in Christ our head. The Lord's Passion depicts for us our present life of trial and shows how much we must suffer, and be afflicted and finally die."

St. Augustine

"How can a man ask for himself what he refuses to give to another? If he expects to receive any mercy in heaven, he should have mercy on earth. Human mercy has compassion on the miseries of the poor. Divine Mercy grants forgiveness of sins. Remember, it was Christ who said: "I was hungry and you gave me nothing to eat. When the poor are starving, Christ hungers. Do not neglect to improve the unhappy conditions of the poor, if you wish to ensure that your own sins be forgiven you. Show mercy, then, while you are on earth, and mercy will be shown you in heaven."

St. Caesarius, Bishop of Arles + 542

"You have conquered your flesh? Then conquer your tongue also. It does you no good to be free from one thing if you are a slave to something else."

"The sister and friend of the Fast is prayer."

"The external Fast is not always necessary. But the internal Fast from iniquities is necessary at all times."

St. Nil

"One will possess the Holy Spirit only in proportion to his reverence for, and adhesion to, the Church of Christ."

St. Augustine

"He who does not have the Church as his mother cannot have God for his father."

St. Cyprian

ON THE DUTY OF THE FLOCK TOWARD THE PASTOR
by St. Tikhon of Zadonsk

"Because the pastor speaks the Word of God, do whatever he teaches, pay diligent heed, all Christians, and do it. Concerning this, the apostle says, "Obey them that have rule over you, and submit yourselves; for they must watch for your souls, as they that must give account, that they may do it with joy, and not with grief; for that is unprofitable for you" (Hebrews 13:17).

The pastor is the messenger of God who is sent to you by God, and He proclaims to you the way of salvation, and invites you in the name of God into His eternal Kingdom. For this reason, revere him as the messenger of God who proclaims to you such great good things, and who invites you to them. "He who receives you, receives me," says the Lord (Matthew 10:40). Receive, then, and revere the pastor as the messenger of Christ.

Because the pastor provides for the common good, and as he looks after you as well as for all, so that all may receive eternal salvation, then love him as your father and benefactor, and be grateful to him. You call him "Father," that is well: he begets you as well as others, not to the temporary, but to eternal life. Then love him, as so great a father to you. You love your own father according to the flesh, how much more ought you love this "Father."

As he takes care and provides for all, and for you, do not leave him in need, but help him in his requests and supply his needs, that he may have time to take care and look after the common good. Thus by mutual love and benediction the common good will not be without success.

Because many among the people are not men of goodwill, and as they do not love pastoral reproof but wish to live according to their own will, they invent and broadcast no little slander and ill report against the pastor.

Then when you hear such slander and ill report against the pastor, do not believe it and guard your lips, lest you say anything about it to anyone else. Otherwise you will sin gravely, as you will return evil for good, which is a great iniquity. It is a serious thing to slander and dishonor a simple person, how much more so a pastor. From this, great discord follows among the people, and disregard and disobedience to the pastor, and thus his labor may end without profit. Pay careful attention to this, avoid evil gossip against the pastor. Most of all do not spread evil gossip about him, lest you feel the avenging hand of God upon you.

If you see in the pastor such weaknesses as occur even among the people, do not be scandalized and do not judge him, but understand that the pastor is a man, just like everyone else, and that he has the same weaknesses as do the rest of the people.

Because the pastor is subject to many temptations, and the Devil, and his evil servants war against him most especially, therefore he also needs the special help and support of God. Then you, and all the people as well, must pray to God for him that He may help him and strengthen him.

The happiness of the household depends on a good householder, the happiness of soldiers depends on a good commander, and the happiness of the sailing ship depends on a good helmsman. Pray then that the pastor may be wise and good, and that Christian society may be happy.

When a pastor himself does not do what he teaches, but lives contrary to his teaching, heed the word of Christ which He spoke concerning such pastors, "The scribes and pharisees sit in the seat of Moses, therefore all they bid you observe, that observe and do, but do not imitate their works, for they say, and do not do" (St. Matthew 23:2-3).

An excerpt from "Journey to Heaven," Jordanville, NY 1991. Used with permission.

7. THE HOLY MYSTERIES – GIFTS OF SALVATION

THE MYSTERIES (SACRAMENTS) OF THE ORTHODOX CHURCH

A well-known prayer of the Church describes the Spirit of God as "present in all places and filling all things." Since God is intimately concerned with each of His children He is truly near to us in many unseen ways. The Creator is not remote or detached from His Creation. Everything we do and all that is done for us in the Church, is sacred and reveals the love of Almighty God. He made us for Himself and we find our only true destiny in returning His great love for us. Therefore, simply put, the Mysteries of the Church are ways in which God shows forth His very special concern, that He does not abandon us in our earthly struggle. God's spirit works in, and through, the Mysteries and we are drawn ever-closer to God in these visible actions of the Church.

The Mysteries take place within the community of the Church, just as our individual salvation finds itself in the whole Church, not in isolation to others, or via selfish man-made schemes. The Mysteries of the Church are gifts from God whereby we are made holy while drawing closer to Our Heavenly Father. They are sacred acts shown forth through material means such as water, bread, wine, oil and other elements.

THE MOST COMMON HOLY MYSTERIES:

1. Holy Eucharist
   1 Corinthians 11:23-25

2. Baptism
   St. Matthew 28:19, Romans 6:4

3. Chrismation
   St. John 14:16, Acts 2:38, Acts 2:16-21, John 7:37-39

4. Confession (Penance)
   1 John 1:9, St. Matthew 18:15-17, James 5:16, St. John 20:23

5. Marriage
   1 Corinthians 7:4, Ephesians 5:23

6. Holy Orders
   St. John 15:16, Acts 1:26, Acts 6:3-6

7. Holy Unction
   (Anointing of the Sick) James 5:14-15

Note: Each of these most common Mysteries (Sacraments) has a place in this Handbook and can be referred to individually.

The Mysteries – Sacraments – are not limited to seven. This number has its roots in Latin ecclesiology. Orthodox theology, however, knows that God's love cannot be reduced to a set number.

> *"As we acknowledge only one God, so too can there be only one Faith, and one interpretation of the Truth."*
>
> *St. Liberatus*

> *"Heretics think and teach false things about God and religion; then they call this the "New Faith".*
>
> *St. Augustine*

THE MYSTERY (SACRAMENT) OF BAPTISM

The Mystery of Baptism incorporates us into Christ's Church and is the means by which each of us shares in the death and resurrection of Jesus Christ. After becoming members of the Church through immersion in water we begin a new life as a Christian, as one who lives in, through, and for, Christ. We become, in the waters of Baptism, new creatures in the Lord. "Therefore, if anyone is in Christ, he is a new creation, old things have passed away; behold all things have become new" (2 Corinthians 5:17).

Orthodoxy practices the ancient custom of the Church, which calls for triple-immersion in water. Pouring or sprinkling can be used only in emergencies, or at the point of death. We baptize infants, whom God chooses to be members of His People, and adults who have never been baptized in the name of the Holy Trinity.

Scriptural references: St. Matthew 28:19, Acts 2:38-46; 8:14-40, St. Mark 3:11, St. Mark 1:8, St. Luke 3:16, St. John 1: 25-34, St. John 4:1-2, St. John 3: 3-5, Ephesians 5:23-32 , Titus 3:5.

(Also see section on Holy Baptism)

THE MYSTERY (SACRAMENT) OF THE HOLY EUCHARIST

The Eucharist stands at the very heart of the Orthodox Christian's experience of life in the Church. The Eucharist, which comes from the Greek word for "thanksgiving," is sometimes called the "Mystery of Mysteries." It is, like Baptism, a celebration of the death and resurrection of Christ, who commanded us to continue the mystery of our redemption in the meal He ate with the apostles, the night before His death.

We celebrate the Eucharist each Sunday according to the most ancient tradition, and on each major feast day of the Church's calendar. There is no Church without the Eucharist since, from the very first days of the Faith Christians, "Day by day, spent much time in the Temple, and broke bread at home, eating this food with glad and generous hearts" (Acts 2: 46). Any group which does not have the Eucharist at the heart of its worship cannot properly call itself a Christian Church. As Felix, an early apologist of the Church, said quite clearly, "A Christian cannot exist without the Eucharist, neither can the Eucharist exist without Christians."

Scriptural references: St. Matthew 26:26-29, St. Luke 22:14-20, St. John 6:53-59, Acts 2:42-46, 1 Corinthians 11:23-25, Acts 20:7.

(Also see section on the Holy Eucharist)

THE DIVINE LITURGY

Its History and Meaning

Liturgy means the public work of the Church done for the benefit of the people. Since New Testament times "liturgy" has come to mean the sacred functions of the Church such as the celebration of the Holy Eucharist, Baptism, etc. Thus we use the term "Divine Liturgy" for the Eucharistic service which is at the core of our Faith as Orthodox Christians.

The Divine Liturgy is the central act of worship in the Orthodox Church. It is offered to Almighty God for the benefit of the members of the Church, but above all it is the Divine Gift whereby God's People are nourished with the Body and Blood of Christ.

Our Lord, Jesus Christ, is present at the Divine Liturgy which joins heaven and earth. The priest acts as Christ's servant representing the Royal Priesthood of the people. This is in fulfillment of Christ's promise that when two or three are gathered in His name, He is there, mystically, in the New Kingdom (St. Matthew 18:20).

The Gospel reflects the glory of the Word, who is Christ, unseen, though truly present, among His People.

We believe that our Lord cares for us and wants to be with the people He loves. He wants to feed us on our journey through life with His holy Body and Blood, in His holy Word, and through the sacramental ministrations of His Church. Even when Jesus walked upon the earth He was concerned with feeding His flock, as in the miraculous feeding of the 5000 by multiplying five loaves of bread and two fish. The next day He was in Capernaum, where the people asked for more of that wonderful bread. Instead of feeding them with actual food He said to them "I am the bread of life... I am the living bread which came down from heaven, if any man eat of this bread, he shall live for ever, and the bread that I will give is my Flesh which I give for the life of the world" (St. John 6:1-14; 48-59).

The Lord went on, "Truly, truly I say to you, except you eat of the Flesh of the Son of Man and drink His Blood you have no life in you...Whosoever eats my Flesh and drinks my Blood has eternal life, and I will raise him up on the last day. He that eats my Flesh and drinks my Blood dwells in me, and I in him" (St. John 6:34-56).

With the words above, our Lord promised to give His Flesh and Blood to be the food and drink of the world.

Again, on the night before His crucifixion, Christ gathered His apostles together to share a last earthly meal with them. As they were eating, our Lord took one of the loaves of bread, blessed it and said:

"Take eat, this is my Body which is broken for you" (St. Luke 22:19).

Taking a cup He pronounced a blessing and said:

"Drink you all of it, for this is my Blood of the New Testament, which is shed for you" (St. Luke 22:20).

> *"As long as the prayers and invocations have not yet been made, (the Eucharist) is mere bread and a mere cup. But when the great and wondrous prayers have been recited, then the bread becomes the Body and the cup, the Blood, of Our Lord Jesus Christ. The Word descends on the bread and cup and it becomes His Body and Blood."*
>
> *St. Athanasius*

> *St. Ignatius of Antioch said: "Hold one Eucharist, for one is the Flesh of our Lord Jesus Christ, one is the cup of union with His Blood. Then there should be one table as there is one bishop."*

THE HOLY EUCHARIST

The Holy Eucharist, the Divine Liturgy of the Church is the most ancient experience of Christian worship. "Eucharist" means "thanksgiving", and is traced back to the Mystical (Last) Supper which Christ celebrated with the apostles at the beginning of His passion and death.

(Actually, the term "Last Supper" is a misnomer since we have been spiritually fed by, and with Christ since that event countless times in the Holy Eucharist. A more appropriate term is "Mystical Supper.")

At this meal Christ instructed His disciples to offer the bread and wine in His memory, until He comes again. In the Eucharist the Church gathers to remember and celebrate, the life, death and glorious resurrection of Our Lord, as one family. In doing so, we thereby participate in the mystery of our own salvation.

Scriptural references: Acts 2:46, 1 Corinthians 10:14-22, 1 Corinthians 11:17-34.

The word "liturgy" ("the work of the people") serves to underscore the corporate character of the Eucharistic Rites. At the Divine Liturgy the Church assembles to worship the Holy Trinity. The Eucharist is truly the center of the life of the Church and the manner in which we nourish ourselves on our journey through life. The Eucharist, at the core of the Church, is "The Way" to eternal salvation, a term which was first given to the early faithful before they were properly known as "Christian," (Acts 11:26).

To understand how important the Eucharist is in the life of Christians, read the Gospel of St. John, 6:1-71. After reading this section you will gain a new appreciation for the Sunday liturgy and begin to understand more fully why the Eucharist must be at the very center of every Christian's life. If we do not commemorate and celebrate the Holy Eucharist every Sunday, we are denied the very essence of life itself.

Truly then, Christ gave His Flesh as food and His Blood as drink so that He might continue to actually live within us and be intimately present in our lives.

In order to perpetuate His memory Christ commanded His apostles to, "Do this in remembrance of me" (St. Luke 22:19). That is why the Divine Liturgy, the Holy Eucharist, is the highest form of thanksgiving to God that man has in his power to render.

The Holy Eucharist is the repetition of the Mystical Supper. It is also the self-same Sacrifice of the Cross, repeated sacramentally. This does not mean that is "done all over again" but rather, is "once again made actual and present" to those of us living today.

The Divine Liturgy is not a re-enactment of the Eucharistic Mystery, but a timeless, eternal recapitulation, or repetition (in concise form), and a true mystical participation in the Divine Kingdom.

From the very beginning of the Church the Eucharist was at the core of the life of the Faith. At first, it was celebrated as one rite but was later divided into two ritual actions – i.e., the Eucharist began with psalms, hymns and readings celebrated in the early morning hours and then the Agape, or Love Feast, was eaten in the evening. In this way the Holy Eucharist was celebrated as "thanksgiving" and a fellowship meal was eaten as a sign of spiritual nourishment and community with one another. In many parishes today it is usual to meet after the Divine Liturgy to share refreshments, however simple, and to socialize as a sign of our brotherhood before the Lord, and each other.

The Eucharist as Sacrifice

> "On every Lord's Day – His special day – come together to break bread and give thanks , first confessing your sins so that your sacrifice may be pure. Anyone at variance with his neighbor must not join you, until they are reconciled, lest your sacrifice be defiled. For it was of this sacrifice that the Lord said, "Always and everywhere offer me a pure sacrifice; for I am a great King and my name is marveled at by all nations."

The "Didache" (First Century)

"When partaking of the Eucharist you bury your teeth in Christ's Flesh and drink the same Blood that came from His side. He did not say, 'This is the symbol of my Body, and of my Blood, but "This IS my Body and Blood."

St. John Chrysostom

"The priest fulfills the role of Christ when he imitates what He did, and only then does he offer a true, complete sacrifice in the Church to the Father, when he begins to offer it after the pattern of Christ's offering... (in the Eucharist)...it is the Lord's passion that we offer."

St. Cyprian

"Do we offer sacrifice daily? We do indeed, but as a memorial of His death, and this oblation is single, not manifold. But how can it be one and not many? Because it has been offered once and for all, as was the ancient sacrifice in the Holy of Holies. This is the figure of that ancient sacrifice as indeed it was of this one; for it is the same Jesus Christ we offer always, not now one victim and later another. The victim is always the same, so that the sacrifice is one. Will we say that because Christ is offered in many places there are many Christ's? Of course not. We do not offer a different sacrifice, but always the same one, or rather we accomplish the memorial of it."

St. John Chrysostom

SUMMARY OF THE DIVINE LITURGY

The Opening Doxology – "Blessed is the Kingdom of the Father and of the Son and of the Holy Spirit," reminds us that we are in God's Holy House and are preparing to worship Him in glory and thanksgiving.

The Great Litany – during which we pray for the particular needs of our parish and those of the Universal Church.

The Antiphons and the Hymn to Christ – "Only Begotten Son" – expresses our sincere belief in Jesus Christ as true God and true man. We recognize Him as Our Savior.

The Troparia and Kontakia – these are variable hymns which introduce the theme of the day's liturgy.

The Small Entrance – the priest and acolytes proceed with the Gospel Book from the Holy Table to stand before the Royal Doors.

The Trisagion – "Holy God, Holy Mighty, Holy Immortal, have mercy on us" – is sung in praise of the Holy Trinity.

The Prokeimenon – is a psalm response sung before the readings from Holy Scripture.

The Epistle – a reading from the New Testament Epistles.

The Alleluia – psalm verses with the singing of "Alleluia," meaning "Praise the Lord."

The Gospel – selected from the Holy Gospels of Ss. Matthew, Mark, Luke and John.

The Homily or Sermon – delivered by the priest with lessons from the Gospels and how we might apply these teachings to our everyday lives.

THE VALUE OF THE HOLY EUCHARIST

> *"The value of the Holy Eucharist is eternal. We know this because Christ Himself said, "I am the living bread which came down from heaven; if anyone eats of this bread he will live forever; and the bread which I shall give for the life of the world is my Flesh."*
>
> St. John 6:51

> *"He who eats my Body and drinks my Blood has eternal life and I will raise him up on the last day. He who eats my Body and drinks my Blood abides in me and I in him...He who eats this bread will live forever."*
>
> St. John 6:54, 56, 58

> *"For this is my Blood of the New Covenant, which is shed for many for the remission of sins."*
>
> St. Matthew 26:28

The Cherubic Hymn – Great Entrance – while the Cherubic Hymn is being sung, the gifts of bread and wine are brought to the Holy Table.

The Peace – the priest turns to people and offers them the Peace of Christ.

The Creed – is the proclamation of our common and shared belief in what the Church teaches.

The Eucharistic Canon – these prayers recount Our Lord's institution of the Eucharist, the death, resurrection and ascension of Jesus Christ and the proclamation of His Second Coming. We respond with joyful anticipation.

The Consecration – reciting together the words of Our Lord while calling upon the Holy Spirit to change our gifts of bread and wine into the actual

Body and Blood of Christ.

The Lord's Prayer – we say in unison the words of the prayer Our Savior gave us, "Our Father who art in heaven ..."

The Reception of the Body and Blood of Christ – (The Eucharist) - by receiving the Lord's Body and Blood we are united with Him in the most intimate way. He becomes part of us both physically and spiritually.

We Depart In Peace – "In The Name of the Lord" - to proclaim His life and teachings to the world through what we do and say as Christians.

The Prayer Before the Icon of Christ – The Prayer at the Ambo - along with the priest we pray for the Lord's peace, guidance and salvation.

Closing Blessings and Adoration of the Cross. Receiving the Antidoron.

> *"Take care to keep the Eucharist (among yourselves), for there is one Flesh of the Lord Jesus Christ, and one cup to unite us by His Blood. There is one sanctuary, as there is one bishop, together with the priests and deacons, my fellow servants, that all of our acts may be done according to God's will."*
>
> *St. Ignatius of Antioch - First Century*

> *"With full confidence let us partake of the Body and Blood of Christ… so that by partaking of them you might become united with Him. By having His Body and Blood distributed through our bodily members we become Christ-bearers and thus we become partakers of the Divine nature."*
>
> *St. Cyril of Jerusalem*

AN EXHORTATION ON DISCIPLINE IN THE CHURCH
by Rostislav Gan

> *"The Apostle Paul tells members of the Christian community that "everything should be done decently and in order" (1 Corinthians 14:40). That is to say that in everything, just as in the Divine Services, there should be a strict, definite order, and that nothing be arbitrary. Elsewhere he says that God is the "God of peace and not of confusion" (1 Corinthians 14: 33).*
>
> *This same discipline should distinguish our Christian life. Unfortunately, our understanding of this discipline has been virtually lost. We have neither harmony nor order. Each person does as he pleases, whatever he feels to be necessary, and the result is total disarray.*

We have been told repeatedly that as members of the Church we cannot do as we want; we must submit to all of its rules, whether we like it or not. The Church has a certain discipline, which requires submission, and to which people should submit voluntarily. This Church discipline is given to us in childhood.

Today one often hears parents complain that their children are unruly: they can't do anything with them: the children don't obey them and they do as they please. At first it seems that the parents are not to blame, that it is the result of circumstances, of today's environment. But the fact is that parents often allow their children to become spoiled at an early age. Likewise, it is not uncommon to hear parents say about a child, "Let him do what he wants." What are they thinking? Is it right to allow someone, particularly one who is still immature, to do just what he wants? What will come of him in the future? We see what happens!

One must accustom children to discipline from earliest childhood . Many parents bring their children here to church, but they don't look after their behavior, and the children often run around outside more than they stand in church. Do such parents really think that some kind "uncle or aunt," or some stranger is going to look after their children and educate them? Every parent who brings their children to church should make sure that they stand with them. It doesn't matter that they want to run around; they need to be properly trained. We must observe Church discipline and decorum. Each one of us should make this his concern."

Archpriest Rostislav Gan (+1975)

ON ORDER IN THE CHURCH by St. John Chrysostom

"What I am going to say is disagreeable, but I will say it nonetheless. A grievous disease prevails in the Church. When we assemble to hold communion with God, and are in the process of glorifying God, some of you carry on with your own conversations and amusements.

Prayers are going on, and yet some of you are unconcerned. A sleepy indifference and even boredom possesses you. You daydream, and your eyes, and attention, roam all over the place.

Some gossip and even indulge in slander and mockery, thereby desecrating the Lord's House. Even more perverse, while the priest is praying, some people giggle outright, others sneer with contempt.

In the temple we stand in the company of angels, and yet some are laughing. Is the liturgy nothing but a theatrical amusement? Therefore, I solemnly beseech you, refrain from your wicked conduct. Be attentive to Holy Things. Show devotion and reverence to your Lord!"

St. John Chrysostom

PROPER CONDUCT FOR ACOLYTES – AND THOSE WHO SERVE AT THE HOLY TABLE

1. One who is serving in the sanctuary or at the altar, should arrive at the church at least twenty minutes prior to the beginning of Divine Services.

2. Upon entering the altar area, make the Sign of the Cross, and three bows from the waist while facing the Holy Table. At other times prostrations may be in order.

3. Receive the blessing of the priest or bishop to serve at the Holy Table.

4. There should be no unnecessary talking, laughing or running around the church.

5. Chewing gum or eating food of any kind before the services, or during the Divine Liturgy is absolutely forbidden.

6. Acolytes and Readers should wear a sticharion that is cleaned and ironed. Receive a blessing before vesting.

7. Acolytes and Readers should not touch the Holy Table or the Table of Oblation or any items upon them.

8. Hands should be clean. Dress shoes, instead of gym shoes, should be worn. They should be polished and in good repair.

9. Nothing should be in the area of the Holy Table which does not pertain to the celebration of the Divine Services.

10. Acolytes and Readers should always reverence the icons and show the utmost respect for the liturgical items used during the Divine Services.

11. When passing behind the Holy Table one should always make the Sign of the Cross.

12. Make the proper reverences when censed or blessed by the clergy.

13. Acolytes and Readers should always come out to the ambo when the sermon is being preached.

THE FOUR DIVINE LITURGIES

Orthodoxy celebrates the Church Year with four separate Eucharistic Liturgies. They are:

The Divine Liturgy of St. John Chrysostom
This is the normal liturgy on Sundays and weekdays. Also celebrated on various feast days.

The Divine Liturgy of St. Basil the Great
This liturgy is celebrated ten times during the Church Year. While its structure is basically the same as that of St. John Chrysostom, the central (Eucharistic) prayer is longer.

The Divine Liturgy of St. James
This liturgy is used once a year, on October 23rd, the Feast of St. James, Brother of the Lord.

Another "liturgy," which is actually a Vesper Service with the distribution of Holy Communion, is:

The Liturgy of the Presanctified
This liturgy is used on Wednesdays and Fridays in parishes during the Great Fast (Lent), and on the first three days of Holy and Great Week. However, There is no consecration of the bread and the wine. Holy Communion is given from the elements which are consecrated on the previous Sunday.

In some parishes and in monasteries which have daily Divine Liturgy, the Presanctified may be celebrated on each weekday, except for Saturday, or Sunday, or the Feast of the Annunciation.

Worship in the Second Century

"Christians assemble from all places-those who live in the towns and the country, and those in the cities. They read the memoirs of the apostles or the writings of the prophets, as much as time permits. When the reader has finished, the priest gives a discourse, admonishing us and exhort-ing us to imitate these excellent examples. Then we all rise together and offer prayers. The priest offers the gifts and the people respond with 'Amen.' All present receive the Eucharist, and alms are collected to aid the orphans and widows and all who are in want, through sickness or any other cause. We hold our common assembly on the Sun's Day, because it is the first day of the week, on which God put to flight dark-ness and chaos, and made the world. On this same day Jesus Christ Our Savior rose from the dead."

St. Justin Martyr – explaining worship in the early Church

THE FREQUENCY OF HOLY COMMUNION

There has been a movement in recent years toward more frequent partaking of Holy Communion in the Orthodox Church. It was the custom in many places to receive the Eucharist at the Divine Liturgy only three or four times a year. This was due to several reasons which are much too complicated to review at this time. However, the movement toward more frequent reception of the Holy Eucharist has begun, and is supported by many within worldwide Orthodoxy.

Scriptural references: Acts 2:46-47, Acts 20:2

It should go without saying that one should always approach the Eucharist with adequate preparation and a sense of awe that we are receiving the very Body and Blood of Our Lord and Savior Jesus Christ. Keeping oneself in a spiritually prepared state, with regular confession and fasting is an absolute minimum to worthy reception of the Holy Eucharist.

In regard to the more frequent reception of the Holy Eucharist, a name which stands out, is St. John of Kronstadt. St. John insisted on frequent communion and as such he anticipated the contemporary trends some 90-100 years ago.

THE WESTERN RITE IN ORTHODOXY

Most people think of the Orthodox Church from a strictly Byzantine viewpoint. They envision a Divine Liturgy from that stance and are unaware there is a small, yet growing, segment of the Orthodox Church which uses an ancient liturgy that was in place well before the Great Schism of the 11th century. This liturgy of the Western Church, fully Orthodox, is still celebrated today.

Western Rite Orthodox are active in the United States, Canada, Italy, Yugoslavia, Britain and France, although they exist in other places of the world in small numbers. They celebrate the great Western liturgy (Mass) as found in the monasteries of Northern Europe in the 7th-11th centuries. This liturgy , in keeping with the practical nature of Western Orthodox Christians in those times and areas, is not as lengthy as the Byzantine Rite, therefore it is more functional to the Western mind, and purged of all the accretions which were added in later centuries by the Roman Church.

There was also a Western Rite monastery of Benedictines on Mount Athos (Our Lady of the Amalfitans) from 990-1287. It preserved the Western Rite Liturgy within the Orthodox Church, and existed until the 13th century. It was an outpost of a complete Western Rite observance in Orthodoxy until it was disbanded. Later, in the 19th century a revival of interest in the Western Rite began in Europe.

Western Rite Orthodoxy is attractive to converts from an Occidental setting who are unable, for one reason or another, to attach themselves to Byzantine-style liturgies which seem foreign to their particular culture. If Orthodoxy wants to be fully-Catholic then there is definitely room for a Rite which serves the needs of a growing number of people in a Western milieu who find themselves united to the Orthodox Faith.

A few shrill voices in Orthodoxy oppose the Western Rite. It is hard to imagine what justification they have when it is historically clear that the Orthodox Church existed in a Western setting in the first millennium, and continues to do so to this day. And, one may ask in all seriousness, "Is God so parochial that He looks with favor only on prayer in a Byzantine setting, while rejecting other forms of worship?" Or, are they equally pleasing to Him because of the warmth of one's heart and desire, regardless of authentic ritual and custom?

> *"The hour is coming, and now is, when true worshipers will worship the Father in spirit and in truth. For the Father is seeking such to worship Him. God is Spirit and those who worship Him must worship in spirit and in truth."*
>
> *St. John 4:23-24*

SOME COMMENDABLE CUSTOMS

* It is an ancient and commendable custom for the faithful to visit Orthodox monasteries from time to time. While there, it is permissible to arrange for confession, if a hieromonk (priest-monk) is available.

One may seek counsel for any difficulty, need or situation which requires the guidance of a spiritually-gifted monk or nun.

* Customs that show proper reverence to Almighty God include prostrations and metanias:

A **metania** means to make the Sign of the Cross, bend the body forward from the waist, then touch the floor with outstretched hands.

A **prostration** is made after the Sign of the Cross, by kneeling and touching your forehead to the floor. Then rise.

It is customary not to make prostrations on Sunday (since it is the remembrance of Our Lord's Resurrection) or on any of the Twelve Great Feasts, except to honor the Holy Cross on September 14th.

> *No prostrations are made on days when one receives Holy Communion – a metania is made instead.*

THE PROSPHORON - BREAD FOR THE DIVINE LITURGY

The bread used in the Orthodox Divine Liturgy is called the prosphoron. The word means "an offering to God." It signifies that Jesus is, indeed, the "Bread of Life," and that if any man or woman partakes of the Eucharist – he or she will never hunger again. There are over fifty references to bread in the Bible, and it is a very important term to Orthodox Christians. Bread is the "staff of life" as most people know. Bread feeds us on our journey through life and is a food found in every culture of the world. When bread is eaten it becomes a very part of our bodies and sustains us well. Bread is also our gift to God for all His benefits. It is our simple, yet heartfelt, gift of gratitude to an ever-loving Father.

In the Greek tradition the priest cuts one loaf of prosphoron. Slavic traditions use five small loaves to prepare the "Lamb" – one which will be consecrated into the very Body of Christ – and the others which commemorate the Theotokos along with members of the Church both living and dead.

It is a great honor to prepare the prosphoron for the Divine Liturgy. Any priest will give you the directions for preparing the loaves. (A recipe follows)

RECIPE FOR PROSPHORA

For the preparation of a single large loaf measuring about six to eight inches in diameter (or five small loaves of about three inches in diameter) only the following four ingredients are used:

2 cups flour all-purpose, sifted
1 teaspoon of dry yeast or one small yeast cake
3/4 cup warm – nearly hot – water
One pinch of salt

Instructions:

Mix water and salt together in a bowl. Spread flour over the surface of the mixing board or pan and make an indentation in the center of the flour. Into the indentation add some of the salted warm water, take the yeast and dissolve in this water. Start kneading. The dough must become stiff (takes about 10 minutes of kneading). More water can be added if dough becomes too stiff or unworkable. If dough becomes soft, add a little more flour. Place dough in a bowl covered with a damp cloth and let it rise in a warm place for 25-35 minutes.

Flour the baking pan - never to be oiled or greased – and place on it the dough which has first been rolled out and cut into two portions – circular in outline. Place the two layers in the pan one on top the other. Dust the prosphora seal with flour and place it in the center of the top layer of dough.

Press very hard on it until the edges disappear a little below the surface. Flatten the dough around the edges of the seal, press again and, then gently rock the seal from side to side, pulling it, at the same time, up and out of the dough.

Place the pan with dough, which has been covered with a clean cloth, in a warm place for one hour or until it rises to fill a ten-inch pan. It is important after stamping to make small vents around the seal-impression with a toothpick to insure escape of yeast gas which otherwise builds up during the baking and which can burst the sealed impression.

Preheat the oven to 400 degrees, (F). Place pan (with cloth removed) in the oven. If you wish to keep the bread from browning, cover it with non-waxed butcher's paper or the brown paper from a grocery bag. The paper will not burn but you might want to keep an eye on it. Bake for fifteen minutes. Lower heat to 350 degrees and continue baking for an additional fifteen minutes. When done, remove and allow to cool, and be sure to cover it with a clean cloth so the crust will not become too hard. When completely cooled, insert into a plastic bag after covering each loaf with a paper towel. The bags can be placed in a freezer. To thaw, take out of freezer the night before it is to be used.

Prayer at Commencement of Making Prosphoras

Make the Sign of the Cross and say:

"Through the prayers of our Holy Fathers, O Lord Jesus Christ, Our God, have mercy upon us. Amen.

Glory to Thee, Our God, Glory to Thee.

O God whose Only-begotten Son has said, "Without me you can do nothing." My Lord and my God, in faith I bend the knees of my soul to bow before Thy Fatherly goodness and raise my hands to Thee. Help me, a sinner, to do this work in conformity with Thy will. Send down Thy Holy Spirit to guide me in the making of these prosphora that they may be worthy of the use for which they are intended.

In the Name of the Father and of the Son and of the Holy Spirit. Amen... Lord Have Mercy, Lord Have Mercy, Lord Have Mercy.

O Lord Jesus Christ, Son of God, through the prayers of Thy Most Pure Mother, by the power of Thy precious and Life-giving Cross, by the intercessions of Blessed Michael the Archangel, of the Holy Prophet, Forerunner and Baptist John, of the Holy Apostles Peter and Paul, of (Patron Saint or Patron Saint of the Church), of my Holy Guardian Angel, and of all the saints, have mercy upon me and save me. Amen."

The Church Fathers on the Eucharist

"Celebrate the Eucharist as follows: Say over the cup: 'We give Thee thanks, Father, for the Vine of David, Thy servant, which Thou did make known to us through Jesus Thy servant. To Thee be glory, forever.

Over the broken bread say, 'We give Thee thanks, Father, for the life and knowledge which Thou has revealed to us through Jesus Thy servant. To Thee be glory forever. As this broken bread scattered on the mountains was gathered and became one, so to may Thy Church be gathered from the ends of the earth into Thy Kingdom. For glory and power are Thine through Jesus Christ forever. Amen.'

Do not let anyone eat or drink of your Eucharist except those who have been baptized. On the Lord's Day, gather in community to break bread and offer thanks. But confess your sins first, so that your sacrifice may be a pure one. No one who has a quarrel with his brother may join your gathering, not until they are reconciled. Your sacrifice must be made holy."

The Didache c. 120, "The Teaching of the Twelve Apostles"

"What the Lord did not endure on the Cross – the breaking of His legs - He submits to now in His Sacrifice for His love of you. He permits himself to be broken in pieces that all may be filled. What is in the chalice is the same as that which flowed from Christ's side. What is the bread? It is Christ's Body. Not only ought we see the Lord, we ought to take Him and unite ourselves with Him in the closest union."

St. John Chrysostom

"We do not consume the Eucharistic bread and wine as if it were ordinary food and drink, for we have been taught that as Jesus Christ Our Savior became a man of flesh and blood by the power of the Word of God, so also the food that is to become the Flesh and Blood of the incarnate Jesus does so by the power of His own words contained in the Prayer of Thanksgiving."

St. Justin Martyr +165

CONCERNING GODPARENTS FOR BAPTISM

From the first century of the Christian era it has been the custom of the Orthodox Church to require Godparents for those to be baptized or "illuminated". The Godparents "sponsor" the person about to be baptized and are responsible for the religious instruction of this new member of Christ's Church. Writings about the practice of requiring Godparents go back to the 2nd century. The first "sponsors" were deacons, deaconess, virgins, hermits or others who had dedicated themselves to serving the Church and who were able to teach the elements of the Faith to those who accepted Christianity.

It is known that in the Russian Church only one Godparent was needed until about the 14th century. After this time it was customary to require two people, one man and one woman to stand as Godparents. This custom slowly became the standard throughout the Orthodox Church – although even today, it is permissible for one person to fulfill the requirement for sponsorship, a male Godparent for a male and a female for a female. (In an emergency it is always proper for one person to act as Godparent.)

A Godparent must be an Orthodox Christian who knows the truths of the Orthodox Church, the moral teaching of the Faith, and the meaning of the Mystery of Baptism. The sponsor must also recognize the serious obligations of this role and what is required of them until the one baptized reaches a mature age. Therefore, a male sponsor must be no younger than fifteen and a female sponsor no younger than thirteen years of age. They must be people of upright character. (At times, the priest, his wife, the reader, or his wife may be asked to sponsor the one about to be "illuminated in the Faith".) There is no such thing as a proxy sponsor or one "in-absentia". This is not permitted since the sponsor(s) must be present during the administration of Baptism. They must give the answers to the questions asked, read the Creed, and process around the font. The sponsor must also give the solemn promise of faithfulness to Christ – if the newly baptized is unable to do so himself.

In no case may the natural parents be sponsors since this violates a Canon of the Sixth Ecumenical Council, which states that the bond between sponsors is so solemn, and of such a high degree, that it supersedes any other physical union.

OUR BAPTISMAL COVENANT – PROMISE

Although most of us were infants when baptized, our Godparents took the Promise of Faith for us. Now, however, it is absolutely necessary to know what was spoken for us, and what we must profess as adults.

The following are the **Baptismal Promises** used in the Orthodox Church :

Priest:
"Do you renounce Satan, and all his angels, and all his works, and all his service and all his pride?"

Answer: "I do."

Priest:
"Have you renounced Satan?"

Answer: "I have."

Priest:
"Do you unite yourself to Christ?"

Answer: "I do."

Priest:
"Have you united yourself to Christ?"

Answer: "I have."

Priest:
"Do you believe in Christ?"

Answer: "I believe in Him as King and God. I bow down before the Father, and the Son, and the Holy Spirit, the Trinity, One in Essence and Undivided."

We then recite the entire body of truths enumerated in the Creed, our Symbol of Faith.

EMERGENCY BAPTISM

Baptism is normally performed by a bishop or priest. In a dire emergency it may be administered by a deacon, or any man or woman provided they are believing Christians. Unlike the Roman Catholic Church which allows even non-Christians to administer Baptism in an emergency, the Orthodox Church requires that the one who baptizes must be a baptized Christian.

An emergency baptism may be performed by an Orthodox layperson. This is done by sprinkling water on the infant three times and saying, "The servant of God, _____ is baptized in the name of the Father, and of the Son, and of the Holy Spirit." If water is not available raise the infant in the air three times and recite the same words.

THE CHURCHING OF WOMEN

On the fortieth day after giving birth, the Orthodox mother (and her child) must attend church so that the mother may be ceremoniously welcomed in her new role, and the child may be formally received as a candidate for Baptism in the Church. This reception of the child precedes Baptism, and is a reflection of Christ's reception in the Temple at Jerusalem some forty days after His birth – complying with the Law of Moses (St. Luke 2:22-23). This is not a ritual of absolution for the mother – as if giving birth was a sin – but is meant to re-establish communion between the woman and the Church after childbirth, in her new role as mother and teacher.

In this Rite of Reception, if the infant is a male, the priest raises the child in front of the Holy Doors and processes around the Holy Table, reciting the Prayer of the St. Simeon, as found in St. Luke 2:29-38. If the infant is a girl the

same ritual in modern times is performed omitting the ceremony of process-
ing around the Holy Table.

Note: In ancient times, when there was a female diaconate, girls were also carried around the
Holy Table.

THE BAPTISM OF INFANTS

We know that from the earliest times infants were baptized in the Church.
Within the New Testament we read of whole families being "illuminated"
(Acts 16:33, 1 Corinthians 1:16). Also, the children of Christian parents were
said to be "holy" (1 Corinthians 7:14). In the time immediately following
the apostles, St. Justin Martyr speaks of Christians who had been "disciples
since early childhood." St. Polycarp, martyred in 156 A. D. claimed to have
been the servant of Christ for eighty-six years, indicating clearly that he was
baptized as a child. St. Irenaeus speaks of Christ as "giving salvation to those
of every age" and specifically notes that there were infants and little children
among them. Origen, an early teacher, writes that infants may indeed be
baptized and that this was a "truth handed down from the apostles." In St.
Cyprian's Epistle 64, there is a description that infant Baptism was a common
occurrence by the mid-third century. In the Orthodox Church the Mystery
of Baptism with Chrismation and the first reception of the Holy Eucharist
immediately followed Baptism, and at the same ceremony. This was the
custom of the early Church. Therefore, Orthodoxy has imparted the Mysteries
of Initiation (Baptism/Chrismation) from the first days of the Faith.

In the year 200 A.D. Hippolytus, an early commentator on the Faith and
Tradition of the Church noted:

> "Infants are baptized first, then the men, then the women, then they are
> all anointed (Chrismated) with the Oil of Thanksgiving."

It was only in the Middle Ages that the Western Church separated these
initiation rites into three Mysteries (Sacraments) – Baptism, with Chrismation (Confirmation) occurring much later, and the first reception of Holy
Communion between a child's seventh and tenth year. This separation of the
Mysteries into three distinct rites over a period of years impoverishes the
true meaning of Baptism, and is not the tradition of the early Church. This
practice has never been found in Orthodoxy.

> "Do you not know that as many of us who were baptized into Christ
> Jesus were baptized into His death? Therefore, we were buried with Him
> through Baptism into death, that just as Christ was raised from the
> dead by the glory of the Faith, even so we also should walk in newness
> of life. For if we have been united together in the likeness of His death,
> certainly we also shall be in the likeness of His Resurrection."
>
> Romans 6:3-5

THE MYSTERY OF CHRISMATION

The Mystery of Chrismation, (referred to as Confirmation in non-Orthodox Western Churches) immediately follows Baptism. From the earliest days of the Church it was called "Sealing the Spirit" conferred at Baptism. In Chrismation we are strengthened with the life of the Holy Spirit imparted to us in a very special way.

Chrismation marks us as special members of the People of God, each with unique gifts and talents. Our bodies are anointed with Chrism (Holy Oil) blessed by the bishop to remind us that souls, bodies, minds and hearts are involved in our salvation and that our physical bodies (these "Temples of the Holy Spirit" as St. Paul calls them) are truly involved in leading us to eternal life.

To abuse our bodies through improper living is a grave sin against the generosity of God who has endowed us with this physical temple in which to house the Spirit during our earthly journey.

Scriptural references: Acts 2:17, St. John 7:37-39, St. John 14:16, 16:13-14, Acts 1:5, 2:38; 8;14-17, 19:1-6.

An Historical Note About Orthodoxy # 3

From the very first days of the Church there was a "government" or "hierarchy" which kept her from falling into chaos. The Holy Scriptures give the Church authority to "preach the Gospel to all nations" and to maintain an order which is both practical and spiritual. Christ Himself gave the Church the power to forgive sins in His name (John 20:23), and the Epistles speak of "ordaining" men to various offices, each of which has a specific purpose (1 Timothy 3:8-13, 5:17; Acts 20:17,28; 1 Timothy 5:17-22, et al).

This reasonable structure in the Church followed the admonition of St. Paul to "do all things decently and in order" (1 Corinthians 14:40). Therefore, the Orthodox Church has substantially the same worship, with exactly the same Creed and beliefs, as the early Apostolic Church.

As such, because of her hierarchy and faithful, the Orthodox Church was able to withstand the many attacks against her integrity and unity. She alone, among Churches today, is the same today as at the beginning. For those who come to her seeking the Truth, she alone stands as the true reflection of the Church of Christ and the apostles. Yet, she is not the True Faith because of her age, she is the "pillar and ground of truth" because of her teachings, which are the same, yesterday, today and forever (1 Timothy 3:15).

THE MYSTERY (SACRAMENT) OF CONFESSION

When an Orthodox Christian falls into sin, the promises made at Baptism are violated. By sin we separate ourselves both from God and from His Church and, if serious enough, from the right to participate in Holy Communion. But God in His mercy foresaw that weak human beings would have to be cleansed anew from sin and therefore Jesus gave His apostles the right to forgive sin in His name (St. Matthew 16:19) provided we repent and confess our sins before God and the Church. The apostles transmitted this right to their successors, i.e. bishops and priests, who continue to remit the sins of the faithful in God's own name, providing there is sufficient sorrow and a firm commitment on the part of the penitent not to sin again. Confession is therefore referred to as a "Second Baptism".

There is a wondrous promise made in 1 John 1:9, "If we confess our sins, He is faithful and just to forgive us and to cleanse us **from all unrighteousness**." So, from the first days of the Church this has been the custom of all Orthodox Christians, "Confess your trespasses to one another" (James 5:16). It was most likely that the early faithful confessed aloud to each other and were sacramentally forgiven, since we are commanded to "Forgive those who trespass against us."

Also, St. Paul reminds us that we "must examine ourselves, so that we may eat of the bread and drink of the cup" which is why the Church is so strict about regular Confession and frequent reception of Holy Communion.

Sometimes priests are asked if Orthodox Christians cannot just confess to God "in private". While it is certainly permissible to first seek God's forgiveness "in private", we must also seek the forgiveness of the community we offended. We do this by confessing to a priest, who is the legitimate representative of the Church. In addition we must seek the counsel and assistance of the priest who is trained in healing the "diseases" of the soul. It is very easy for us to confess in "private" and therefore never fully admit our sin. Our shame at sinning keeps us from asking others for forgiveness. The Mystery of Confession belongs to the Church, not to the individual conscience, and therefore, as in all Mysteries of the Church, a priest is required for conferring the sacramental love of confession to the faithful of the Church.

> *"You therefore, who laid the foundation of the rebellion, submit to the priests, and be chastened to repentance, bending your knees in a spirit of humility."*
>
> *St. Clement of Rome – First Century*

Confession is a spiritual cleansing and an inventory of our posture before a loving God. And as those who have benefited from Confession know the liberating feeling of the words of the priest as he pronounces the forgiveness promised by Christ, "Go your sins are forgiven", is great and lasting.

Scriptural references: St. Matthew 18:17, James 5:16, St. John 20:23, 1 Corinthians 11:28-31

HOW TO MAKE A CONFESSION

1. Confess your sins openly. You are speaking to God not to a man. Of course, God knows what sins you have committed but wants you to openly confess your sins to the priest. Do not be ashamed to confess to another person. Your spiritual father knows man's weakness, empathizes with you and comes to love you for your honesty. He, too, is a sinner and under stands your needs and concerns. He wants to help, and bring you back to God's grace.

2. Confess your sins one by one. Do not generalize and say things to the priest such as, "I was disobedient," "I sinned" or "I was impure." Just as you would enumerate your physical infirmities to a doctor, do the same to the physician of your soul.

3. Do not involve other people in your confession. The priest is not interested in the sins of others. He wants to help you alone. To blame others is a form of judgment which is another sin altogether.

4. Do not feign forgetfulness. Honesty is a prerequisite to a good confession. If you knowingly conceal something, your confession is worthless and you add further sin to yourself.

5. You should have contrition and sorrow for your sins. To approach the Mystery of Confession with no concern for the state of your soul, is to add even more to your inventory of sins.

6. Have confidence in Christ's mercy, and approach Confession knowing that we are assured, by the words of Holy Scripture, of the mercy and love of Jesus Christ:

   "If we confess our sins, He is faithful and just to forgive us our sins and to cleanse us from all unrighteousness" (1 St. John 1:9).

Prayer Before Confession of St. Symeon the New Theologian

"O God and Lord of all, Who has the power over every breath and soul, the only one able to heal me, hearken unto the prayer of me, the wretched one, and having put him to death, destroy the serpent nestling with me by the descent of the All-holy and Life-giving Spirit. And vouchsafe me, poor and naked of all virtue, to fall with tears at the feet of my spiritual father, and call his holy soul to mercy, to have mercy on me. And grant, O Lord, unto my heart humility and good thoughts, becoming a sinner, who has consented to repent unto Thee, and do not abandon unto the end the one soul, which has united itself unto Thee and has confessed Thee, and instead of all the world has chosen Thee and has preferred Thee. For Thou knows, O Lord, that I want to save myself, and that my evil habit is an obstacle. But all things are possible unto Thee, O Master, which are impossible for man. Amen."

THE QUESTION OF SIN - WHAT THE CHURCH TEACHES

Sin is disobedience to Almighty God. In Holy Scripture it is an important and continual concept in man's relationship with His Creator. The New Testament places the question of sin directly at the core of man's character, i.e. in his pride, his will and conscience . In St. John's Gospel we are taught that sin is the product of disbelief in Jesus Christ :

> *"You are of your father, the devil, and the desires of your father you want to do."*
>
> St. John 8:42-47

With sin, death entered into the human condition. Man was created immortal but because of the Fall in the Garden of Eden, sin entered the world, and death by sin, so "Death passed upon all men, for all have sinned" (Romans 5:12). St. Paul calls death "the wages of sin", or the payment extracted for sin (Romans 6:23).

Christ, by his death and resurrection, stopped the tyranny of sin. By His passion and death Christ revealed a great love for all mankind. St. Cyril of Alexandria says, "With such a love for mankind the judge has canceled the chastisement."

Even though we are sinful men and women, the love of Almighty God will cancel the consequences of sin if we are sorry for our transgressions and come to Him with true repentance.

Scriptural references: Romans 5:12, St. John 5:14, Romans 3:9-18

THE MARKS OF REAL SORROW FOR SIN

Contrition - to be truly sorry for one's sins while recognizing the need for confession to God and the Church.

Confession - to go before the priest, who represents the Church, confess your sins and ask the forgiveness of God and the Church-at-large.

Amendment - to make reparation for sin, to undo any wrong, to repay any debts, to make amends for any hurts or evil inflicted on others. Christ said, "I will give you the keys to the Kingdom of Heaven, and whatever you bind on earth will be bound in heaven, and whatever you loose, or forgive on earth, will be loosed in heaven" (St. Matthew 16;19).

WAYS OF PARTICIPATING IN ANOTHER'S SIN

1. By counsel - encouraging others to commit sinful acts.

2. By command - forcing another into sinful actions.

3. By consent - agreeing to participate in sinful action.

4. By provocation - placing another in an occasion of sin.

5. By praise or flattery of another's sinful actions.

6. By concealing another's sin from lawful authority.

7. By partaking in the actual sin itself.

8. By silence - refusing to stop another from sinning.

9. By defense of the sin committed through rationalization.

"ORIGINAL SIN" – MORE PROPERLY KNOWN AS 'THE ANCESTRAL CURSE'

The Orthodox teaching about the "Ancestral Curse," i.e. called "Original Sin" in other Churches, is that grace is always found in fallen mankind. We are all subject to the sin of Adam and it is impossible for anyone, except Christ, to be free from sin. Yet, by His death and resurrection Christ restored mankind to what it was before the Fall.

The Fall of Adam (and Eve) consisted essentially in disobedience to Almighty God. Adam set his own will against the Divine will and chose to separate himself from God. Because of the Fall a state of death, disease, and human suffering of all kinds entered the world. Human beings were henceforth in an unnatural state leading to sin, disobedience, human suffering, and eventually death.

We know that if one member of the body suffers the entire body is affected. St. Paul mentions this in 1 Corinthians 12:12-26, "If one member of the body suffers, all suffer together with it and if one member is honored, all rejoice together with it."

The results of Adam's sin have come down to his descendants so we are now under the influence of sin and evil. Each of us then, is subject to the spiritual effects of the original sin of our first parents. "Therefore , just as sin came into the world through one man, and death came through sin, so death spread to all because all have sinned" (Romans: 5-12).

Orthodoxy views the human species before the Fall in a less exalted state than does the Western Church. Therefore, the consequences of the Fall did not devastate the human race, as taught in Western theology, and are less severe.

True, our minds and wills have become weakened and impaired so that we find it extremely difficult to attain to the likeness of Almighty God, yet we do not teach that God's grace is entirely lacking, nor that mankind lacks freedom to attain to good as the Augustinian Theory of the West teaches. God's Divine image within us is distorted but not destroyed. Human beings still have a free will and we reject any theory that holds men to be totally lacking in responsibility.

Orthodoxy also rejects the theory of "Original Guilt" which says that mankind inherited the very guilt of our first parents because of their sin. The Orthodox Church teaches that mankind may, as partakers of the Fall , inherit all the consequences of that first act of disobedience but we do not inherit Adam and Eve's guilt – and we do not teach that our noble actions cannot in any way be pleasing to God.

Certainly there was a barrier between God and man because of the First Sin. Human beings could not break through this obstruction to achieve union with God – so since man could not come to God – God came to us in the person of Jesus Christ. Adam caused death and the chaos of sin; Christ brings new life and order so that we can exist in the power of the Spirit.

Scriptural references: Genesis 3:1-24, Romans 5:12-16.

CONSEQUENCES OF THE FALL by St. John of Kronstadt

"Why did God allow the Fall of man, His beloved creation and the crown of all earthly creatures? To this question one must reply thus: If a man is not allowed to fall, then he cannot be created in the image and likeness of God, he cannot be granted free will, which is an inseparable feature of the image of God; but he would have to be subject to the law of necessity, like the soul-less creation – the Sun, sky, stars, the circle of the earth, and all the elements – or like the irrational animals. But then there would have been no king over the creatures of the earth, no rational hymn-singer of God's goodness, wisdom, creative almightiness and Providence. Then man would have had no way to show his faithfulness and devotion to the Creator, his self-sacrificing love. Then there would have been no exploits in battle, no merits and no incorruptible crowns for victory; there would have been no eternal blessedness, which is the reward for faithfulness and devotion to God, and no eternal repose after the labors and struggles of our earthly pilgrimage."

Repentance

"Through this man (Jesus) is preached to you the forgiveness of sin.
Him, God has exalted to His right hand to be Prince and Savior, to give
repentance to Israel and the forgiveness of sins."

Acts 5:31

"And that repentance and remission of sins should be preached in His
name to all nations, beginning at Jerusalem."

St. Luke 24:47

"But if a wicked man turns from all his sins which he has committed,
keeps all my statutes, and does what is lawful and right, he shall surely
live; he shall not die."

Ezekiel 18:21

"He who sins is of the devil: for the devil has sinned from the beginning.
For this purpose the Son of God was manifested, that He might destroy
the works of the devil."

1 John 3:8

AN EXAMINATION OF CONSCIENCE BEFORE CONFESSION

With a sincere heart and conscience ask yourself the following questions to
prepare yourself for receiving the Mystery of Confession.

You and your relationship with Almighty God

Do you truly believe in God and His goodness? Do you believe in the Trinity:
Father, Son, Holy Spirit? Do you believe that the Church is the way to salvation and that there is a heaven for those who love God, and an everlasting hell
for those who reject Him?

Do you pray to God, knowing that your petitions will be heard? Do you
blame God for your misfortunes? Do you often get discouraged and enter into
temptations which show a lack of faith?

Do you consult psychics, card readers, fortune tellers and horoscopes? Do you
honestly believe in their power and take refuge in mediums? Or do you trust
God in all things?

Are you ruled by superstitions and the belief in "luck" or "fate"?

Do you say your prayers in the morning, before meals, and in the evening?

Do you cross yourself in public, or are you embarrassed to be known as a
Christian?

Do you read and study Holy Scripture? Do you regularly read religious books, magazines and tracts?

Do you attend Divine Liturgy on Sundays and feast days? Do you arrive on time and stay for the entire liturgy? Do you dress appropriately and refrain from all unnecessary talking or gossiping?

Do you present a hindrance to those who wish to attend Church services, or encourage people not to attend religious events?

Do you receive Holy Communion regularly and confess to a priest on a regular basis? Do you use profanity, blaspheme the name of Christ, the Theotokos or the saints?

Do you fast on Wednesdays and Fridays, and during regular Fast periods?

Your relationship with others

Do you harbor a strong dislike or hatred toward some person who insulted or harmed you?
Do you distrust people, suspecting that they may be talking about you, or seeking to do you harm?

Do you get jealous often and envy the happiness, the beauty, or the possessions of others?

Do you remain unmoved when you see a person in real need? Do you ignore the distress of others?

Are you honest, trustworthy, sincere and straightforward in your dealings with others?

Have you ever slandered or told deliberate lies about others?

Do you belittle or speak with sarcasm about others who are trying to live a Christian life? Do you make fun of those with physical or emotional disabilities?

Have you ever damaged the reputation of others or failed to defend those you know are innocent of what others are saying about them?

Do you pass judgment on the actions of others, the mistakes, shortcomings, or faults of those around you?

Do you curse those who hurt you? Or have you ever cursed your situation in life, or the fact that you were born?

Do you send people to hell with your words or gestures? Do you use insulting gestures or signs which have inappropriate meanings?

Do you respect your parents? Do you try to care for them and look out for their welfare? Do you help them with their physical, emotional or spiritual needs? Have you ever deserted them in real need or found excuses not to help them when they are in trouble?

Have you influenced your parents to give an inordinate amount of their resources to you, while ignoring your siblings?

Have you ever struck anyone in anger, misused them verbally, cursed them to their face, or behind their backs?

Do you conduct all your affairs with integrity and sincerity?

Do you steal? Have you knowingly swindled someone out of what they deserve? Have you unnecessarily reported co-workers to your supervisor for an infraction of policy? Have you ever covered up for theft or received stolen goods knowingly?

Are you grateful to God and to people who are generous or good to you?

Do you associative with evil people, or are you involved in sinful relation-ships? Have you ever talked someone into sin or led them to it by your example?

Have you ever committed forgery or taken advantage of your employers trust?

Have you borrowed money and then failed to repay it? Have you taken objects belonging to others and kept them for your own use?

Have you ever taken the life of another, or assisted in murder? Have you ever secured an abortion, or counseled someone to obtain one?

Do you interfere with the lives of others, or their work, or their families or been the source of strife and arguments?

Do you give generously to the poor, orphans, elderly, the homeless or poor families whom you know?

Relationship with yourself

Are you attached to earthly goods, money, material things?

Have you been greedy or stingy, keeping as much for yourself as possible?

Are you a spendthrift, forgetting that your surplus means belong to those in desperate need?

Are you conceited or do you think of yourself as better than others?

Do you show off your possessions, clothes, cars, your wealth, or your children's successes?

Do you love attention and praise from those around you?

Do you get angry when someone points out your mistakes and do you get hurt when corrected by those in authority?

Are you stubborn, obstinate, self-absorbed and proud?

Do you have an inordinate desire for pornography or watch obscene TV shows-movies? Do you read obscene books?

Have you ever considered suicide?

Do you overeat – gluttony? Are you lazy, insolent and do you neglect work?

Do you use insulting, obscene, or improper language to show off, insult, or humiliate others?

Do you dress to show off your body or provoke indecent thoughts in others?

Do you listen to, or sing indecent songs with vile lyrics?

Do you drink heavily, do drugs, or associate with people who do? Do you consider illegal drugs to be harmless or recreational?

Relationships for married couples

Are you loyal to your spouse? Have you ever been guilty of extramarital relationships?

Do you insult, offend or humiliate your spouse in the presence of your children or others?

Have you been insensitive to the faults of your spouse?

Do you neglect your family to go to parties, recreational events, or occasions of gambling?

Do you support your spouse in his-her occupation? Are you encouraging when your spouse is weary from work, or has to work irregular hours?

Are you overly commanding as a spouse?

Do you attend Church services with your spouse and do you take your children to Church-sponsored events? Or do you neglect their spiritual upbringing because of indifference or laziness on your part? Do you raise children in the teachings of the Lord? Do you see to their religious education and do you read Holy Scripture as a family?

Are you a good example to your children? Do you inspire them with your words or actions?

Are you aware of what your children read or watch on TV, what movies they attend, or the type of parties to which they go?

Are you aware of your children's friends, and with whom they associate?

Do you take them to indecent shows, or allow them to dress improperly?

Do you curse them, or use foul language in their presence?

Do you beat them or hit them for no reason? Are you cruel either with your fists or your words?

Do you as spouses share the workload at home? Do you share duties both in taking care of the home and rearing your child(ren)?

Do you respect and speak decently of each other's parents and relatives.

Do you show respect toward your parents to set an example for your own children?

Do you interfere, as a parent, in the home life of your married children?

> *"The sins of those who ask for pardon are forgiven. But see that you do not harbor hatred for your brothers when you ask forgiveness of your sins."*
>
> *St. Ephraim the Syrian +372*

SACRAMENT OF PENANCE (CONFESSION) by Metr. Innocent of Moscow

Read now what Innocent, Metropolitan of Moscow said about the Mystery of Confession.

What is Confession? Confession is the oral avowal of the sins which lie heavily laden upon one's conscience. Confession, however, only empties the soul from sin but repentance cleanses and makes it ready to receive the Holy Spirit.

Let us present an example and a comparison to Confession. Suppose you had only one utensil of some kind, which you, through negligence or laziness, let reach a stage where little by little it accumulated all sorts of dirt so that your utensil becomes unusable and even unbearable to look at without repugnance. But what if a king wanted to give you a gift of fragrant and costly Balsam, one drop of which could heal all infirmities and protect your health – what then? Would you refuse such a costly gift only because you had no other clean vessel in which to put it? No! It would be very natural for you to accept such a gift and you would try to clean your utensil. How would you start? Naturally, before anything, you would rid it of all uncleanness by washing it with water and, perhaps, would burn it so that it no longer retained any of its former odors.

Let the utensil represent the soul given to you by God, which you have brought to such a state that it has been filled with all kinds of transgressions and untruths: and let the sweet-smelling Balsam signify the Holy Spirit, who heals all infirmities and calamities and which the King of heaven and earth, Jesus Christ, freely bestows upon us. To examine your utensil or vessel signifies feeling your guilt before God and recalling all sins which have stolen into your heart. To clean out the vessel typifies the confession of your sins before your confessor; the washing with water and burning with fire signifies a contrite and even tearful repentance and a good-willed resolution to endure all disagreeableness, wants, insults, misfortunes, and even calamities which happened to us.

Is Confession worthwhile; is it of any use? Certainly it is worthwhile and even absolutely essential because just as it is impossible to cleanse the vessel without ridding it of all uncleanness, so it is impossible to purge your soul of sins without Confession. But is Confession alone enough for the reception of the Holy Spirit? Certainly not, because to receive the sweet-smelling and priceless Balsam into the defiled vessel it is not enough to just empty it, but it is necessary to wash it with water and burn it with fire. To receive the Holy Spirit it is not enough just to confess or recite your sins before your Father Confessor, but it is also necessary to purge your soul with repentance or contrition and humiliation of the soul and to burn it with the free-willed suffering of insults. Thus we have the meaning of confession and repentance.

Of what does a true and rightful confession consist? When we want to cleanse our conscience from sins in the Sacrament of Penance it is necessary:

1. To believe in the Lord Jesus Christ and strongly hope that He is ready to forgive all sins no matter of what magnitude, if only the sinner will repent open-heartedly. It is necessary to believe and hope that the God of all things wants and seeks our return. Of this He has assured us through the prophet thus, "As I live, says the Lord God, I desire not the death of the wicked, but that the wicked turn from his way and live" (Ezekiel 33:11).

2. To have a contrite heart. Who is God and who are we? God is the Almighty Creator of heaven and earth. He is the great and righteous judge. And we, we are weak and insignificant mortals. All people, even the greatest people, before God are less than the earth. Yet we weak and insignificant mortals dare to insult Him – the All-Good One – by besieging Him with transgressions. We are such debtors before God, such transgressors, that not only should we not dare to call ourselves His children, but are not even worthy of being His lowliest servants.

Picturing all this, you see what contriteness, what lamentation is necessary when we want to purge ourselves of all sins. And such a feeling must be had not only before Confession, and during Confession, but also after Confession. And even more important, do you want to bring a sacrifice to God such as will be acceptable to Him? Naturally all gladly want this and in the measure within our power do bring it. But what can we bring Him that is really acceptable? A contrite heart! "A sacrifice to God is an afflicted spirit: a contrite and humbled heart" (Psalm 51:17). Here is an offering to God more priceless than all offerings and oblations.

3. To forgive all of our enemies and humiliations – all they did wrongly and insultingly to us. What does it mean to forgive? To forgive means never to avenge, neither secretly nor openly, never to recall wrongs but rather to forget them and above all, to love your enemy as a friend, as a brother, to protect his honor and to treat him honestly in all things. It is a hard matter to forgive wrongs, but he who can forgive wrongs – is for this reason great!

Though it is hard to forgive our enemy, it is truly great, before both God and before man – and very necessary to forgive. Otherwise, God Himself will not forgive. Jesus Christ said: "If you will forgive men their offenses, your heavenly Father will forgive you also your offenses. But if you will not forgive men, neither will your Father forgive you your offenses" (Matthew 6:14,15). Opposite to this, however, even if you frequently pray to God, even if you have such faith that you can move mountains, even if you give away all of your belongings to the needy, and give up your body at the stake – if you do not practice forgiveness and refuse to forgive your enemy, then all is in vain. For in such circumstances prayer will not save us, neither faith, nor charity, or, in a word, nothing will help you.

But if it is needful to forgive our enemies, so it is indispensable to ask forgiveness of all those people whom we have offended. Thus, have you insulted anyone by word – entreat forgiveness of him. Come and bow down before his feet and say, "Forgive me." Have you offended anyone by deed? Endeavor to expiate your guilt and offenses and compensate his damage. Then be certain that all of your sins, no matter how heavy they be, will be forgiven you.

4. To openly reveal all of your sins without any concealment. But some say, "For what reason should I reveal my sins to Him, who knows all of our

secrets?" It is true that God knows all of our sins, but the Church, which has the power from God to forgive and absolve sins, cannot know them, and for this reason cannot without confession pronounce her absolution.

Finally, set forth a firm intention to live prudently in the future. If you want to be in the Kingdom of Heaven, if you want God to forgive your sins – then stop sinning. Only on this condition does the Church absolve the penitent. He who does not think whatever about bettering himself confesses in vain, for even if the priest says, "I forgive and absolve," the Holy Spirit does not forgive and absolve him.

Metropolitan Innocent

These things does the Lord hate –

> *"A proud look, a lying tongue, and hands that shed innocent blood. A heart that devises wicked imaginations, feet that be swift in running to evil, a false witness which speaks lies, and he who sows discord among his family."*

Proverbs 6:16 -19

> *"He who does not acknowledge his sinfulness, his fall, his perdition, cannot accept Christ, cannot come to believe in Christ, cannot be a Christian."*

St. Ignatius Brianchaninov

THE MYSTERY (SACRAMENT) OF HOLY ORDERS – ORDINATION

The Mystery of Ordination, which means "to set in place," is offered to men who feel called to service in the Church and who, after proper training, are deemed worthy ("Axios") to have hands set upon them by a bishop. They thus follow Christ as a servant of God's People. Ordination is seen as an eternal "setting apart" and cannot be revoked. This calling is so sacred that the very souls of God's People are entrusted to men in Holy Orders.

The Divine Priesthood of Christ is divided into three ranks: bishop, priest, and deacon. The bishop is given the full power of the priesthood, while priests or "presbyters" and deacons are representatives of the bishop. Priests bring the Life-giving Mysteries to the people and are the leaders of the local Church. Their ministry is specific in that they are responsible for the welfare of souls, as men who will have to give an account (Hebrews 13:17). The faithful are commanded to be obedient to their pastors since Christ said, "He who hears you (the presbyters) hears me, and he who rejects you, rejects me and Him who sent me" (St. Luke 10:16).

Deacons assist the bishops and priests in their sacred ministry. The very word "diakonia" means "service" and the deacon's ministry is laid out quite clearly in Acts, Chapter 6, which names the deacons as those who served the poor, the widows, and saw to the daily distribution of food to the faithful.

Actually, each of us is called by our Baptism to serve the Church in a sacred capacity. All of us have a role to play in God's Kingdom and to neglect it is to deny that we have been called to service and set apart in the "ecclesia" (the assembly), more commonly known as "the Church."

Scriptural references: St. John 15:16, Acts 1-26, Acts 6:1-6, Acts 14:23, Titus 1:5-9, Romans 11:29, St. John 20:21-26, St. Matthew 18:18, 1 Tim. 5:17, 2 Tim. 4:1-5.

> *"It behooves those who have received from God the power "to loose and to bind" (i.e. priests) to consider the quality of the sin and the readiness of the sinner for conversion, and applying medicine suitable for the disease, lest if he be not thoughtful in each of these respects, he should fail in regard to the healing of the sick man. For the disease of sinning is not simple, but various and multiform, and it germinates many mischievous offshoots, from which much evil is diffused, and it proceeds further until it is checked by the power of the physician."*
>
> *Fathers of the Sixth Ecumenical Council 680 A.D.*

ON THE PRIESTHOOD by St. John Chrysostom

"Do you not know what the priest is? He is an angel of the Lord. Are they his own words that he speaks? If you despise him, you cannot despise him, but God who ordained him. If God does not work through him, then there is no Baptism, nor communion in the Mysteries, nor blessings: you are no longer Christians.

Why then, you say, does God ordain all, even the unworthy? God does not ordain all, but He works through all, though they themselves are unworthy, that the people may be saved. For if God spoke, for the sake of the people, by an ass, and by Balaam, a most wicked man, (Numbers 22) much more will He speak by the mouth of the priest. What indeed will God not do for our salvation? By whom does He not act? For if He worked through Judas and through those others who "prophesied," people to whom He will say, "I never knew you, depart from me, you evildoers" (Matthew 7:23), and if others cast out devils, will He not much more work through His priests?

Reverence him, because every day he ministers to you – prays for you, and offers supplications for you – say not, he is unworthy. How does that affect the matter? Does he that is worthy bestow these great benefits on you of himself? By no means. Everything comes about because of your faith. Not even the righteous man can benefit you, if you lack faith, nor the unrighteous harm you, if you have faith. God made us "oxen" to save His People with the ark (1 Sam. 6:12). Is it the good life of the priest or his virtue which confers so much on you? The gifts that God bestows are not such as to be effects of the power of the priest. Everything springs from grace. The priest has only to open his mouth, but God it is who works all things. The priest only performs the sign. The offering is the same whether it is offered by common man or by Peter or Paul. Christ gave the same thing to His disciples which the priests now minister. One is not less than the other, for it is not men who consecrate it, but Christ Himself who bestows sanctification. For as the words which God spoke are the same which the priest now utters, so is the offering the same."

Second Homily on 2 Timothy 2-4 by St. John Chrysostom

"This is the essence of the priesthood in my mind: preaching and announcing the good news. I offer the sacrifice; no one will blame a priest if he wishes to offer an immaculate victim. My purpose is not to achieve my own glory, nor that I may attain the splendor of honors and renown, but that the offering of the Gentiles may be acceptable and sanctified in the Holy Spirit. It is my wish that the souls of those taught by me may be acceptable. This mission has not been given to me in order to bring honor on myself, but to assure your welfare."

Homily 29 on Romans 1 by St. John Chrysostom

"The priest fulfills the role of Christ when he imitates what Our Lord did, and only then does he offer a true complete sacrifice in the Church to the Father, when he begins to offer it after the pattern of Christ's offering."

St. Cyprian (Third century)

THE MYSTERY OF MARRIAGE - HOLY MATRIMONY

Holy Matrimony is the Mystery which shows forth the union of Christ with His Church. Since men and women make up the Church their marriage union is immensely important for the well-being of the Faith and for their own salvation. During the marriage ceremony a blessing is imparted to the couple. This blessing asks that the grace of the perfect love Christ has for His Church be granted to the couple and that, through their love, a family will be formed which will mirror the Church itself. Marriage is permanent. It is holy and everlasting in both the sight of God and the Church. There is also equality and order in marriage. In the Sacrament of Matrimony the new couple is reminded of their duty to be equal and responsible partners in this union, the wife to love and honor her husband, and the husband to love and cherish her as Christ loves His Church.

The marriage ceremony consists of two rites, that of the Betrothal and that of Marriage. In the Rite of Betrothal the bride and groom are blessed with rings that signify mutual support and equality within marriage itself. The Rite of Marriage follows immediately during which the new couple stands with lighted candles symbolizing purity. They are then crowned, which signifies they are a royal couple and that someday by the virtue of their marriage they will be blessed with the crown of everlasting life. They then share a common cup to show forth equality of purpose and responsibility. Finally, the couple is led around the wedding table three times to signify that they will preserve their marriage bond until death and that the Holy Trinity is called upon to witness these oaths.

Scriptural references: St. Matthew 5:32, 19:4-6, St. John 2:1-12, Ephesians 5:22-33, 1 Corinthians 7:4.

> *"God created Adam and Eve that there might be great love between them, reflecting the ministry of the Divine unity."*
>
> St. Theophilus of Antioch c. 180

> *"That is to be called love which is true, otherwise it is desire; so that those who desire are said improperly to love, just as they who love are said to desire. But that is true love, that living in the truth we may live righteously, and so may despise all mortal things in comparison with the love of men, whereby we wish them to live righteously."*
>
> St. Augustine + 430

> *"Marriage is arranged by the Church, confirmed by the Holy Eucharist, sealed by the blessing and inscribed in heaven by the angels."*
>
> Tertullian c. 223

When marriages are not permitted:

On the eves of Wednesdays and Fridays. During the Great Fast from Dairy Sunday up to the first Tuesday after Pascha.

During the Falling Asleep of the Theotokos Fast, which consists of a two week period from August 1-15.

During the Holy Apostles' Fast: Monday after All Saints to June 28.

During the Nativity Advent, the period before Christ's Birth.

On Saturday, on the eves of the Twelve Great Feasts, on the day before the Feast of the Beheading of John the Baptist, (August 29th), and the day before the Exaltation of the Cross (Sept. 14th).

Some jurisdictions exclude other days as well. Check with your priest.

Note: In extraordinary cases the bishop may grant a dispensation for a wedding during any of the prohibited days except during the Great Fast.

DEGREES OF KINSHIP IN MARRIAGE AND IMPEDIMENTS

Parents are not allowed to marry their children, grandchildren or great-grandchildren. Also, a brother may not marry his sister, or vice-versa.

A brother-in-law may not marry his sister-in-law and vice versa.

Uncles and aunts may not marry their nieces and nephews.

First cousins may not marry each other.

Foster parents may not marry their foster children, nor may foster children marry the children of their foster parents.

Godparents may not marry their Godchildren; nor may Godparents marry the parents of their Godchildren.

> *"When husband and wife are united in marriage they no longer seem like something earthly, but rather like the image of God Himself."*
>
> St. John Chrysostom + 407

> *"Marriage is more than human. It is a 'micro-basileia,' a miniature Kingdom, which is the little house of the Lord."*
>
> St. Clement of Alexandria +223

MIXED MARRIAGE LAWS OF THE CHURCH

A mixed marriage is that of an Orthodox Christian with a non-Orthodox Christian. The following are the current practices of Orthodox jurisdictions in regard to mixed marriages:

The Orthodox Church will bless a mixed marriage if the non-Orthodox is a member of a Church which practices Baptism in the name of the Father, Son and Holy Spirit. The party who is not Orthodox, and who has not been properly baptized , must become Orthodox by way of Baptism in the Church.

A non-Orthodox Christian does not become a member of the Church simply by being married by an Orthodox priest.

A non-Orthodox Christian may not receive Communion in the Church, or any other of the Holy Mysteries, or receive an Orthodox burial.

The non-Orthodox party, who is properly baptized, may become a full member of the Church by receiving the Mystery (Sacrament) of Chrismation.

The non-Orthodox party, if not a member of the Church by Baptism/Chrismation, may not serve as a sponsor at Baptism or be a best man/woman at a marriage performed in the Church.

An Orthodox person who has been married in a non-Orthodox Church may not receive the Holy Mysteries in the Orthodox Church. His, or her, marriage is not recognized by the Church, and membership in the Church is suspended until the marriage is properly blessed by an Orthodox priest.

The Orthodox Church requires that the non-Orthodox party give a written statement promising to raise any children from the union in Orthodoxy.

Children must be baptized and receive religious education in the Church. This may differ in some jurisdictions. Check with your priest.

> *"Two souls united in matrimony have nothing to fear. With harmony, peace and mutual love, husband and wife possess every possible wealth. They can live in peace behind the impregnable wall which protects them, which is love in accordance with God's will. Thanks to love they are harder than a diamond, stronger than iron; they have everything they need as they steer their course towards eternal glory, and enter more and more fully into God's grace."*
>
> *St. John Chrysostom*

THE MYSTERY OF HOLY UNCTION

The Mystery of Holy Unction refers to the Sacrament whereby the sick are anointed with oil, and the Holy Spirit is called upon to heal the body and spirit of the afflicted. Oil is blessed and consecrated by prayer and the faithful are anointed as needed. There is also the special celebration of the Mystery of Holy Unction on Wednesday of Holy Week, performed by seven priests-but when impossible, by one or more priests.

The Sacrament of Holy Unction is based on the words of the Epistle of St. James, 5:14-15, where it is commanded that the sick call upon the elders of the Church to pray over them, and anoint them with oil in the name of the Lord.

The Orthodox Church believes in the healing power of the Holy Spirit and invokes His aid and comfort for the people of faith.

Holy Unction consists of an anointing, with Confession and Communion, performed for the healing of sickness, recovery of health and forgiveness of sins.

The Service of Anointing is for the recovery of health and not a preparation for death. However, if death occurs the priest may still be called and asked to read the "Prayers for the Departure of the Soul from the Body." The laity should then read the psalms appointed until the time of the funeral.

If Holy Unction, commonly performed in church, is requested to be performed in the home for one unable to move around, the family should provide a table covered with a clean white cloth, seven tapers (thin candles), or in an emergency – a lighted vigil lamp, and wine with pure olive oil in a bowl set on the table. There should also be flour or wheat in an appropriate container signifying eternal life.

An icon of Our Lord, and the Mother of God, should be displayed in a prominent place. When the priest arrives he should be met at the door and escorted to the sick room where family members are gathered. They should participate reverently and thoughtfully in the ritual without conversation among themselves, or any other distractions such as TV, radios, etc.

Scriptural references: James 5:14-15, St. Matthew 4:23, I Corinthians 12:9

> *"Let us then, so long as we are in this world, repent of whatever evils we have done in the flesh, so that we might be saved by the Lord while we yet have time for repentance. For after we have departed from this world, it will no longer be possible to confess, nor will there then be any opportunity to repent."*
>
> St. Clement of Rome-(First century)

8. THE BIBLE AND ORTHODOXY
The Gift of His Word

The Church as Guardian of Holy Scripture:
The Holy Bible

HOLY SCRIPTURE IN THE ORTHODOX CHURCH

The Orthodox Church is the Mother of Holy Scripture. It is she who protects this supreme manifestation of God's revelation to all mankind. Orthodox are "People of the Book"and Scripture is lived within the Church, from which it receives its authority and meaning. For without the Church and her guidance, the Bible would be a very confusing book indeed! As noted in the New Testament, Philip the deacon met an Ethiopian man reading the book of the prophet Isaiah and inquired, "Do you understand what you are reading?" The eunuch replied:

> *"How can I understand (the Scriptures) unless some man guide me"*
> *(Acts 8:31).*

The Orthodox Church then, is guardian of Holy Scripture, but she is also the protector of the Tradition in which the Bible's teachings are maintained and promulgated. She is the repository of all Scriptural truth. In short, Orthodoxy sees the Christian Faith as composed of Holy Scripture, the teachings of the Fathers, the liturgy of the Church throughout the centuries, the Creeds of the Church, and the Holy Mysteries. Orthodox Christians believe that Almighty God has revealed Himself in these many wondrous ways, and has enriched the life of His people in doing so!

Scriptural reference: 2 Thessalonians 2:15, 3:5.

DEALING WITH "DOOR-TO-DOOR" EVANGELISTS

Note:
How can Orthodox Christians deal with the proclamations of the "Pentecostals" and other sects, that preach a Faith unknown to the early Church?

1. Be knowledgeable and confident with your own Faith. Do not be intimidated by other contemporary teachings, some of which are totally inconsistent with traditional Christian belief.

2. Do not become defensive or argumentative. Listen politely but be firm in stating your views.

3. Know your Bible. Avail yourself of every opportunity to learn more about your Faith. Explain that the Orthodox Church is enriched by Tradition, and know what the Church teaches.

4. Ask the Pentecostal about his or her Church and how they explain its traditions. In this way you can redirect focus on what may be an attack on your personal beliefs.

5. Know Holy Scripture but do not attempt to counter the Pentecostal's Bible quotes with your own. This takes the dialogue to a level of mere words and "argument for argument's sake."

6. Live a life which is commendable and worthy of imitation. This can be the most powerful statement of your Faith and what the Church teaches, since it is a bit disconcerting to hear an Orthodox Christian, who has not practiced his or her Faith for years, arguing with a Fundamentalist about who is right or wrong in matters of religion.

Since Scripture is inspired by the Holy Spirit, it is also considered "infallible." This means that everything in it is entirely true and real, even though it may be difficult for us to understand exactly what it means without the guidance of the Church.

Holy Scripture sets forth this truth with the following words: "Holy men of God spoke as they were moved by the Holy Spirit" (2 Peter 1:21). This means that the Holy Spirit inspired human authors who placed their talents in writing and linguistic abilities at His disposal. The same authors were illuminated to protect them from error, so they would write only the truth of Almighty God for all time.

The Books of the Old Testament written before the time of Christ are 39 in number. These books contain the truth as revealed by God and the events of Salvation History which occurred before the birth of Our Lord. All the books of Holy Scripture written after the time of Christ comprise the New

Testament. There are 27 books in the New Testament which contain the truths Jesus Christ revealed to His followers.

The books of the Old Testament are arranged according to the following categories: Historical, Teaching or Didactic, and Prophetical books.

HOLY SCRIPTURE

A. BOOKS OF THE OLD TESTAMENT

Historical Books

Genesis – this is "the book of beginnings" in the Bible. The stories are about God creating the universe and the early relationships He forged with His people. There is also the significant promise God made with Abraham and the generations that followed him.

Exodus – this is the book that relates how God led His people, the Israelites, out of bondage and slavery in Egypt. "Exodus" means "to leave, depart." In this book God makes an eternal promise, or covenant, with His people and gives them the Ten Commandments to set standards in their lives.

Leviticus – this is a book of ritual for the priests of Israel, the tribe of Levi. It is basically a book of rubrics and liturgical customs.

Numbers – this book relates the wanderings of the Israelites in the deserts of Sinai before they came to the "Promised Land" (Canaan). The name of the book is taken from the two censuses conducted during the forty years of wandering in the desert.

Deuteronomy – this book relates the three "farewell discourses" Moses gave to his people shortly before his death. In the account , Moses reviews the Laws of God for the people, hence the name Deuteronomy, or "Second Law."

Joshua – in this book an account is given as to how Joshua led the people into victory over the Canaanites. The book concludes with the division and establishment of the twelve tribes of Israel.

Judges – throughout their history the Israelites often turned from God and were bound in slavery and oppression. The "judges" were sent by God to lead them from bondage.

Ruth – Ruth and her mother-in-law Naomi are featured prominently in this book of love and faithfulness.

1 Kings – (a.k.a. 1 Samuel) – Samuel was the ruler of Israel between the era of the "Judges" and Saul (first king of the land). When Saul proved unfaithful and failed in his task, David was anointed by Samuel to be the new king.

2 Kings – (a.k.a. 2 Samuel) – the saga of Israel under King David tells of a time of strength and prosperity. However, David proved unfaithful and committed adultery/murder. The nation then suffered and fell into decline.

3 Kings – the book relates the history of Solomon's reign in Israel. After his death however, the nation split in two, with Israel in the North and Judah in the South. Subsequently a time of conflict and slavery ensued.

4 Kings – Israel was overthrown by Assyria in 721 B.C. and Judah was conquered by Babylon in 586 B.C. These events were seen as punishment upon the nation because of their unfaithfulness to the law of God.
1 Chronicles–this book lists the genealogies from the time of Adam to King David whose reign is recorded in the Book of Chronicles.

2 Chronicles – this book relates the history of Israel/Judah from 721-586 B.C. with an emphasis on the southern Kingdom of Judah.

+ 1 Esdras – 2 Esdras – God's people return to the Holy City of Jerusalem after bondage in Babylon. The most influential leader of the time was Ezra, who insisted that the people be faithful to their covenant with Almighty God.

Nehemiah – after the restoration of the Temple in Jerusalem, the city was again fortified. Nehemiah and Ezra were influential in this rebuilding and bringing the people back to God.

+Tobit – a book found in the Apocrypha relating the trials and tribulations of life in the non-Palestinian areas inhabited by the Jews. Its message is that God will protect and heal those who are prayerful and compassionate.

+Judith – the story of the widow Judith and her role in the history of the Jewish people.

Esther – this book relates the story of the Jewish queen of Persia who saved her people from destruction when she discovered a plot against them.

+1,2,3 Maccabees – histories of the Maccabeans and their revolt against forces hostile to the Jewish people. The histories cover the period from about 200 years before Christ.

Didactic or Teaching Books

Psalms – the Psalter (containing 150 Psalms) is a book of prayer and song used by the Hebrews to tell of their covenant and relationship with God. The psalms relate the entire range of human feelings and emotions from joy, anger, conflict to love, hope and despair.

Job – the famous story of Job's immense suffering in spite of the fact that he was a faithful servant of God. It seeks to answer the question of "Why does God allow suffering, especially among the innocent and young"?

Proverbs of Solomon – a.k.a. "Proverbs"– is a book of wisdom along with ethical and practical teachings on living a life in union with God's teachings.

Ecclesiastes – the writer of this book, known as "The Philosopher" raises age-old questions about the meaning of life.

Song of Songs – this love poem relates the love of God for Israel as His chosen people.

+Wisdom of Solomon – a poetic discourse written by a Jew who knew Greek. It is in praise of wisdom and righteousness while condemning oppression and idolatry.

+Wisdom of Sirach – a.k.a. "Ecclesiasticus"– a book of wisdom and proverbs written in Hebrew about 180 B.C. It provides a history of Judaism just before the Maccabean revolt in 167-64 B.C.

Prophetical Books

Amos – the Prophet Amos warned the wealthy not to ignore the poor and dispossessed. He warned of a judgment against the leaders of the land who ignored the pleas of the poor.

Hosea – illustrated the unfaithfulness of Israel towards God by using his own wife's adultery as an example.

Micah – this prophet's message to Judah was a warning of both judgment and forgiveness by God for the people going astray.

Joel – after a plague of locusts decimated the land, Joel urged the people to repent.

Obadiah – related a prophecy against Edom, a nearby country.

Jonah – resisted the command by God to preach to the Ninevites, enemies of the Jews. After Jonah's preaching mission the Ninevites repented of their sin.

Nahum – this prophet announced God's ultimate judgment of Nineveh

Habakkuk – Habakkuk's book features a dialogue between the prophet and God about the meaning of suffering and justice.

Zephaniah – the Prophet Zephaniah foretold the "Day of the Lord" which would bring God's judgment on Israel and other unfaithful nations. Doom would come to many but out of this tragedy a faithful remnant would rise from the ashes.

Malachi – after the Jews returned from exile in Babylon, they again fell into a lukewarm devotion to God. Malachi attempted to restore their vibrant faith by speaking of "The Day of the Lord."

Isaiah – the great Prophet Isaiah pronounced the message of God's judgment upon the nations that ignored Him and predicted a future king such as David. Isaiah also prophesied a time of comfort and peace upon the land.

Jeremiah – prior to the destruction of Judah by Babylon, Jeremiah prophesied God's judgment on the people. The prophesy was ignored for the most part. Jeremiah also spoke of a new covenant with God.

+Baruch – a short collection of various prayers, poems and other verses to comfort the people. Baruch was the scribe of Jeremiah.

Lamentations of Jeremiah – as the prophecy of Jeremiah was fulfilled, Babylon conquered the land and city of Jerusalem. The book of his name includes the five "laments" for the captured city.

+Epistle of Jeremiah – written to give the Jewish people an argument against their neighbors who practiced idolatry.

Ezekiel – the message of the Prophet Ezekiel was mainly for the conquered Jews held hostage in Babylon. Ezekiel used several forms of literature such as parables to tell of judgment, hope and the restoration of the People of God.

Daniel – the prophet remained steadfast in his devotion to God, even though he was a captive in Babylon. The Book of Daniel includes noteworthy visions and prophecies.

Haggai – the Prophet Haggai told the people to rebuild God's Temple in Jerusalem before rebuilding their own homes. In this way God was given first honor.

Zechariah – like Haggai, Zechariah urged the people to rebuild the Temple. His prophecies point to a grand and glorious future for the Israelites.

+ Deutero-Canonical Book

The Church stands as guardian and interpreter of the Scriptures. This is because there are many passages within the pages of the Bible which are difficult to understand and for which Christians need a guide, however devout or sincere they may be. As we have seen, when Philip asked the Ethiopian "Do you understand what you are reading?" He replied, "How can I, unless someone guides me? And he invited Philip to sit beside him" (Acts 8:31).

All Orthodox Christians must accept the Holy Scriptures in accordance with what the Church teaches. These are teachings which never have, nor will, change. It is this assurance which makes the Church the vessel that leads us to the Truth.

The Old and New Testaments are the written record of what God wants to say to us. The Old Testament leads to the birth of Christ, while the New Testament brings us to a full revelation of what God wishes for His people. The Bible is the very word of Almighty God and if one professes to be a Christian he or she cannot ignore the Holy Scriptures. To do so invites sure disaster to a "follower of the Lord", since the Bible leads us to Christ and salvation. The Scriptures are a product of Holy Tradition and have come to us from the earliest days of the Faith. Therefore, the Word of God is at the very core of our lives as faithful followers of the Lord.

The Orthodox Church recognizes 39 books in the Old Testament and 27 books in the New. The Septuagint is the standard translation used in Orthodoxy. It differs somewhat from the so-called "Hebrew version", in that the Septuagint contains an additional 10 books in the Old Testament called the Deutero-Canonical Books. They are part of the Scripture, yet stand on the different level than the books of the Hebrew Version.

B. BOOKS OF THE NEW TESTAMENT

Gospel according to St. Matthew – this Gospel contains many quotations and prophecies from the Old Testament. It is meant for a Jewish audience and it presents Jesus as the promised Messiah. The stories of Christ's life from His birth to resurrection are related in Matthew's account.

Gospel according to St. Mark – this is short, concise and perhaps the first Gospel written. Mark noted the miracles of Christ along with His sufferings. The Gospel was intended to solidify the faith of the people along with a commitment to Jesus Christ.

Gospel according to St. Luke – this Gospel presents salvation to all mankind. It includes Christ's concern with those on the fringes of society, the poor, dispossessed and lonely.

Gospel according to St. John – John's Gospel is arranged around the seven signs of Christ as the Son of God. John's Gospel is more theological than the others and the pages are filled with powerful imagery.

Acts of the Apostles – this book relates the coming of the Holy Spirit when Christ returns to His Father. It is a sequel to the Gospel of St. Luke. The book reads like a history of the early Church as the disciples attempted to spread the Faith throughout the known world.

Epistle of St. Paul to the Romans – St. Paul writes about life in the Holy Spirit, which is imparted to true believers through faith. It is a comforting book telling of God's great love for us and His ever-abiding forgiveness which is both strong and deep.

First Epistle of St. Paul to the Corinthians – this book addresses the problems found in the Church at Corinth which include immorality, dissension, and a confusion about the role of faith in the lives of the believers.

Second Epistle of St. Paul to the Corinthians – Paul tells of his connection with the Corinthian Church and how the teachings of certain false apostles are dividing that Church.

Epistle of St. Paul to the Galatians – this letter relates freedom from the Law through faith in Christ. Paul underscores that it is by faith that man is reconciled to God.

Epistle of St. Paul to the Ephesians – shows how God's purpose is to unite the Church of Christ , and bring together men and women from all nations.

Epistle of St. Paul to the Philippians – this is an Epistle of joy through belief in Christ and His teachings.

Epistle of St. Paul to the Colossians – Paul advises the faithful at Colossae to put aside their superstitions and make Christ the core of their faith.

First Epistle of St. Paul to the Thessalonians – this Epistle teaches about Christ's return to earth.

Second Epistle of St. Paul to the Thessalonians – this Epistle relates how believers should prepare for Christ's eventual return.

First Epistle of St. Paul to Timothy – this letter advises Timothy about worship, ministry and how the Church should work together for the common good. Timothy was a leader of the early Church.

Second Epistle of St. Paul to Timothy – the last letter of St. Paul. He again advises Timothy about the challenges of discipleship.

Epistle of St. Paul to Titus – Paul advises Titus how to minister to the faithful in Crete.

Epistle of St. Paul to Philemon – Paul urges Philemon to forgive his errant slave Onesimus and accept him as a believer in Christ.

Epistle to the Hebrews – this letter shows the early believers how to move from their traditional rituals and believe that Christ is the fulfillment of all things.

General Epistle of St. James – James teaches that Christ's followers must put beliefs into practice using good works as a way to live out their faith.

First General Epistle of St. Peter – a letter of comfort to persecuted Christians.

Second General Epistle of St. Peter – Paul warns against false teachers and urges Christians to remain loyal to Christ.

First Epistle of St. John – this letter covers basic teachings about Christianity and the command to love one another.

Second Epistle of St. John – warning against false teachers.

Third Epistle of St. John – tells of the need to grant hospitality to those who believe and preach Christ.

General Epistle of St. Jude – warning about those who are unbelievers outside the Faith.

The Revelation of Jesus Christ – this book, full of symbolism, encourages per-secuted believers and affirms that God will indeed care for them. It promises victory of good over evil and the creation of a new heaven and earth.

On Reading Scripture

"One of the great obstacles to preserving inner peace, my brother, is binding yourself as by some immutable law, by a set rule, to read so many psalms and so many chapters from the Gospels and Epistles. Those who set such rules to themselves, are usually in a hurry to com-plete the reading, not concerning themselves as to whether the heart is touched by it or not, or whether spiritual thoughts and contemplation arise in the mind; and when they fail to finish the reading, they are agi-tated and worried, not because they were deprived of the spiritual fruit of reading, which they need in order to create a new man in themselves, but simply because not everything was read. Listen to what St. Isaac has to say about this – (Chapter 30) – 'If you wish to gain delight in reading texts and understand the words of the Spirit you utter, brush aside the

quantity and number of verses, so that your mind may be absorbed in studying the words of the Spirit, until, filled with wonder at the Divine dispensation, your soul is incited to a lofty understanding of them and is thus moved to praise of God or to sorrow that profits the soul. Slavish work brings no peace to the mind and anxiety usually deprives the reason and understanding of the power of taste, and robs the thoughts like a leech, which sucks life from the body along with the blood of its members.'"

"Unseen Warfare" Chapter 20

A Prayer Before Reading Holy Scripture

"Illumine our hearts, O Master, who loves mankind, with the pure light of Thy Divine knowledge. Open the eyes of our mind to the understanding of Thy Gospel teachings. Implant also in us the fear of Thy blessed Commandments, that trampling down all carnal desires, we may enter upon a spiritual manner of living, both thinking and doing such things as are well-pleasing unto Thee. For Thou art the illumination of our souls and bodies, O Christ Our God, and unto Thee do we send up glory, together with Thy Father, who is from everlasting, and Thine All-holy, Good and Life-creating Spirit, now and ever, unto ages of ages. Amen."

HOW TO READ HOLY SCRIPTURE

Short Statements About the Word of God

- One cannot be a good Christian without a knowledge of Holy Scripture. The Bible is God's word for everyone, meant to inspire us to a decent life, while strengthening our union with our heavenly Father.

- Scripture tells us the story of God's great love for us. The saga of our salvation is found within its pages and the purpose of knowing the Bible is so that we might be converted to God's saving Truth.

- We learn the Bible best when we have a desire to know its riches and want to be closer to Our Lord. We gain the most from Holy Scripture when we read it regularly, i.e. on a daily basis, not just sporadically.

- After we read and study Holy Scripture we must meditate, and wait for God to speak to us in our minds and hearts.

- Holy Scripture is meant to be lived. After we discern its truths we must put them into action. Holy Scripture should change our lives for the better.

- The liturgy of the Church is steeped in Holy Scripture. Our teachings and prayers are based on Holy Scripture, therefore God speaks to us in our worship.

- When we read the Bible we begin a conversation with Almighty God. We read, meditate, listen and then act on what we have read in order to turn our lives around in accordance with God's Holy Will.

Scriptural references: 2 Timothy 3:16, Galatians 3:22.

On Reading Holy Scripture

"If now we will search the Holy Scriptures, exactly and not carelessly, we shall be able to attain to our salvation. If we continually dwell upon them we shall learn right teaching and a perfect life. For it cannot be that one who speaks with God, and hears God speak, should not profit."
St. John Chrysostom

"The best way to find out what is fitting for one's life is the meditation of the Divinely-inspired Scriptures. For in these are found counsels for our actions, and the lives of blessed men, though transmitted in writing, are put before us, like living images of a godly life, for our imitation of their good works."
St. Basil

"For whatsoever things were written previously were written for our learning, that through patience and comfort of the Scriptures we might have hope."
Romans 15:4

Christianity involves more than just obedience to external laws or canons. Those who truly wish to become one with Jesus Christ must take up their Cross daily and experience internal struggle and pain. The Beatitudes are a capsule listing of sufferings to endure – and difficulties to surmount. The rewards for such faithfulness are noted by Christ after each virtue and are, in effect, a summary of His blessing on our efforts to remain faithful Christians.

THE BEATITUDES (Matthew 5:3-12)

In Thy Kingdom remember us, O Lord, when Thou comest into Thy Kingdom.

Blessed are the poor in spirit, for theirs is the Kingdom of Heaven.

Blessed are they that mourn, for they shall be comforted.

Blessed are the meek, for they shall inherit the earth.

Blessed are those who hunger and thirst after righteousness, for they shall be filled.

Blessed are the merciful, for they shall obtain mercy.

Blessed are the pure in heart, for they shall see God.

Blessed are the peacemakers, for they shall be called sons of God.

Blessed are they that are persecuted for righteousness sake, for theirs is the Kingdom of Heaven.

Blessed are you when men shall revile you and persecute you, and shall say all manner of evil against you falsely for my sake. For they also persecuted the prophets who were before you.

Rejoice and be exceedingly glad, for great is your reward in heaven.

WHERE TO FIND WHAT HOLY SCRIPTURE SAYS ABOUT...

The Bible is a precious book which fills the need of every soul. The messages found in it provide spiritual nourishment for all Orthodox Christians. There are chapters exactly suited for your particular need or inquiry. The following are places in the Bible where you can find events related to the life of Jesus Christ, and assistance for living your lives as faithful Orthodox Christians.

God as Creator, Father and Redeemer
Birth of Jesus . . . . St. Luke, Chapter 2
Creation of the world . . . . Genesis, Chapter 1
God's People are comforted . . . . Isaiah, Chapter 40
The Good Shepherd . . . . St. John Chapter 10
Our Redemption . . . . St. Luke, Chapter 23
For those who suffer . . . . Isaiah, Chapter 53

Your Spiritual Needs
The Beatitudes . . . . St. Matthew, Chapter 5
For comfort . . . . 2 Corinthians, Chapter 1
Endurance in difficult times . . . . Hebrews, Chapter 12
For those in prison . . . . Acts, Chapter 23
Dealing with temptation . . . . Epistle of St. James, Chapter 1

Salvation
Atonement of Christ for our sins . . . . Hebrews, Chapter 9
Gift of courage . . . . Joshua, Chapter 1
Invitation to abundant life . . . . Isaiah, Chapter 55
New birth . . . . St. John , Chapter 3
How to pray . . . . St. Matthew, Chapter 6

How to Find Happiness

> *"Do not think to maintain the true Gospel of Christ, if you separate yourselves from the flock of Christ."*
>
> St. Cyprian

> *"Know this first: no prophecy of Holy Scripture is a matter of one's own interpretation, for prophecy never came by the will of man, but that men moved by the Holy Spirit may speak from God."*
>
> 2 Peter 1:20-21

Practical Directions for Living

When You Have Fallen

Life after Death

CHRIST'S PARABLES AND MIRACLES

Jesus taught in parables, or stories with familiar themes and experiences for the listener, which challenged them to make suitable responses in faith and action.

Over thirty parables have been recorded in the Gospels. In them, Jesus used realities of day-to-day life to reveal God's love in His Kingdom. However, when one is either disbelieving or indifferent, he or she is unable to discover the real meaning behind parables.

Miracles were not performed so that Jesus could simply dazzle crowds. His miracles reveal God's everlasting love and compassion for His people. God does not want mankind to dwell in loneliness, therefore Jesus' miracles show forth God's desire to reunite men and women with Him, whatever else has gone before to separate the Father in heaven from His children on earth.

Scriptural references : St. Matthew 13:1-3:10-17, St. Mark 4:11.

Doing Good To All

"Grow rich, not only in substance, but also in piety; not only in good but also in virtue; or rather only virtue. Be more honored than your neighbor, by showing more compassion. Be as God to the unfortunate, by imitating the mercy of God. For in nothing do we draw closer to God as in doing good to men. Though God does the greater things, and man the less, yet each man, I believe, according to his capacity. God made man and when man is undone, He remakes him. Never despise fallen man, never refuse to do good to those who have need of you. Give help. Help others to live. Give food, clothing, medicine, apply remedies to the afflicted, bind up their wounds, ask about their misfortunes, speak with them about patience and forbearance, come close to them; you will not be harmed, you will not contract their affliction, even though the timid believe this, misled by foolish talk. Have confidence! Let compassion overcome your timidity, the fear of God your softness. Let the love of your fellow man rise above the promptings of self-love. Do not despise your brother, do not pass him by! Do not turn away your face from him, as from something terrible, something fearful to be shunned and disowned. He is your own member, though this calamity has deformed him. The poor man has been left to you as to God: though you should pass by, over-proud in spirit. Perhaps I have shamed you, saying these things to you. But I have set before you the rule of the love of your neighbor, even though those who are hostile turn you away from accepting it. Whoever journeys on the sea is close to shipwreck, the nearer the shore, the more boldly he navigates."

St. John Chrysostom

THE TEN COMMANDMENTS (Exodus 20:1-17 and Deuteronomy 5:6-21)

I   I am the Lord your God; you shall have no other gods before me.

II   You shall not make unto yourself any graven images.

III   You shall not take the name of the Lord your God in vain.

IV   Remember the Sabbath Day, to keep it holy.

V   Honor your father and mother.

VI   You shall not kill.

VII   You shall not commit adultery.

VIII   You shall not steal.

IX   You shall not bear false witness against your neighbor.

X   You shall not covet your neighbor's goods nor wife.

9. THE CHURCH TEACHES MORALITY

TEACHING THE GIFT

WHAT THE CHURCH TEACHES IN REGARD TO SOCIAL PROBLEMS

Abortion – the Orthodox Church is unyielding in her opposition to abortion. At no time may Orthodox Christians secure an abortion, assist another in obtaining one, or support causes which promote abortion as a "right" of the parents, and as the natural consequence of a woman's desire to control her own body. Orthodox Christians may never destroy human life in any form.

Orthodox bishops have often restated the Church's stance against abortion by saying that it is an act of murder for which those involved, voluntarily, will answer to Almighty God.

However, the bishops show true compassion for those confronted with tragic circumstances where the lives of mothers and their unborn children are threatened and where painful decisions of life and death have to be made, such as those involving rape, incest and sickness.

Yet, the bishops are adamant that those considering abortion must resist this evil act. Adoption, rather than abortion, is the answer to unwanted pregnancy and those who secure an abortion must sincerely repent of the decision, in order to gain the assurance of God's mercy.

Orthodox Christians are urged to become politically involved so that proper laws may be enacted to protect the lives of unborn children while being sensitive to the complexities of life in contemporary society.

> *"As for women who furnish drugs for the purpose of procuring abortions, and those who take fetus-killing poisons, they are made subject to the penalty for murders."*
>
> Sixth Ecumenical Council – Canon XCI 681 A.D.

Suicide – is condemned by the Church as the ultimate breakdown of hope in God's Providence. Those in good mental health want to live according to God's plan for us. We trust in God to care for us in good times and in bad. To take one's life is to show contempt for God, as a Father, who cares for us with an infinite love. We, as Christians, should show our faith by believing that even personal suffering has a place in our life, and that we must accept adversities for our spiritual benefit.

Note: Usually the Church refuses a burial, memorial service or funeral service under her auspices to one who has committed suicide. However the Second Canon of the Trullan Council says that the priest should discover the aberrant mental condition of the person who commits suicide, and with the testimony of qualified personnel, a Church burial is allowed-if the person is found to be mentally deranged at the time of the suicide.

Homosexuality – is forbidden by the Church as contrary to moral law. Certain Scriptural texts proscribe carnal relations between members of the same-sex. Regardless, we must never withhold our love for those who struggle with this condition.

If homosexual Orthodox faithful are struggling with their situation, and have a firm determination to avoid carnal relations, they may receive Holy Communion, predicated upon personal repentance and a desire for spiritual growth.

In relation to this topic the Orthodox bishops, at every opportunity, defend marriage against continued attack and ridicule. Recently a Synod of Orthodox bishops, in a pastoral letter, noted: "Sexual intercourse is to be protected as a sacred expression of love within the community of heterosexual, monogamous marriage-for which God has given it to human beings for their sanctification. Sexual love is to be chaste and pure, devoid of lewdness, lechery, violence or self-gratification."

Extramarital Sex – is also condemned by the Church. Sex is a true gift from God, but a gift to be used only within marriage. Any sexual intercourse outside marriage is condemned as sinful, even if the couple has the firm intent of someday getting married (Exodus 20:14, St Matthew 5:28; Galatians 5:19; 2 Peter 2:14). Again, it must be stated that Christians are called upon to exhibit compassion and sensitivity in such matters. To condemn outright, without helping individuals reform themselves, is to write-off sinners as "lost," clearly contrary to the example of Christ who would not condemn the woman caught in adultery, yet reminded her of her sin (St. John 8:11).

Birth Control/Contraception – different opinions exist within the Orthodox Church regarding the question of birth control and contraception. While in past years there was a condemnation of anything which diminished the "natural order" within marriage, today the question of birth control is left largely to the consciences of the husband and wife – who alone determine how many children they can responsibly bring into the world. Of course, couples confused in this matter, or unable to make an informed decision, are advised to consult their priest for guidance on what the Church advises regarding the issues of parenthood and family.

Artificial Insemination – the procreation of children is not to be detached from the marital union. Married couples may use medical means to enhance conception of their common children but the use of semen or ova, other than that of the married couple who take responsibility for the offspring, is expressly forbidden to Orthodox faithful.

Divorce – divorce is permitted within the Orthodox Church and remarriage may be allowed for serious reasons. Certainly the Church upholds the sanctity and indissolubility of the marriage bond, however she is compassionate as regards situations where two people can no longer live peacefully or provide children with a healthy and nurturing home life. The Church bases her teaching of the words of Christ in St. Matthew 19:9 where our Lord says: "Whoever divorces his wife, except for fornication, and marries another commits adultery." So the Church offers those who are suffering in a bad marriage, a second chance rather than insisting that a marriage exists, when it does not! In theory , the Church permits divorce for adultery, but in practice she grants divorce and permits remarriage for anything which seriously "adulterates" a marriage. Some Orthodox jurisdictions require an ecclesiastical divorce. Check with your priest

The Family's Welfare – Orthodox teaching states that single parent families which exist due to death, divorce, or desertion are to be supported and honored.

Abuse in the family and society in general is strongly condemned. Any form of physical, psychological, spiritual and emotional abuse of men, women and children is not allowed under any circumstance. Abuse of subordinates by those in positions of authority is also censured while the abuse of those in supervisory roles by peers and subordinates is similarly condemned. Unjust criticism, uninformed judgments, ungrounded accusations, careless talk, malicious gossip, disrespect, disdain and outright insubordination of peers and/or those in authority is strictly forbidden to Orthodox Christians.

Cremation – because of the Church's reverence for the human body as a "Temple of the Holy Spirit" (1 Corinthians 6:19), the Orthodox Church prohibits cremation for her members.

Autopsy – When the causes of one's death have not been determined accurately, then doctors, with the permission of one's relatives, may perform an autopsy. Often the results of an autopsy are very beneficial.

The Orthodox Church does not encourage the unnecessary autopsy of the dead, and a body should not be given over merely for medical research or experimentation. Also, a routine autopsy should not be performed. It should be done only if required by civil law.

Orthodox Christians believe the human body is a repository of the Holy Spirit and insists that those who are responsible for the autopsy should accord the utmost respect for the remains of the deceased.

Circumcision – Jesus was circumcised in accordance with the Jewish Law. Some physicians believe circumcision is necessary for proper health and hygiene. The Orthodox Church does not prohibit circumcision as long as it is not mandated for strictly religious reasons, or as a cultic ritual.

Scriptural reference: St. Luke 2:21

Euthanasia/Prolonging Life – The Orthodox Church intends, in all its teaching, to affirm the right to life, the violation of which is an offense against the human person and against Almighty God, the author of all creation.

The Gospel of Christ is a "Gospel of Life", not of death, and so Orthodoxy proclaims this to every person. Often, she stands alone, or with a decided minority, in her opposition to the culture of death which prevails in our modern society. Yet it is a stance she gladly accepts for the love of Christ, and His message on the dignity of human existence.

As to the question of Euthanasia the Orthodox Church stands completely and unalterably opposed to this ever-increasing solution to human suffering and aging. Euthanasia is a dangerous "playing at God" by fallible human beings, where we place our will in direct opposition to the Almighty. There is never any situation where Euthanasia is acceptable as a convenient "way of death", or a "solution" for the suffering of a loved one.

As for prolonging life by extraordinary means, such as an artificial lung or kidney, we must understand that it is acceptable to use these artificial means, if life will be enhanced or prolonged, or where a weakened organism is allowed time and energy to recuperate by using these devices. Wherever life is enhanced or preserved, the means used are ordinarily allowed.

As for keeping an organism alive when the body's functions completely break down, there is the question of common sense and integrity. Where machines will keep the "dead body" functioning as if it were alive there is no teaching which commands that we use extreme and extraordinary means to maintain life. It is noteworthy that there are even prayers of the Church which call upon God to take a life unto Himself once again – and where the Church helps the dying person to face death with dignity and compassion.

In such cases, Euthanasia et al, the following guidelines from the book Contemporary Moral Issues by Fr. Stanley Harakas*, are to guide the Orthodox Christian faithful in making a decision as to matters of life-and-death:

Clear Orthodox Christian guidelines in these cases are available to us.

1. *We have the responsibility, as a trust from God, to maintain, preserve and protect our own lives and those lives entrusted to us.*

2. *In case of illness, we are obliged to use every method available to us to restore health, both spiritual and medical.*

3. *Life is so precious and to be so respected that even when health cannot be fully restored, it should be protected and maintained.*

4. *When, however, the major physical systems have broken down and there does not seem to be any expectation that they can be restored, Orthodox Christians may properly allow extraordinarily medical devices to be removed. When the body is struggling to die, when its numerous physical systems break down, and when it cannot be reasonably expected that the bodily systems will be able to regain their potential for life, the Orthodox Christian is no longer obligated to continue the use of extraordinary medical devices.*

5. *The decision should never be taken alone. It should be shared by the family, if possible. And, certainly, it should be made on the basis of expert medical opinion in consultation with the physician in charge of the case. It should also be made with the advice, counsel and prayer of an Orthodox priest.*

This action should never be confused with Euthanasia which brings to an end, deliberately and consciously, a life which is capable of maintaining itself with normal care. It is one thing to kill and murder, it is quite another to allow the peaceful separation of soul and body.

*"Contemporary and Moral Issues Facing the Orthodox Christian", by Stanley Harakas. Light and Life Publishing Co., Minneapolis, Minnesota 1982.

Capital Punishment – The issue of Capital Punishment is not an easy one to resolve. On one hand, punishment for breaking the law of the land has not been uniformly enforced, nor consistent in nature. Others believe that Capital Punishment does not serve as a deterrent to crime and should be replaced by life in prison or serious, on-going rehabilitation efforts.

It is clear that the State has the right to employ Capital Punishment as a deterrent to crime, if it so chooses. Yet, if capital punishment is employed then it must be done consistently. Capital Punishment is not just for the poor or those who are unable to afford legal assistance while the wealthy escape with life in prison or other compromises.

We know that there are Orthodox Christians who oppose Capital Punishment and believe instead in prison reform or rehabilitation. Active voices in this direction have been heard in Orthodox circles for some years. Yet it appears there is no one teaching of the Church in this regard. For the Orthodox believer, whatever his or her conscience dictates, the result must be clear, consistent, and coupled with the proper punishment for the person committing the crime, whether that is permanent imprisonment, rehabilitation, or death from State-sponsored legal means.

Note: Also involved in the question of Capital Punishment one must never forget the rights of the victim's families or survivors of brutal acts. How will these very real rights be addressed and will the families of victims also receive counseling, legal and material help for suffering the crimes of others?

Gambling – It is only common sense that a person who is addicted to gambling has a serious disorder which must be treated by professional counseling. The arguments for and against gambling are complicated. Can buying a raffle ticket be compared to losing hundreds of thousands of dollars because of an uncontrollable "urge"? Of course not! But one must seriously confront the dignity of having bingo, Las Vegas Nights, or carnivals with gambling and drinking to raise money for the parish. These efforts are seriously misguided and are certainly inconsistent with giving funds for the Church to continue her mission in the world. Giving must be motivated by love for God and with a clear sense of the Church's place in the salvation of souls.

More and more Orthodox parishes are abandoning crass and vulgar methods of fund-raising and accepting the responsibility of giving from motives of charity and love. This is certainly a hopeful sign within the Church and must be encouraged.

Other Questions – Other movements within contemporary society which must be approached with great caution and care are, Charismatic Christianity an emotional and "quick fix" to serious issues of salvation; Astrology and the Occult which are extremely dangerous contacts with Satanic forces, to be avoided at all costs; and using salacious publications for "entertainment" along with movies which glorify lust and exploitative dealings with the opposite sex. All these approaches to life are demeaning to the human spirit.

Drugs - Use of illegal drugs is condemned at all levels of Church teaching. An Orthodox Christian would be hard-placed to accept the use of drugs as "recreational or harmless fun", which is sometimes used as an excuse for smoking marijuana, or using other drugs. The Orthodox Christian must understand that these artificial ways of producing a "high" are certainly against the law of the Church and the will of Almighty God. Most Orthodox faithful are well-versed in the problems we face as a society, most of which are fueled by the use of many illegal drugs. Can anyone then, defend their use in the hard light of the varied and serious social problems they engender?

Stem Cell Research – "The Orthodox Church firmly rejects any and all manipulation of human embryos for research purposes as inherently immoral and a fundamental violation of human life… Embryonic stem cell research results in unmitigated harm. It should be unequivocally rejected in the interests of preserving both the sacredness and dignity of the human person." (Holy Synod of the Orthodox Church in America-October, 2001)

PSALM 103

Bless the Lord, O my soul, and all that is within me, bless His Holy Name.

Bless the Lord, O my soul, and forget not all His benefits.

Who forgives all your iniquities.

Who heals all your diseases.

Who redeems your life from destruction.

Who crowns you with loving kindness and tender mercies. Who satisfies your mouth with good things; so that your youth is renewed like eagles.

The Lord executes righteousness and justice for all who are oppressed.

He made known His way to Moses, His acts to the Children of Israel.

The Lord is merciful and gracious, slow to anger, and abounding in mercy.

He will not always strive with us, nor will he keep His anger forever.

He has not dealt with us according to our sins, nor punished us according to our iniquities.

For as the heavens are high above the earth, so great is His mercy towards those who fear Him.

As far as the East is from the West, so far has He removed our transgressions from us.

As a father pities his children, so the Lord pities those who fear Him.

For He knows our frame.

He remembers that we are dust.

As for man, his days are like grass. As a flower of the field, so he flourishes.

For the wind passes over it, and it is gone. And its place remembers it no more.

But the mercy of the Lord is from everlasting to everlasting, on those who fear Him, and His righteousness to our children's children.

To such as keep His covenant, and to those who remember His commandments to do them, the Lord has established His throne in heaven, and His kingdom rules overall.

Bless the Lord, you His angels, who excel in strength, who do His word.

Heeding the voice of His word. Bless the Lord, all you His hosts.

You ministers of His, who do His pleasures.

Bless the Lord, all His works. In all places of His dominion.

Bless the Lord, O my soul!

THE ROLE OF WOMEN IN THE ORTHODOX CHURCH

Throughout the history of the Church women have always served and ministered to the faithful. The Holy Gospels and The Acts of the Apostles testify to this fact (Acts 16:1; St. Matthew 27:55). The role of women as mothers and guardians of families is a sacred calling to be sure. Women have also been at the forefront of education whether it be in the home, or in Church-sponsored schools. Women have been a holy, leavening-agent in society and have taught the Church much by their witness and service to those in need.

Throughout history women in Orthodoxy have served the Church as enlightened empresses, as abbesses in monastic communities and as holy women who have guided both individuals and nations in their spiritual lives, an example very common in traditionally Orthodox countries.

As wives, women must complement their husbands as husbands must support their spouse. Their role is increasingly important in a society where families are being fractured at a frightening rate. In Orthodox society the home is a "little Church" and it is here where women enjoy an exalted place as mentors and teachers. Woman are also taking leadership roles in home-schooling , Church-sponsored educational institutions, and as writers and speakers.

The question of women serving as priests in the Orthodox Church is inappropriate. It is not a question of their worthiness or unworthiness which prevents a ministry at the altar. All of us , men or women, are unworthy of the sacred priesthood. Simply put, the clerical state is a matter of the majesty of the Divine, not a question of "human equality."

Therefore Orthodoxy offers women a traditional, dignified and complementary witness in Christian society. The idea of superiority of males, competition for office, or a "right" to the priesthood has no place in the Orthodox Church. While the voice of Orthodox women must be heard and respected in our Church life, service in other capacities will come at the right time, and in the correct manner.

We know that Orthodox women are students at Church-sponsored theological schools and there are active and growing associations of priests wives. Women have also become involved in publishing efforts, and are at the core of the educational ministry of the Church. They are speakers and writers and generally conduct the local educational efforts in parishes. All these roles are to be welcomed because the Church always has need of the exceptional gifts women bring to the Faith. The primary role of women, however, is that of a Christian mother and the first educator in the home, not necessarily involved in the lives of families other than their own.

The Royal Martyr Empress Alexandra once said, "No work any woman can do for Christ is as important as what she can, and should do, in her own home."

> *"Every Christian mother considers it one of her primary obligations to teach her child prayer as soon as his consciousness begins to awaken, prayer that is simple and easy for him to understand. His soul must be accustomed to the warm and fervent experience of prayer at home, by his cradle, for his neighbors, his family. The child's evening prayer claims and softens his soul, he experiences the sweetness of prayer with his heart, and catches the first scent of sacred feelings."*
>
> *Father Michael Pomazansky*

DEIFICATION

Most Christians just assume that the Christian life consists of going to Church, saying prayers, observing the Commandments and doing good works. Yet these are only the means to a Christian existence. The true aim of the Christian life is Deification, or union with Almighty God by acquiring the Holy Spirit. Our call in the Christian life is not just to be good but to be perfect, to be "Gods by grace." We "are called to ascend the ladder to heaven." As St. John Damascene writes, "Since the Creator bestowed on us His own image in His own spirit, and we did not keep them secure, He Himself took a share in our poor and weak nature so that He might cleanse us and make us incorruptible, and reinstate us as participants in His Divinity."

St. Maximos the Confessor states: "A sure warrant for looking forward with hope to the Deification of human nature is provided by the incarnation of God, which makes man God to the same degree as God Himself became a man. For it is clear that He who became without sin will divinize our human nature without changing it into the Divine nature, and will raise it up for His own sake, and to the same degree, as He lowered Himself for man's sake."

"When man cleanses himself from human passion, Christ comes to abide in him, making him light from light, true God from true God."
St. Simeon the New Theologian

"The human family constitutes the primary and essential element of human society. Peace in society will be a direct result of peace in the family: order and harmony in the secular, political realm will be the direct result of the order and harmony which arises out of creative guidance and the giving of real responsibility to children by assigning specific tasks to the trial."
St. John Chrysostom

"Marriage is more than human. It is a 'micro-basileia,' a miniature kingdom, which is the 'little house' of the Lord."
St. Clement of Alexandria (3rd century)

THE FAMILY AND ORTHODOXY

The Orthodox Church highly values the family. The faithful should live as a Christian community whether that community is a formal group of monastics (monks and nuns), a diocese, a parish, or a nuclear family of husband, wife and children. Each member of a family, whether monastic, in a parochial setting , or domestic home, accords respect to each other as a precious part of God's earthly ensemble.

In any Church setting the elderly are treated with special respect for their wisdom and experience.

In the family, whatever its nature, men and women are both distinct and equal. Neither sex has the right to disrespect or defraud the other. Male and female complement one another, each has their own role, and each stands equal and fully responsible for fulfilling their role as parent or child, before Almighty God.

The Family

"O God, our Father, bind together in Thine All-embracing love every family on earth. Banish anger and bitterness within homes, nourish forgiveness and peace. Bestow upon parents such wisdom and patience that they may gently exercise the disciplines of love, and call forth from their children the greatest virtue and highest skill. Instill in children such independence and self-respect that they may freely obey their parents and grow in the joys of companionship. Open hearts to hear the truth within the words another speaks. Open eyes to see the example of virtuous parents, open hearts to complete forgiveness and understanding of all things willed by Thee, O Creator and Sustainer of families."

St. Augustine

"Those who have devoted themselves to the Almighty Father have proved to be good parents to their children. Those who know the Son are good parents to their sons. Those who remember the Bridegroom-Christ are good husbands to their wives."

St. Clement

10. THE SETTING FOR WORSHIP

RETURNING THE GIFT

ORTHODOX CHURCH ARCHITECTURE – The Setting for the Worship of God

Orthodox churches are basically square in shape with a large central area surmounted by a dome. This contrasts with churches in the West that have long and narrow naves. In the past, Orthodox churches usually did not have permanent pews but contained benches along the walls for the elderly or infirm. This allowed churchgoers freedom to move around the sanctuary, an arrangement that secured pews would prohibit. In North America, these permanent pews have replaced the traditional open spaces imparting a more formal and structured feel to worship. Yet, Orthodox worship still allows a certain informality, which means that the faithful are free to move about at certain times during the services. This is fitting as we are children in our Father's house. Orthodox worship is family-oriented and more natural than some rigidly structured Western rituals. This also gives one a profound sense of being at home with God, comforted by a loving Father.

Iconostasis
In every Orthodox Church the sanctuary – where the altar, or Holy Table stands – is separated from the congregation by a screen called an Iconostasis covered with icons of Our Lord, the Mother of God, the angels, saints and apostles. The Iconostasis has three sets of doors. The central doors are the

Royal Doors, the openings on either side are the Deacon's Doors, one which leads to the area where the priest prepares the bread and wine, and the other to the place where the sacred books and relics are kept in a place of honor.

The Deacon's Doors are opened when needed during the Divine Liturgy, the Royal Doors are also opened and closed at appropriate times during the liturgical services.

The Church Edifice
The interior of the church building represents the universe. The ceiling recalls heaven, and the dome is actually adorned with an icon of Christ to remind us of His All-powerful presence in this world.

The Narthex: Entrance or Vestibule
The vestibule of the church represents the world in which man is called to serve Almighty God and to continually repent of sin.

The Nave: the Body of the Church
The nave represents the Kingdom of Heaven. When we pass from the narthex (the world) into the nave (heaven) we pass from this existence into the everlasting Kingdom of God.

The Icons in the Church
Icons remind Orthodox Christians that the Church is the abode of Christ and His saints. We venerate the icons and light a candle to remind us that Christ is the "Light of the World" and we are called to reflect His light in our everyday lives.

The Cathedral
The Cathedral Church in Orthodoxy is the main church in a diocese. It is usually the seat of the bishop in that it contains his "Cathedra", or throne. This signifies the unity that must exist in the Church, as the faithful gather around the bishop who is the icon of Jesus Christ.

The Cathedral is the church in which the bishop celebrates the official services of the year and this reminds the people that he is the chief hierarch (clergyman) of the diocese.

The Candelabra
The candelabra represent the columns of light with which God led the Israelites through the desert to the Promised Land. We too, are led to the Kingdom through the Holy Mysteries (Sacraments), and the teachings of the Gospels.

The Royal Doors

The doors in the center of the Iconostasis remind us that Christ is King. He is carried through these portals during the Great Entrance since Christ is the door leading to everlasting life. In some traditions the Royal Doors are referred to as the "Beautiful Gates."

The Holy Table-Altar

The Holy Table, or altar, in the Orthodox Church comes to us from the Holy of Holies found in the Jewish Temple. The sanctuary (the area where the Holy Table is found) is a sacred space which should be treated with the utmost care and respect.

The Royal Doors and curtain maintain an atmosphere of sanctity which cannot be violated . The altar area is not a meeting place, it is not common space. No informal talking of any kind should occur there. It must always be kept tidy and clean since it is the abode of Our Lord and His angels. Upon entering the sanctuary which should be done only by those who have been blessed for this purpose, one makes three prostrations, kisses the Gospel Book and the Holy Table, and then goes quietly about his duties.

The custom of holding business or social meetings inside the church building, in front of the Holy Table is a most unseemly one and should never be allowed! To use the church sanctuary as a common hall is to show disrespect for this sacred space, a space which is set aside for the worship of God alone.

The Table of Oblation

This is the table behind the Iconostasis and to the left of the altar where the priest prepares the gifts of bread and wine during the Service of Oblation (Proskomedia). Later, during the Great Entrance, the gifts are carried in procession through the Royal Doors to the Holy Table.

The Tabernacle

The Tabernacle is a wooden or metal object, made to represent a small church, which is kept in the middle of the Holy Table. Sometimes it is very elaborate since this is where the Lord's precious Body and Blood are kept in reserve for emergencies such as sick calls. Jesus Christ indeed dwells in the Tabernacle at all times. We should show the utmost respect for his Divine presence every time we enter the church building.

The Eternal Light

This is the large votive light which is suspended above the Tabernacle or the Royal Doors. It symbolizes two things, 1. Jesus Christ is the "Light of the World." 2. God created light before all else and without both the light of the Gospel and the Mysteries of the Church, we would surely dwell in spiritual darkness, selfishness and sin.

The Gospel Book
The Gospel Book is kept in a prominent place on the Holy Table. The Gospel is enthroned, representing the presence of Christ as the "Word of Life." It is also placed before the Tabernacle to remind us that Christ is the "Bread of Life", food for our earthly journey.

The Cross
The Cross reminds us that Christ died for our sins. Because of His suffering, death and resurrection we are redeemed in the eyes of Almighty God and able to reach everlasting life in heaven. The Cross is also symbolic of the words of Christ, "Greater love has no man, than that he would lay down his life for his friends" (St. John 15:13).

The Seven-branch Candelabrum
The Candelabrum represents the Seven Gifts of the Holy Spirit and the Seven Mysteries of the Church, which bring us true life in Christ. The Candelabrum also represents the seven days of creation according to the Book of Genesis (Genesis 1:1-31; 2:1-3).

The Fans (Ripidia)
The Ripidia are usually metal or wooden fans upon which are carved two six-winged angels, the Seraphim. These ranks of angels according to Psalm 91, 2 Thessalonians 1:7, Isaiah 6:1-3, surround the throne of God in heaven, continually singing His holy praises. In the sanctuary the fans are placed in back of the Holy Table to signify that angels are with us at all times, most significantly, at the celebration of the Divine Liturgy.

The Bishop's Throne (Cathedral)
The bishop's throne is situated behind the Holy Table or to the right of the Iconostasis. The bishop is considered the local head of the Church and he represents the presence of Jesus Christ. The bishop occupies his throne during all major liturgical services.

The Pulpit
The pulpit is located to the left of the Iconostasis near the center of the nave. It is used for the reading of the Gospels and preaching the sermon. It represents the stone used to seal the tomb of Christ from which the angel proclaimed the good news of the resurrection to myrrh-bearing women. The pulpit is sometimes decorated with icons of Christ and the Four Evangelists.

The Antimens (Antimension)
The word Antimens simply means "in place of the table." The Antimens was originally made of wood or cloth. Today it is a cloth stamped with the icon of the burial of Christ into which relics of a saint are sewn, and upon which the Eucharist is celebrated. The Antimens is consecrated by a bishop and kept on the Holy Table at all times. It represents the tomb of Our Lord, and the tombs of the holy martyrs of the early Church.

Relics

The Orthodox Church has venerated relics since the very first days of the Faith. St. Polycarp's body was shown great reverence from the early second century and there were many reports of miracles because of the first Christian's devotion to his remains. The early faithful noted "his relics were more valuable than precious stones and finer than refined gold."

Also, in Acts 19:11-12, the cloth which had touched the body of St. Paul, was responsible for the exorcism of evil spirits and curing the sick.

Relics are still honored in remembrance of Christ, for whose witness the saints lived and died. Also, one's body, according to St. Paul, is the "Temple of the Holy Spirit" (1 Corinthians 6.19). The early believers concluded that since the bodies of the saints served them while they lived (as organs of the Spirit), they should be precious to all Christians as well. As long as relics do not degenerate into superstition they are a valuable witness to those who were saints of God and served as instruments of many miracles.

> *"Many people erect high 'temples' and decorate them. They build tall belfries and cast great bells. They sew rich vestments for the churches and frame the sacred books, the icons and the Cross with gold and jewels. With these material gifts they wish to please the immaterial God: but they despise the poor and leave them to their fate; and thus they do what God has not ordained and do not what He has ordained. I do not condemn the building of churches. I only condemn neglect of the work of God. Churches are necessary, but not the magnificence of churches. Public worship can be held in any place, provided it is clean. But people-the living temples of God-cannot exist without food, clothing and rest."*
> *St. Tikhon of Zadonsk*

ICONS

It has been said that an Orthodox parish church is a tiny part of God's Kingdom that has been reclaimed so that He might truly dwell there. Subsequently, a proper etiquette must be observed when entering a church building.

Since the parish church is a part of the Kingdom, it holds representations of angels and saints who have served God so well. Churches are full of icons and the first action of an Orthodox Christian upon entering the sanctuary is to reverence the Holy Table and the icons of our Lord, His Mother, various apostles, and saints. As one does this a candle is lighted and left to burn as a remembrance. Prayers are also said at this time and often the faithful will approach the icons during the Divine Liturgy when they feel the need to communicate with the Holy Ones and offer a prayer for some special need.

It is important to remember that icons and murals are not mere decorations but form an integral part of what the church building represents. Icons fill the church building and are places where heaven meets earth. At a traditional Sunday liturgy, or during festive times, the icons of Christ, the Theotokos, saints, and angels lit by flickering candles, create a true and valuable portrait of the whole Church being present, i.e. the earthly Church at worship, and the heavenly Church represented by the icons. Thus we see the Church truly as "Heaven on Earth."

Often services take place in front of the Iconostasis. They are usually unhurried, and of greater length than in Western Churches. The Holy Mysteries are celebrated in close proximity to the congregation rather than at a high altar or dozens of feet away from the participants, as in a Gothic cathedral.

In all, one must admit that the mystical quality, the beauty, the employment of all our senses, and even the repetitions of the litanies serve to impart a timeless, wondrous, and utterly sacred sense to Orthodox worship.

Scriptural references: I Kings 6:29-35. 2 Chronicles 2: 12-13, Acts 2:46.

As Orthodox Christians we venerate and honor icons and other objects of our Faith. No one would ever think of desecrating an icon, the Gospel Book, or the Cross. However, we must remember that these items are not magic. We venerate and honor them because of whom and what they represent. They are material things that have been elevated to a special place in our lives. The Cross, for example, represents the redemption of the human race, and it is therefore accorded the greatest dignity and honor. When we bow and kiss an icon, or any religious object, we are showing our love, devotion and thankfulness to Almighty God for the saints, who were great examples of what all Christians must aspire to be.

Some say, quite erroneously, that Orthodox Christians "worship" icons. This is certainly untrue. We give honor to icons, or venerate them, because of what they represent. **We worship only Almighty God!**

Throughout the pages of the Old Testament, prohibition against the worship of idols was strictly enforced because people actually believed a god or goddess lived inside the wood, stone or metal, and that the idol had power in and of itself.

Orthodox Christians, however, understand that the material in religious objects is powerless to work of itself. Therefore the Church teaches us to venerate – not worship – symbols because of what they represent, not what they actually are.

ICON CORNERS

It should be the custom of every Orthodox home to construct an Icon Corner. On this table or shelf there should be the icon of the patron saint of the person/family, a lampada or vigil light, copies of the prayers that the family prays together, a Bible, and holy water. A small censer might also be added.

Icons should be placed in the family car and in bedrooms, to act as the point where the living members of the Church meet those who have gone on to be with the Lord. Saints should be our friends and helpers, not just distant figures from antiquity about which nice stories are passed on from generation to generation.

HOW TO VENERATE ICONS

It is the traditional custom of the Orthodox Church that worshipers should venerate icons upon entering a church or chapel. We venerate icons by bowing from the waist, with our hand lowered to touch the floor. We repeat this, rise, kiss the icon, and bow a third time.

We must always keep in our thoughts that we do not give honor, or venera-tion, to the wood but to the actual prototype that is represented on the icon. In other words we give adoration only to the person depicted.

Note: One thing is important to remember. It has become fashionable for women to wear lipstick when they venerate an icon or approach the chalice. This is a custom that should be discouraged since it shows disrespect to sacred and holy things and other worshipers in the church.

> *"Enter into the church and wash away your sins. For here there is a hospital and not a court of law. Do not be ashamed again to enter the church: be ashamed when you sin, but not when you repent."*
> *St. John Chrysostom 347-407*

THE MEANING AND LANGUAGE OF ICONS

The word icon, so badly misused in today's culture, means "image." The icon is one of the most distinctive features of the Eastern Church. The use of sacred icons, as representatives of individual piety and spirituality, goes back to the earliest days of the Christian Church.

The icon is sometimes referred to as a "Window Into Heaven." Icons are also called "Doorways into stillness, unto closeness with God." Whatever name you wish to give to the icon it stands for something other than itself. The icon is a representation of a real person, or event, in Christian history and it is designed to lead us to remember that person/events' purpose and the part they played in our eternal salvation. The icon is supposed to uplift us, by honoring a sacred thing, while instructing us in the truths of our Faith, and arousing us to a blessed appreciation of the way in which God works miracles in our lives. The icon keeps these truths alive.

Icons can be painted images on wood, frescoes or mosaics that bear witness to the reality of God's Kingdom on earth. Icons proclaim the Gospel in a very special way. Using line, form, and color, icons show sacred persons and events not as they appear to be, but as a reality that has been changed, transfigured and made holy by the power of God. Icons are to be honored and venerated , but never worshiped, for this is something reserved to God alone!

Herein we try to present a practical study of the icon, showing what forms the figures represent and how color, position and clothing can have a deep and significant meaning in interpreting this sacred art.

Icons in a church are arranged on an Iconostasis, which is the large screen stretching across the front of a church building. The Iconostasis has three doors, the middle set is called the Holy Doors and the two side doors are referred to as Deacon's Doors. A typical Iconostasis may be very elaborate with many tiers, or a simple arrangement according to local custom.

In Russian churches the Iconostasis sometimes reaches the ceiling of the sanctuary. Iconostasis is the common term employed for this significant portion of Church architecture, however the word "Templon" is also used.

> *"When at prayer in church it is profitable to stand with closed eyes in eternal mindfulness, and to open your eyes only when you become downcast, or when sleep should weigh you down and incline you to doze, then you should fix your eyes upon an icon and the candle burning before it."*
>
> *St. Seraphim of Sarov*

The act of painting an icon is a definite experience of worship and service. Before beginning an icon the painter must fast for a specified time and involve oneself in a period of prayer. He or she is also bound to follow a definite, and quite ancient, pattern in painting.

Icons do not attempt to copy nature. Instead of portraying the natural world which will "pass away" the iconographer attempts to show the spiritual nature of God's creation and the person who is now triumphant in God's eternal, unchanging Kingdom of Heaven. Earthly time, space and emotion are meaningless in the icon. There is a definite sense of timelessness and spiritual truth portrayed in this religious art form that has no equal in our secular world.

The following listing shows what the various elements of icon painting mean and how the construction of an icon imparts a Godly sense of wisdom and truth. It has been said that, "through icons, heaven reaches down to the worshiper."

ELEMENTS OF ICONOGRAPHY

The nose on an icon is thin and elongated. It is no longer needed for detecting smells. The senses usually associated with the human body are now unnecessary.

The mouth is small, there is no need for language. Communication comes from the visual senses and we know everything we need to know through contemplation of the icon-in mental prayer.

The eyes of the icon are very large. They have seen Almighty God and have been opened to the "ultimate reality." They are aware of the Divine and are now "Windows into Heaven."

The person in the icon is made holy because of the presence of the Holy Spirit.

Full or three-quarter figures are portrayed as having a conversation with the world. They are in the process of communication with us and are relating God's presence in our lives.

A large forehead signifies wisdom.

Subdued colors are indicators of a spiritual victory. The person portrayed has acquired God in a very special sense and is no longer bound by earthly things or conventions.

The * is an indicator of virginity. It appears on the veil of the Theotokos and sometimes on the garments of a virgin or martyr.

Early bishops are portrayed in their episcopal phelonions and stoles. In later centuries they are shown in the sakkos.

The crown is a symbol of martyrdom, but there is no suffering ever depicted in an icon, in relation to one's giving his/her life for Christ.

Faces on icons are emotionless to show an ascetic lifestyle, since there can be no range of emotions in a heaven where love rules supreme.

Wrinkles are used to indicate both age and suffering.

Prophets are usually painted with white hair and brown or olive tunics. Occasionally dark hair is used if the prophet is "young" or has escaped unusual suffering.

Overshadowed eyes are indicative of a person observing the world and its activities.

There are never shadows in iconography because shadows are the result of light from outside (the world.) Illumination, or the experience of the Holy

Spirit, emanates from within and shines on the face of the saint.

The Theotokos often looks past the Christ Child, which indicates a vision of the forthcoming passion of Jesus. It is almost as if the Virgin is contemplating the suffering which is to come into her life.

There are several types of Marian icons: the Theotokos or Birth-giver representations, i.e. the Mother of God. The Mother of God at prayer, with outstretched arms, is called the Orans Icon.

On one famous icon, the Mother of God contemplates the passion of Christ with two angels in the upper corners holding the instruments of the crucifixion.

Ranking of the Saints
The saints of the Church have a special ranking, according to their place in God's plan of salvation. The ranking begins, after Christ and the Theotokos with:

1. St. John the Baptist
2. St. Michael the Archangel
3. St. Gabriel the Archangel
4. St. Peter the Apostle
5. St. Paul of Tarsus
6. St. Basil, Saint and Bishop
7. St. John Chrysostom, Saint and Bishop
8. St. Nicholas, Saint and Benefactor
9. St. Gregory of Nazianzus, Saint and Bishop
10. St. George, Saint and Martyr
11. St. Theodore
12. St. Demetrius, Saint and teacher

The sadness on the face of the Virgin Mary indicates future sorrow, as she contemplates the passion and death of Jesus Christ.

Weeping angels indicate anticipation and participation in the passion of Christ.

The Nimbus or Corona (Halo) portrays holiness, and sainthood.

Realistic gestures, such as resting the head on the hand or touching the thumb to the nose are human touches.

A covered face means extreme sorrow.

Raised hands indicate an attitude of prayer.

Frontal views indicate high-ranking in the listing of saints.

The Imperial chair, the "Sella Curulis" shows an imperial, kingly position. A saint who was once royalty, or Christ the King, is portrayed in glory!

Bowing to one another shows repentance and the need for mutual forgiveness.

> *"Those who can read learn by means of writing. The uneducated learn by looking at holy icons."*
>
> *St. Gregory of Rome*

Coloring System of Icons:

Green and brown represent the earth/vegetation.
Blue is a sign of heaven and contemplation.
Scarlet/red means strength, or the blood of martyrs.
Deeper red stands for the blood of Christ/imperial concerns.
White indicates purity, and the invisible presence of God.
Gold represents magnificence, the Sun, or Divine energy.

Whoever accepts the Holy Scriptures will accept icons since they are both revelations of the same Truth.

In iconography there is a definite distinction between the body and the flesh. The icon painter reproduces the human body without drawing attention to the flesh. Icons present the spiritualized, transfigured body to the faithful.

The Icon Has Three Levels of Meaning

First, the icons remind us of certain Biblical texts and the occasions, or individuals, which they represent.

Secondly, the icon represents the life of Almighty God, and how God uses individuals and events to show forth His glory and power.

Thirdly, one's salvation is available for those who pray and recognize God's unending love for mankind, and that each of us is infinitely precious in the mind and eyes of the Creator.

Note: Icon Corners are featured in many Eastern Christian homes. Icons, candles and censers are included. Icons are kissed as an expression of the love we have for Almighty God, and all His saints.

St. John of Damascus wrote: "If I have no books, I go to the church. The flowers of the paintings make me look, charm my eyes as a flowering meadow does, and softly stir the glory of God in my soul."

BLESSINGS IN THE ORTHODOX CHURCH

Orthodox faithful are very familiar with blessings, such as those bestowed on food, houses, water, crosses, medals, and persons.

Blessings are not superstitions. They do not transfer something that is unholy into the realm of the sacred. Everything that comes from God is good and to bless something is done with the knowledge that it is a gift from God. It means that when we bless something it is the recognition of God's presence among us. To bless a medal, a cross, food, etc. means that what we have on earth is actually a gift of the Almighty One.

Blessing water, fruit or people gives acknowledgment to these persons and things as visible signs of God's presence in our world. Through things which are blessed we see the world with new eyes, and view creation as God's gift to us, as His loving concern for the struggles and joys of our everyday lives.

Blessing of Bread, Wheat, Wine and Oil
On the eve of every great holy day and feast, loaves of bread, wheat, wine and oil are blessed. These gifts of God are traditional signs of prosperity, therefore we both ask God to multiply His gifts to us and thank Him for His goodness.

Blessing of water
On Jan. 6, the Feast of the Baptism of Our Lord is celebrated. It is also known as the Feast of the Theophany, or Epiphany. When St. John the Baptist baptized Jesus Christ in the Jordan River, the water became sanctified. In remembrance of this event the Church blesses water, once again calling upon God to be present and sanctify it, while manifesting His Divine love for us.

This blessed water is taken home by the people to drink and becomes a vehicle whereby we are cleansed. God once again becomes intimately present in our lives. Water is also blessed on the first day of each month.

Blessing of Palms and Pussy Willows
On the "Feast of the Entrance of Our Lord into Jerusalem", or "Palm Sunday", we recall how the people waved palm branches to welcome Our Savior. If palms are not available then we use what God has provided by blessing pussy willows, the first signs of Spring, for Christ is truly "Spring," or "new life" for us.

The Paschal Basket
Orthodox Christians fast from many foods during Great and Holy Lent. This time offers us the opportunity for spiritual refreshment by focusing on what is truly important in our lives.

To prepare for Holy Pascha , Orthodox people bring a basket filled with certain foods to be blessed in church. (Traditions vary as to when this is done.)

The foods in these baskets are traditional and include, "Paska" a rich sweet bread into which a candle is inserted (and on which the symbol for "Christ is Risen" is impressed), red-dyed eggs, meats such as lamb, ham and various sausages, cheese, butter, boiled beets, horseradish, salt and wine.

In this way the Paschal celebrations in church are tied to the observances in the home, which is, after all, a little church. These wonderful customs also bring forth the idea that everything we do should be for the glory of Almighty God and serve as a way to observe traditions that have been in the Orthodox Church for centuries.

Our blessed food becomes a sign that Our Lord, indeed, restored all things by His Holy Resurrection and that He is now with us in glory, continuing to sustain us with His gifts of food and drink.

Blessing of Fruit
On August 6th the Feast of the Transfiguration of Our Lord is commemorated. This feast falls during the harvest season signifying that all we have depends on God's great goodness. All blessings come from God and we are reminded once again that through the fruits of the harvest, God is present in our lives.

Blessing of Flowers
Flowers are brought to the church on the Feast of the Dormition ("The Falling Asleep of The Mother of God"). Tradition says that when the Virgin Theotokos fell asleep in the Lord, the apostles placed her in a crypt. St. Thomas, not present for the burial, begged to see the Mother of His Lord one more time. When the apostles went to her tomb it was empty. Only flowers were present where the Mother of God had been placed.

On August 15th, as a reminder of this event, flowers are brought to the church to be blessed. When they are taken to one's home they are no longer just flowers, they are tangible evidence of the beauty of all things that come from Almighty God.

House Blessings
It is a pious and beautiful custom for Orthodox Christians to ask the priest to bless their house, especially at the time of Epiphany. However, it is also customary to bless a new home, thereby placing it in the care of the Lord, or to bless one's family on special occasions. Consult your priest in advance as a courtesy, and invite him to invoke the blessing of the Lord on your family or home, as a sign of your faith in the loving protection of Almighty God.

Requesting a Blessing
When an Orthodox Christian approaches a bishop, or priest, it is customary to request a blessing. A bow, accompanied by reaching down and touching the floor with the right hand-and the words, "Father, or (if a bishop "Your

Grace"), Bless" is common etiquette. Placing our right hand over our left, the priest, (or bishop), will bless us with the words, "May the Lord Bless You" and place his hand in ours. We then kiss his hand in thanksgiving.

Greetings to Fellow Christians
It is an ancient and beautiful custom Orthodox Christians to greet one another with "holy words" which bind us together as believing members in the Faith.

For example, at Pascha, the Lord's Resurrection, it is customary to greet one another with the spoken or written words, "Christ is risen. Truly, He is risen." We do this from Pascha to the Eve of the Ascension of Our Lord. Also, at the Feast of the Nativity, one should greet others with the words, "Christ is born. Glorify Him." Words are an outward expression of our inner feelings. Faithful Orthodox Christians show forth their faith in both words and noble actions.

> *"Lord, as the first martyr, Stephen, prayed before his murderers, so do we fall before Thee and pray, forgive all who hate, slander and maltreat us, and let not one of them perish because of me, but may all be saved by Thy Grace, O God most bountiful."*
>
> *A Desert Father*

Other Mysteries and Blessings
It may come as a surprise that the Orthodox Church has never formally limited the Holy Mysteries to just seven in number. This listing is used basically as a convenient teaching tool. However, there are certain actions which we might call "Mysteries" which are used in the life of the Church to draw us closer to God. They are of a sacred nature, and may vary from the Rite of Monastic Profession, to the blessing of fruits, fields, farms, homes, babies or any object which one wishes to set aside for the glory of God and as a thanksgiving for His benefits.

> *"We are commanded to worship, not only on special days, but continuously – all our life through, and in all possible ways."*
>
> *St. Clement of Alexandria*

> *"Thou did form us and place us in the paradise of pleasure... Thou did not cast us off forever, yet continually visited us through the holy prophets and, in these last days, Thou did manifest to us who sat in darkness and the shadow of death, Thine Only-begotten Son. He showed us the ways of salvation, granted us to be reborn by water and the spirit, and made us a people by His own possession, sanctifying us by His Spirit. He loved His own who were in the world, and gave Himself for our salvation unto death which reigned over us and held us down because of our sins."*
>
> *St. Basil*

Orthodox Greetings
Glory to Jesus Christ! Glory forever! (General)

Christ is among us! He is and always will be! (General)

Christ is born! Glorify Him! (At the Nativity of Christ)

Christ is risen! Truly He is risen! (At Paschal Time)

Exorcisms
People who have not been properly taught have a very warped view of exor-cisms. By definition, exorcisms are the casting out of evil spirits by the means of prayer and fasting. Christ and His apostles cast out evil from people who were "possessed" (St. Matthew 10:1, St. Luke 11:14-23, Acts 16:18;19:13-20) and the Church still prays for those who are afflicted by the Evil One.

The most common exorcisms in the Church are those used before the Mystery of Baptism. These exorcisms denounce Satan, accept the Lordship of Jesus Christ, and are four in number. After praying to avert the influence of evil spirits in the life of the newly-illuminated , the sponsors/candidate recite the Affirmations in Christ and the Nicene Creed as a symbol of their Orthodox Faith.

Along with the exorcisms of Baptism, there are certain prayers in the sanctifi-cation of water, blessing of oils, or consecrating sacred vessels that are part of the life of the Church. What should be avoided, however, is not the denial of evil and the influence of Satan in our lives, but the pagan rituals for exorcisms that have taken on a popular life of their own, and are currently practiced in some Churches by uninformed clergy. Casting out evil needs the assistance of the Church through her corporate prayers, and accomplished through the faith and the exemplary spiritual life of her members. This prevents Satan and his legions from gaining hold of individuals or groups who may be sorely lacking in holiness.

Scriptural references: St. Matthew 10:1, St. Luke 11:14, Acts 16:18,19:13, Acts 16:16-18.

The Sign of the Cross
Orthodox Christians, from the very first days of the Faith, have used the Sign of Christ's Cross as a blessing. We make the Sign of the Cross by joining our thumb and first two fingers, touching our forehead, right shoulder then the left.

The three fingers that we bring together represent the Holy Trinity and the two fingers we touch on the palm of our hand represent the Divine and human natures of Christ, in that He was both God and man. The three fingers (joined) show that we believe in God the Father who loves us, God the Son who saves us, and God the Holy Spirit who lives in us. The remaining two fingers are lowered to the palm of the hand to show that "Jesus came down from heaven" to save us. Bishops and priests bless others with the "Christogram" making the Sign of Christ with their right hand.

It is customary for any Orthodox Christian to bless children, food or oneself, placing the sign of the Cross on the person or object.

A Most Powerful Weapon – Holy Water
There is a wealth of material in Orthodox literature, prayers, Church services and the lives of saints that refer to the power of the Sign of the Cross.

It is known, by what the Fathers write and the Holy Saints relate in their testimonies, that the demons flee from the Sign of the Cross as they are unable to withstand its power or its spiritual effect. Even the prayers of the Church reflect this fact, as in the verse:

> "Thou gave us Thy Cross as the weapon against the might of Satan, O Lord, for he trembles and quakes at its sight, unable to bear the sight of its awesome strength."

Also, in the prayers of Vespers we read:

> "Let the demons perish from the presence of those who love God and sign themselves with the Sign of the Cross and say with joy, 'Rejoice, most precious and Life-giving Cross of the Lord, for thou drives away demons by the power of Our Lord Jesus Christ who was crucified on thee'."

> "The Cross is the crown of victory. It has brought life to those blinded by ignorance of its power. The Cross has released those enslaved by sin. Indeed, it has redeemed the whole of mankind. Do not, then, be ashamed of the Cross of Christ: rather, glory in it. Although it is a stumbling block to the Jews and folly to the Gentiles, the message of the Cross is our salvation. Of course it is folly to those who are perishing, but to us who are being saved, it is the power of God. For it was not a mere man who died for us, but the Son of God, God made man."
>
> From "The Catechesis"
> St. Cyril of Jerusalem (4th century)

The saints taught their disciples about the power of the Holy Cross. For example St. Anthony the Great, admonished his monks to "Fortify yourselves and the house by the Sign of the Cross and immediately turn to prayer, then the demons will vanish, for they are filled with fear when they see the Sign of Our Lord's Cross."

Also, St. John Chrysostom advises that, "When you make the Sign of the Cross make it not only with your fingers but with your faith. If you engrave its image onto your forehead no impure spirit will dare to attack you. He sees the blade with which he has been wounded, this sword with which he has received his death blow."

Concerning the Use of Holy Water in the Church

When water is blessed at the Feast of Theophany, and other times during the year, a wondrous thing happens.

We call on the Holy Spirit to come over the waters and change them so that they become an agent for healing sickness, driving away evil, and sanctifying both people and their dwellings.

We call upon Christ to help us, and the Church responds by giving us this marvelous blessing in the form of Holy Water. We know that God will protect us and that He sanctifies even the most common of natural things. The use, then, of Holy Water is a good and commendable tradition. It is not to be disparaged. We should always have a supply of this water in our homes to drink, i.e. an Agiasma (Holy Thing) as the Greeks refer to it, and make use of it whenever it becomes necessary. This could be at the time of illness, when traveling, when one is anxious or depressed, and for blessing children, the aged or infirmed or any Orthodox believer.

Drinking Holy Water strengthens the soul. If used with prayer, and belief in its power, it will serve us well. Used mechanically, or believing it to be magic, will do no good and quite possibly harm one spiritually.

Maintain this wonderful tradition in your home to express your belief, and show forth your faith in Almighty God and His glorious providence in our lives.

11. THE KINGDOM ON EARTH

THE CHURCH

CHRIST'S TRUE CHURCH

We know that many Churches call themselves Christian. This implies that they are "of Christ" claiming the title of being "His Church." Therefore we hear people speak of the Roman (Papal) Church, the Protestant Church, i.e. the Methodist, Baptist, Presbyterian Church, and so on. Which of these is the "Church of Christ", the One, Holy, Catholic and Apostolic Church of Christ? Which of these constitutes the Church and is alone, "the pillar and ground of the truth", and which of these stands as the Divine ark of our salvation? (1 Timothy 3:15).

Although the members of these confessions are our brothers and sisters, and we respect them as fellow pilgrims to eternal life, we must be truthful in saying that because they are so many and varied, (in fact thousands of individual denominations and sects, each with its own Confession of Faith, dogmas, and religious rites), they cannot all constitute the One Church of Christ. In fact, we must not technically speak of a Protestant Church, but confessions within the Protestant Church.

Where then is the Church of Christ? It is not misplaced arrogance to believe the claims of the Orthodox Church that she is the One, Holy, Catholic, and Apostolic Church since she has preserved the Apostolic Faith in its entirety. She alone, faithfully preserves the correct interpretation of Holy Scriptures, the traditions of the apostles transmitted by the Holy Fathers, and she has protected the pristine Faith from being polluted by new or strange doctrines. Holy Orthodoxy preserves the dogmas and canons of the Seven Councils. She is the Faith of the martyrs, the Church of the God-bearing Fathers, her worship is unadulterated and un-compromised, and her teaching is unchanged from the first days of Christianity.

ECUMENISM

Ecumenism to some, is a belief that the Apostolic Faith is not to be found in any one Church, but partially in all the Churches. Ecumenists teach that if we were to take some teachings from this Church and some from that Church and put them altogether we create an Ecumenical Church, melded by the things we have in common, which is actually a contradiction of the Truth.

Ecumenists believe that the Church is a tree with countless branches. Yet, Orthodox Christians believe Truth can only be one. We cannot amalgamate the teachings of the Churches, by taking the basic truths of Christianity along with all the heresies and false teachings of participating Churches and somehow - by combining the best of all of them - come up with one Church.

True Ecumenism sees the Church as that which existed before the schisms of the late first millennium and beyond. Heresy and untruth cannot stand aside the Truth! How can Orthodoxy stand side-by-side with false teaching, faith with unbelief, Truth with error?

Since Truth cannot tolerate untruth, it suffices to say that false Ecumenism, i.e. compromising the Truth simply for organic unity, is in no way acceptable to the Orthodox Church.

How the Roman Catholic Church Views Ecumenism
Regardless of the Roman Catholic Church's participation in numerous activities devoted to Ecumenical contacts some in which the Orthodox Church has refused to participate, this participation by Roman Catholics is not an indicator of their belief in the equality of the Churches!

One of the most telling statements made about Ecumenism, as practiced by Roman Catholics, was that of Cardinal Heenan, one-time Archbishop of Westminister and the Primate of All-England, who said:

"Ecumenism to Roman Catholics does not mean pretending that all denominations are equally true. It does not mean that the (Roman) Catholic Church has nothing more than other churches. The ultimate object of Ecumenism is to unite all Christians under the 'Vicar' of Christ – the Pope of Rome."

This particular statement was underscored in September, 2000 when the papacy issued the encyclical "Iesus Christus" in which the official teaching of the Roman Church was proclaimed in the words:

"The Church of Christ continues to exist fully ONLY in the Roman Catholic Church. Catholics may not subscribe to the idea that one religion is as good as another… If it is true that the followers of other religions can receive Divine Grace it is also certain that they are in a gravely deficient situation in comparison with those who, in the Catholic Church, have the fullness of the means of salvation. There exists only a single Church of Christ which subsists in the Catholic Church, governed by the successor of St. Peter (ed. the pope) and the bishops in communion with him."

In spite of Rome's contacts and public affirmations in many Ecumenical functions (devoted to bringing Churches together) it is noteworthy to realize that the stance of Rome, regarding the "True Church", can be summarized in statements such as the following:

"Christian unity will not become a reality unless all churches accept the authority Christ entrusted to St. Peter and his successors. This unity will not be fully manifested until all churches accept Christ's will for His Church and acknowledge the apostolic authority of all bishops in communion with the successor of St. Peter, the pope. For true unity, all churches must accept papal authority."
(Pope John Paul II in "Catholic Movement," August 10, 1995)

Note: Response to these statements of triumphalism by the Roman Catholic Church is no call for meanness or uncharitable attitudes by Orthodox Christians. Orthodoxy knows who she is and is not persuaded by such proclamations from Rome, seeking hegemony and ultimate power. Orthodox Christians are called to be respectful and tolerant of all persons in other Churches. Kindness, patience, and a friendly attitude are hallmarks of Christians, despite our obvious differences in belief. Also, the Orthodox Church has been quite clear in her teaching, that she considers herself the Church of Christ. She has not pretended to take part in Ecumenical endeavors saying one thing and meaning another! For this she has often been criticized, but no dispassionate person could ever accuse her of falsehood.

THE ORTHODOX CHURCH – A CONSTANT FAITH

The Orthodox Church has always been very clear in her teaching about the "truth" of Ecumenism:

According to the Gospel of Matthew 16:18 , we know the Orthodox Church is a constant Church built on Christ "the Rock." The Orthodox Church is not built on any one apostle , she stands firmly on the one "Rock", Jesus Christ, and the profession that He is "The Christ, the Son of the Living God." She can hardly be otherwise since she is the custodian and overseer of Divine salvation. It is she who acts as guardian of our relationship with Almighty God. She does not involve herself in the modern-day wars of Fundamentalism or religious liberalism. The faith she espouses and teaches is fixed for all times.

Embedded in Orthodoxy is every piece of Rome's true Catholicism, rejecting the innovations Rome has added to the Faith since breaking off from Orthodoxy during the first millennium, (with the definitive break occurring in 1054). The Orthodox Church also maintains the affirmations of Protestantism that are authentic interpretations of ancient Christianity. The Reformation, being a uniquely Western event, never directly touched Orthodoxy, although there is within her much of Calvin's teaching about God as the supreme end of all human endeavor, the Quaker's sense of the immanence of God, Luther's opposition to all the innovations of Rome, the Baptist's belief in total immersion at Baptism, and a fervor of worship found in the Methodist/Evangelical bodies.

The Orthodox Church has all of these things, within the boundaries of her Holy Faith and doctrines, because she is the undivided Church of the first millennium and she has taught these truths from the earliest days-to the present time

The Orthodox Church is truly the Church of Christ, authentic Christianity, and the way of salvation. She is the Mother of all Churches.

> *"The Church is one. However widely she has spread among the nations, through her fruitful growth… the Church is bathed in the light of the Lord and pours her rays over the whole world. It is one light that is spread everywhere and her unity is undivided."*
>
> *St. Cyprian of Carthage*

TRADITION

Orthodoxy often speaks of Tradition. It is a difficult concept to convey since it often is misunderstood outside the Orthodox ethic. Simply put, however, Tradition is the living continuity with the past, the link we have with the Church of ancient days. Tradition cannot change, it is Truth! This is because Tradition is the faith and practice which Christ imparted to His apostles, and which has come down to us throughout twenty centuries. But it is more! Tradition includes the books of Sacred Scripture, the creeds, the Church Fathers and their teachings, the decisions of the Ecumenical Councils, the liturgy of the Church, the Canons and the entire system of Church government and worship which are given us to preserve, protect and defend.

Tradition, it has been said, is a witness of the Holy Spirit since Christ promised that "when the Spirit comes He will guide us to the Truth" (John 16:13). Since Truth cannot change and Tradition is Truth, it is evident that Tradition is of utmost importance in maintaining the golden link with the Church that comes to us from the apostles.

FOUR MARKS OF THE TRUE CHURCH – THE ORTHODOX CHURCH

ONE – the teachings of the Church have remained unchanged since the time of the apostles.

HOLY – established by Christ for the salvation of mankind: a Church guided by the Holy Spirit whose purpose is to make us holy.

CATHOLIC (UNIVERSAL) – the Church remains the same in all ages, for all people.

Catholic means distinguishing the true Church from heretical groups that have been founded since the earliest days. The Orthodox Church has preserved the teachings of Jesus Christ from the beginning. She possesses the wholeness of the Christian Faith, since other groups have either added or subtracted from the totality of the apostolic witness over the centuries.

APOSTOLIC – the Orthodox Church has an unbroken connection with the apostles. She possesses "Apostolic Truth" (teachings which were believed by the earliest Christians) and she possesses the priesthood that has been passed down through the centuries, from the early Church to the present time.

"The Church, instituted by the Lord and confirmed by the apostles is one for all men."
                                                            St. Hilary of Poitiers

"Wherever Jesus Christ is, there is the Church."
                                                            St. Ignatius of Antioch

ORTHODOXY – THE CHURCH OF CHRIST

The Orthodox Church is THE authentic voice of Christianity because her teachings are true. This is the very meaning of the word Orthodox, or TRUE BELIEF AND TRUE WORSHIP. St. Paul says that the Church, the household of God, "is the pillar and bulwark of the Truth" (1 Timothy. 3:15).

So we are the Church, not just because we are ancient-many heresies are also ancient – but because we teach the Truth! Orthodoxy preserves the Faith of the Apostolic Church that she has guarded throughout the centuries. Orthodoxy maintains the living Faith of the apostles, and is the very criterion of Christianity that was established by Jesus Christ Himself.

To be members of the Church we must accept all the teachings of the Church with its unbroken Tradition. Truth is unchanging. Therefore we are Orthodox because our teachings are immutable. We are nothing less than the Church of Christ in heaven and on earth.

A Prayer for the Church

"O God of power unchangeable, and light unquenchable. Look favorably upon Thy Church, that sacred and excellent mystery. By the tranquil working of Thy Providence, carry on the work of our salvation.

Let the whole world, and every person, feel and see that the things once cast down are being raised up.

The things that were old are being made new, and all things are returning to their perfection, through Jesus Christ, through whom they had their beginning.

He is Lord for ever and ever. Amen"

8th Century Prayer

The Signs of the Church

"Remain steadfast, unshaken, immovable in the Orthodoxy of Christ's Faith, as the Eastern Orthodox Church has educated you. Let no man lead you astray into thinking that the affliction and the sorrows of the Church may be a sign that a Church, subjected to temptations and sufferings, is not the true Church. In fact, a most true sign of the Church of Christ is her sufferings, her headaches, her troubles. The Savior Himself said, 'In the world you shall have tribulation.'"

Meletios Pegas in Cavernos , New Library Vol. II

"One ought to remain in the Church which having been founded by the apostles, exists even until this day."

St. Jerome

"Not only are we in this assembly (the Church) but also the prophets, apostles and all the saints. And what is most important of all – among us is Jesus Christ Himself, the maker of everything."

St. John Chrysostom

CANONS OF THE CHURCH

Canons are mileposts for observing the basic tenets of the Faith. They support one on a Godly-journey through life. Canons were written by the Ecumenical Councils, local councils/synods, and individual bishops in response to the practical needs of the Church and her faithful.

Canons are the guideposts to spiritual growth as determined by the Orthodox Church. They were composed throughout the ages in response to the need for guidance of Orthodox believers. Canons show the sense of the Church to protect her members from spiritual ruin. They are reliable barometers and measuring devices whereupon we can determine our relationship to Almighty God, with the advice and accumulated wisdom of the Church. Ignorance of the most basic standards that are measured by the Canons will certainly lead to spiritual disaster, and will surely place the welfare of one's immortal soul in jeopardy.

Some of the Canons are very ancient and some are quite strict, requiring special effort on the part of individual Orthodox Christians. But the Canons were codified for the spiritual and material benefit of the faithful, not as some impossible demands to be met. They are guideposts to a full and beneficial Christian life. Yet, Canons of the Orthodox Church have nothing to do with the severe legal system determined by the Church of the West. We must realize at all times that in the words of Patriarch Ignatios IV of Antioch, "the canons were made for the Church and not the Church for the canons."

Canons refer to the whole code of ecclesiastical conduct that has been issued by the Orthodox Church in matters of faith, morals and discipline. Again, let us repeat, that they were codified out of love, not as threats of punishment. They were natural laws which must be understood in the light of the Church's mission in this world, a mission that is centered on bringing men and women everywhere, and at all times, to salvation in Christ.

The Canons of the Church are not the same as the doctrinal definitions of the Faith, or what the Church teaches in regard to eternal Truths about Almighty God. Canons show the way to apply dogmatic teachings of the Church to our day-to-day struggle towards perfection. They must be seen as a way to salvation, not as a hindrance to real sanctity or an impossible dream to be achieved. Yet it must be stated that society has changed so much since many of these canons were codified that many need to be updated.

Canons have a very practical importance although some may not impact us in today's world. Yet, it would be a mistake not to take them seriously or to acquire a cafeteria mentality in regards to the teachings of the Faith. Shopping around for those Canons that suit our fancy, or to interpret them in a frivolous manner, is counter to what the Church really meant when she established these standards for our behavior.

COUNTERING THE CLAIMS OF FUNDAMENTALISTS

Orthodox Christians believe that Sacred Tradition is the true witness of the Holy Spirit. Holy Scripture is part of that Tradition. Some Fundamentalist Christians believe that the Bible is the only source of normative ethics and behavior. For them, the definitive answers to life are to be found in the pages of Holy Scripture. They believe that the Bible is the sole way in which God has revealed Himself to the world.

Orthodoxy looks upon the claims of Protestant Fundamentalists as too narrow and confining, often giving the impression to believers that salvation is brought about by emotions and a much too simplistic view of what it means to be an authentic Christian.

Now clearly the Orthodox Church has taught for the twenty centuries of her existence that Truth is to be found in Holy Scripture as interpreted by Holy Tradition and in the writings of the Church Fathers. It is also to be found in the Creed and statements promulgated by various Church councils. Orthodoxy wisely sees Truth as protected in the Canons and Divine worship, since it is an ancient axiom that you can tell what people believe by the way they pray.

As for the "born again phenomenon", so prevalent today, we need only to look back to the statements of the Church Fathers to see that this simple reliance on the confession of belief and a "once saved, always saved" theology is both false and extremely dangerous. It is a phenomenon which is not only ancient but one which threatened the life of the Church many centuries ago after which it was roundly condemned by the Fathers as a pernicious danger to the life of authentic Orthodox believers. (*See also: Section on Holy Scripture–"Dealing With Door to Door Evangelists"*)

In the Seventh Century, St Gregory the Great said this:

> *"For many come to faith, but few are brought into the Heavenly Kingdom. For many serve God with their tongue, but turn from Him in their lives. From this we should reflect on the following. First, that no one should presume concerning his own salvation, for though he is called to*

the Faith, he knows not whether he will be chosen to enter the Kingdom of Heaven. The second is that no one should take it upon himself to despair of his neighbor, when he sees him steeped in vice, because no one knows the richness of Divine mercy.

Perhaps each of you will say to yourself: I have believed therefore I shall be saved. He speaks what is true if to his faith he joins good works. This is indeed the faith that does not deny in work what it professes in word.

For this, St. Paul says of certain false faithful: "They profess to know God but by their lack of works they deny him" (Titus 1:16). St. John also says: "He who says that he knows God, and keeps not His commandments, is a liar, and the truth is not in him" (1 John 2:4).

DIFFERENCES BETWEEN EASTERN ORTHODOXY AND ROMAN CATHOLICISM

The Orthodox Church is not the Roman Catholic Church without the pope. This fallacy is sometimes bandied about as a prelude to Ecumenical contacts between the Churches, yet it is far from accurate.

There are some very major differences between Orthodox and Roman Catholic theology that have not been resolved, and which the Orthodox Church will never abandon. These differences remain serious obstacles to reunion.

Orthodoxy considers herself to be the pristine Apostolic Church of Christ believing none of the innovations that have been added by the Roman Church throughout the centuries. However, the Orthodox Church is not the true Church of Christ simply because she is ancient. She is the Church of Christ because she maintains the Truth in all its integrity and teaches what the Church has always taught, without any major omissions or additions. This is what makes Orthodoxy the Faith of Christ.

The following are some of the major differences which mark the deep divide between Orthodoxy and Roman Catholicism. They are:

> The Papacy
> The Filioque
> Purgatory
> Indulgences
> The Immaculate Conception

and other variances in practice and discipline.

The Papacy

The Roman Catholic Church teaches that Christ's words to St. Peter, as found in St. Matthew 16, give her the sole right to hegemony over Christendom. The Orthodox Church, however, teaches that when Christ said, "You are Peter and upon this Rock I will build my Church" (Matt. 16:18), the "Rock" He referred to was not Peter but the confession which Peter had just made in the previous verse, "You are the Christ the Son of the living God" (Matt. 16:16). In other words the "Rock" was Christ, not Peter, and it is a perversion of Holy Scripture to maintain otherwise.

We can search the Scriptures and see that in every instance where the word "Rock" is used it always refers to Almighty God. So the Church is built upon Christ as "Rock" not on a mere man such as Peter, since any Church built on a man would be built on too faulty a foundation.

The Orthodox Church is grounded on Christ as her one foundation and where the Church was given authority to act, such as to forgive sins, (Matt. 18:18), it was given to the apostles as a group, and not to St. Peter alone.

The Orthodox Church has no single, earthly head. One's Orthodoxy is determined and defined by adherence to the Tradition of the Faith and our common unity, or "communion" with one another. We, as Orthodox Christians, hold a common witness to the Faith, and this becomes the benchmark of canonicity.

The early Fathers of the Church were unanimous in their judgment, that it was Peter's confession of faith in Christ as the Son of the Living God, and not Peter's person, which is the true foundation of the Church.

Below are a few of many comments of the Church Fathers on the Roman Papacy:

> "The 'Rock' on which Christ will build His Church means Peter's confession OF FAITH IN CHRIST."
> > St. John Chrysostom, 53rd homily on St. Matthew

> "The Church, the House of the Lord, is built upon the foundations of the faith of the apostles and prophets."
> > St. Basil of Caesarea, Second Chapter of Isaiah

> "If you believe that God has raised the whole building of His Church on Peter alone, what would you say of John, the 'Son of Thunder?' What would you say of each of the apostles? Would you venture to say that the gates of hell shall not prevail against Peter in particular, but shall prevail against the others-are not the words addressed to them all?"
> > Origen "Commentary on Matthew"

"Jesus Christ is the 'Rock.' He did not deny the grace of His Name to Peter because he borrowed from the Rock the constancy and solidity of his faith. Thy Rock is thy faith and faith is the foundation of the Church. If thou art a Rock, thou shall be in the Church, for the Church is built upon the Rock-and the Rock is the profession of faith in Christ Jesus."

St. Ambrose

Note: St. Ambrose often spoke disparagingly of the Bishop of Rome as usurping the legitimate rights of other bishops in the Church c.f. "On the Incarnation", "On St. Luke", and "On the 69th Psalm."

St. Ambrose, writing in "On the Incarnation", sums up the entire matter when he declares:

"Faith is the foundation of the Church, for it was not of the person but the faith of St. Peter of which it was said, 'The gates of hell shall not prevail.' Certainly it is Peter's Confession of Faith in Christ which has vanquished the powers of hell. The rock is the unity of faith, not the person of Peter."

St. Cyprian writing in "De Catholicae Ecclesiae Unitate," cap. 4-5

"Thou art Peter... but the Rock was Jesus Christ. Peter, having confessed Him as all the Church confesses Him , he then called Peter 'a Rock' for his faith. Between these two sentiments let the reader choose the most probable."

St. Augustine "Retractations," 13th Sermon; "Contra Julianum" 1:13

"Christ said to Peter... I will build thee upon Myself , I will not be built upon thee. Those who wish to be built among men said... I am of Paul, I am of Apollos, I am of Cephas. However, those who did not wish to be built upon Peter, but upon the Rock say, I am of Jesus Christ."

St. Augustine "Retractations," 13th Sermon

"Behold how Peter does all things by common consent, and decides nothing by his own power or authority."

St. John Chrysostom

THE FILIOQUE ("and the Son")

In the 9th century the Roman Church changed the Creed of Nicaea/Constantinople that was the foundation of the ancient Church's teaching. The Eastern Church could not accept this tampering with ancient doctrine and never allowed the "Filioque" (the words "and the Son") to be added to the Creed.

The original Creed stated:
"I believe in the Holy Spirit, the Lord, and giver of life, who proceeds from the Father."

This is what Jesus taught in John 15:26, *"When the Comforter comes, whom I shall send to you from the Father, this Spirit of Truth **who proceeds from the Father,** will testify of me."*

Also, Pope Hadrian I, in the eighth century, refused the request of the Emperor Charlemagne to add the Filioque to the Creed, proclaiming it was inappropriate to tamper with the ancient Creedal statement of the Christian Church. Later, however, with political pressure applied on the papacy, the Filioque was accepted at Rome even though it altered apostolic witness to the Faith.

PURGATORY AND INDULGENCES

Roman Catholic doctrine teaches that even after a sinful action is forgiven, there still remains some punishment that must be expiated. If, after death, there is still temporal punishment remaining it must be satisfied in Purgatory – before a person will be admitted to heaven.

In this regard the Roman Catholic Church believes that it alone, holds a vast "Treasury of Merits," i.e. the merits of Christ and saints which will be applied toward any punishment due to sin. The Orthodox Church believes that no Christian, however saintly, can ever perform more good works than are necessary for one's salvation. These are the so-called extra merits that the Pope places in a book and applies to those in purgatory to shorten their suffering. Jesus spoke specifically about this when he said, "So you also, when you have done all that you were ordered to do, say, 'we are worthless slaves; we have done only what we ought to have done'" (Luke 17:10).

The Orthodox Church finds these teachings regarding Purgatory and Indulgences to be contrary to the atoning death of Jesus Christ and the teachings of Holy Scripture. They seem too harsh, too mechanical and legalistic although Orthodox faithful do believe in an Intermediate State between this life and Paradise, a state of existence that will remain until the last day. Here the souls of the faithful departed are at rest awaiting the Second Coming of Jesus Christ and the Last Judgment. However, Orthodox Christians reject completely the so-called "excess merits" of the saints, or the scorecard of piling up good works to obtain indulgences in order to exit Purgatory.

Indulgences and Purgatory therefore, seem a way of extracting additional punishment for sin that had been completely forgiven, and which Christ promised would be totally forgotten, with no further debt owed. This is contrary to the ancient Orthodox teaching that Christ gave Himself once, and for all time, as satisfaction for sin.

To demand punishment in Purgatory devalues the death and resurrection of Jesus Christ (Acts 3: 17-26). Christ did not say to the thief crucified next to him, "Today you will be with me in Purgatory." Instead, He said, "Today you will be with me in Paradise."

> "Blessed are Thy saints, O God and King, who have traveled over the tempestuous sea of this mortal life, and have made the harbor of peace and felicity. Watch over us who are still in our dangerous voyage; and remember such as lie exposed to the rough storms of trouble and temptations. Frail is our vessel, and the ocean is wide, but as in Thy mercy, Thou has set our course. So steer the vessel of our life toward the everlasting shore of peace, and bring us at length to the quiet haven of our heart's desire, where Thou, O God, are blessed, and lives and reigns for ever and ever."
>
> St. Augustine

THE IMMACULATE CONCEPTION AND ASSUMPTION

The Roman Catholic doctrine of the Immaculate Conception was first proclaimed in 1854. From that day all Catholics were required to believe in a "sinless" Virgin Mary from the very moment of her conception in St. Anne's womb. And they are required to believe this in order to be saved! However, until that time a Roman Catholic could be in good standing in his Church without assenting that Mary was "immaculately conceived." This is a innovative doctrine that was never taught in the early Church and up to 1854 it was contested by many within Roman Catholicism itself.

Orthodoxy believes that Mary, the Theotokos or "Birth-giver of God," is All-holy, Most-blessed and even All-pure. But Orthodoxy cannot accept the new dogma of the Immaculate Conception invented by the Roman Church. We know from Holy Scripture that "All have sinned and come short of the glory of God, and that there is no one righteous, no not one" (Romans 3:10).

In the hymn of the "Magnificat" the Virgin Mary even calls upon God as "my savior" (St. Luke 1:47). If she was without sin from the moment of her conception, as Roman Catholicism says, then why would she need a savior? Orthodoxy teaches, however that the Theotokos is the first of the redeemed and the first human being to receive God's wondrous blessing of salvation, now open to all mankind.

The error behind the Immaculate Conception is due to the fact that Roman Catholics believe that each of us has inherited the sin of Adam and the guilt associated with this "original sin." Orthodox view this as another Western innovation simply because one cannot inherit the guilt of another person. Rather, Adam's sin was more of an ancestral curse by which men and women were alienated from God's Divine life and therefore were subject to sin, suffering, and physical death.

The Assumption of Mary is another new dogma thrust upon Roman Catholics in the 1950's. Roman Catholics say that Mary, "having completed the course of her earthly life, was assumed body and soul into heavenly glory." It was defined as dogma in the early 1950's by Pope Pius XII. Until that time it had never been the official teaching of the Roman Catholic Church.

Catholics were not obliged to believe in this dogma before the 1950's, but after its definition they were required to give full assent to it in order to gain eternal salvation.

Orthodox say that the Virgin Mary "fell asleep in the Lord." This is called Mary's "Dormition." However, it has never been proclaimed as official dogma by the Orthodox Church since we do not concern ourselves with the mechanics of the Virgin's repose. We consider it a mystery. Moreover, the scripture says nothing about the Assumption of Mary. The Assumption remains as a "pious belief" but not as a dogma in the Orthodox Church.

Orthodox give respect to such a belief , but cannot see that it is equal to Christian doctrines such as the Incarnation, Resurrection, Trinity, Virgin birth, the humanity and Divinity of Christ, etc.

DIFFERENCES IN PRACTICE

There are certain differences in Orthodox and Roman Catholic practice that are not as serious as the above dogmas, but which set us apart from our Roman brothers and sisters. They are briefly:

1. Orthodox administer the Eucharist (or Holy Communion) under both species, i.e. both consecrated bread and wine. This is in keeping with the most ancient practice of the Church. Roman Catholics almost always administer just the bread, even though Christ said: "Unless you eat my body and drink my blood you shall not have life in you." (St. John 6:53).

Scriptural reference: St. John 6: 51-58

2. Orthodox administer the Mysteries of Initiation,(Baptism, Chrismation and the Eucharist)   at the same time, i.e. on the day of one's Baptism-as was the normal practice in the early Church. Roman Catholics, however, separate them into three distinct occasions.

Note: In some areas of the world these Mysteries (Sacraments) are again being administered as one in Roman Catholic parishes which recognize the ancient custom of the undivided Church.

Scriptural references: St. John 3:5; St. Matthew 28:19.

3. Orthodox Christians administer Baptism through immersion, placing the child or adult under the water, rather than just sprinkling or pouring. Immersion is the ancient practice of the Church and some Roman Catholics are re-instituting the custom by constructing large baptismal pools within their church building.

Scriptural references: Acts 1:5, Acts 2:17, Joel 2:28, St. John 14:16

4. The Orthodox Church allows married man to be ordained priests, although a man may not marry after he has been ordained. Monks are unmarried, and bishops are chosen from monastic rather than from the married clergy. Priests whose wives have died may be elected bishops. The Roman Catholic Church imposes mandatory celibacy which was a practice begun later in the medieval age. This was not so in the early Church when married men were commonly ordained into the priesthood and served also as bishops.

   The reasons for prohibiting men from marrying and ministering as priests in the Roman Catholic Church were based on political and economic reasons. A married priesthood is not prohibited by Holy Scripture, since some of the apostles, such as St. Peter, were married men.

Scriptural references: Titus 1:5, Acts 1:20-26, St. John 15:16, Acts 1:26, Acts 6:3-6, Acts 14:22-29

> *"The Church is the Ark of Salvation. In her bosom, we find Our Lord, and make our sure, humble way to salvation. Is it any wonder, then, that the Evil One will do everything in his power to subvert the Church and seek to undermine both her authority and her sacred power? Yet we have Christ's solemn promise that nothing will overcome the Church. Even though she is battered and bruised in this world, her mission will not be denied."*
>
> *The Church Fathers*

THE SEVEN ECUMENICAL COUNCILS

First Ecumenical Council: Nicaea 325 A.D.
318 bishops mostly from the East were present. Called by the Emperor Constantine, presided over by Bishop Hosius of Spain.

Combatted: the Arian heresy which taught that the Son (Christ) is not equal to the Father. Arianism declared that the Son was a mere creature although more holy than ordinary men.

Decreed: that Jesus Christ is truly God, of one substance with the Father and begotten, not made, from all eternity.

Second Ecumenical Council: Constantinople I 381 A.D.
150 bishops present
Called by: Emperor Theodosius I, presided over by St. Meletius, Bishop of Antioch and by St. Gregory Nazianzen.

Combatted: the teaching that the Holy Spirit was inferior in essence to the Father and Son. Also, that Jesus Christ had no human intellect and that his flesh was one substance with His Divinity. This heresy deprived Christ of His true humanity.

Decreed: that the Holy Spirit proceeds from the Father and that He is to be worshiped and glorified with the Father and the Son.

The Third Ecumenical Council: Ephesus 431 A.D.
200 bishops present
Called by: Emperor Theodosius II

Combatted: the heresy of Nestorianism which taught that just the human body of Jesus was born of Mary. Therefore, Mary was not to be called "The Mother of God," simply the "Mother of Jesus".

Decreed: that Divinity and humanity were complete in Christ. Therefore Mary is able to be named "The Mother of God".

Fourth Ecumenical Council: Chalcedon 451 A.D.
650 bishops present
Called by the Emperor Marcian who refused the Roman Pope's request that the Council be held in Italy. To combat the ever-increasing claims of the Roman patriarch (Pope) to hegemony over the Church, the Council decreed that Constantinople be elevated to a similar and equal dignity as Rome. It also:

Combatted: the heresy of Monophysitism which claimed that Christ had only a Divine nature, not a human nature.

Decreed: that there are two distinct natures in Jesus Christ both Divine and human.

Fifth Ecumenical Council: Constantinople II 553 A.D.
165 bishops present
Called by: Emperor Justinian

Combatted: the heresy of Monophysitism and "The Three Chapters," a radical document.

Decreed: that Monophysitism is a heretical teaching. (*See: Fourth Ecumenical Council*)

Sixth Ecumenical Council: Constantinople III 680-681 A.D.
170 bishops present
Called by: Emperor Constantine IV

Combatted: the Monothelite heresy which declared that while Christ had only a human body, He did not have a human will but possessed only a Divine will.

Decreed: that Christ did indeed have two wills, with the human will being subject to the Divine. The Council also condemned Pope Honorius of Rome for teaching the Monothelite heresy.

Seventh Ecumenical Council: Nicaea II 787 A.D.
367 bishops present (This was the last Ecumenical Council)
Called by: Empress Irene

Combatted: the Iconoclastic heresy which outlawed any veneration of the Holy Cross.

Decreed: that the Church should encourage veneration of icons and the Cross. Veneration is not worship, since worship is due to God alone, but the "honor paid to the images passes on to that which the image represents, and the one who shows reverence to the image shows reverence for the subject represented in it."

Note: In some Roman Catholic literature the pope's name is given instead of the Emperor or Empress who actually did convene a Council. This is an historical falsehood and should never be accepted as fact.

MONASTICISM IN THE ORTHODOX CHURCH

Men and women who enter monastic life in Orthodoxy devote their entire life to God.

The word monastic means "solitary" and in the monastery one focuses soley on union with Almighty God. Monastics follow what is called the Evangelical Life.

Formal monasticism goes back to the fourth century, when those who felt a call to extensive prayer and devotion, fled into the deserts of Egypt, Palestine, and Syria to be alone with God. Even today, Orthodox monastic life is referred to as "the desert."

Traditionally monastics are guardians of the Faith, and even priests in secular life regularly go to monasteries for spiritual guidance, because they under-stand the value of the monastic witness. As guardians of the Faith monks and nuns have often been called the "Beacons of Orthodoxy."

Monks and nuns devote their lives exclusively to God , yet one is never really able to be alone with God without extreme labor. Therefore, monks and nuns face enormous spiritual struggles while combating the great enemy-Satan. However, monasticism is seen as the jewel of Orthodoxy, and it would be unthinkable to imagine the Church without the witness of those in monastic life.

Male monastics are either simple monks or "hieromonks." The latter may celebrate Holy Liturgy and other Mysteries (Sacraments) because they are ordained priests. There are three types of monastic life in Orthodoxy.

1. One type is where monks and nuns live in community and pray, work and do all things as a family.

2. Yet another is where monastics meet regularly for prayer and Divine Liturgy, but spend most of their time secluded with God.

3. The third type is where monks or nuns live in total seclusion and prayer. These monastics meet others only on rare occasions, and are called hermits.

There are no religious orders in Orthodoxy as found in the West. In Orthodoxy, monasteries are noted for their "charism" and each monastic house has an important gift, or dedication, to a particular aspect of Christian spirituality which they share with the world-wide Church.

A monk was once asked, "What do you do in the monastery?" He replied: "We fall and get up, fall and get up, fall and get up again."

Monastics in the Orthodox Church do not take "vows" as practiced in the Western Church. Instead they make solemn promises of growth in spirituality, as well as a life-commitment to a particular monastic family. Orthodox bishops and other senior clergy are drawn from monasteries. In Orthodoxy, since bishops are monks their lives mirror a special vocation to Christ.

While monks and nuns withdraw from the world, paradoxically they become responsible for it at the same time. Often the larger monasteries send out monks as missionaries to teach a life of prayer and total dedication to God. In this way monastics become teachers, around whom the laity can learn the spirit and riches of this very special life of dedication.

Scriptural reference: St. Matthew 19:16-30

Mount Athos – Center of Monasticism
Since the 9th century the center of Orthodox monasticism has been the Holy Mountain, or Mount Athos. Located on a peninsula in Northern Greece, the Holy Mountain contains twenty monastic communities, a number of

smaller "sketes", as well as places for those who have chosen the solitary life as hermits.

Mount Athos attracts many visitors who wish to learn more about Orthodox monasticism. It is a place of prayer and pilgrimage. Although women are not allowed on the Holy Mountain, Athos has exerted a strong influence on Orthodox thought and life for over 1,100 years and is thankfully undergoing a period of renewal and growth in these sad, materialistic times.

Mount Athos is called "The Garden of the Theotokos." Monks firmly believe that the Holy Virgin will never abandon her mountain , or its humble inhabitants.

> *"A monk is a mourning soul that both asleep, and awake, is unceasingly occupied with the remembrance of death."*
>
> *St. John of the Ladder*

FATHERS OF THE CHURCH

The Four "Great" Fathers of the Church
St. Athanasius: Alexandria . . . . . . 4th century
St. Gregory of Nazianzus . . . . 4th century
St. Basil the Great of Caesarea . . . 4th century
St. John Chrysostom . . . . 4th century Archbishop of Constantinople

Greek Fathers of the Church
St. Amphilocius of Iconium . . . . . 4th century
St. Anastasius of Sinai . . . . 8th century . . . . Apologist, Bishop
St. Andrew of Crete . . . . 7th/8th century . . . . Archbishop
St. Anthony the Great . . . . 4th century . . . . Founder of
                                                                   Easter Monasticism
St. Athanasius . . . . 4th century . . . . . . Patriarch of Alexandria
Athenagoras . . . . 2nd century . . . . Apologist
St. Basil the Great . . . . 4th century . . . . . Archbishop of Caesarea
St. Clement of Alexandria . . . . 2nd/3rd century . . . . Theologian
St. Clement of Rome . . . . 1st century . . . . Bishop
St. Cyril . . . . 4th century . . . . Bishop of Jerusalem
St. Cyril . . . . 4th/5th century . . Patriarch of Alexandria
Didymus the Blind . . . . 4th century . . . . Theologian
Diodore . . . . 4th century . . . . Bishop of Tarsus
Dionysius the Pseudo Aeropagite . . 5th century . . . . Theologian
St. Dionysius the Great . . . . 2nd/3rd century . . Patriarch of Alexandria
St. Epiphanius . . . . 4th century . . . . Bishop
Eusebius . . . . 3rd/4th century . . . . Bishop
St. Firmillian . . . . 3rd century . . . . Bishop
St. Gennadius . . . . 5th century . . Patriarch of Constantinople
St. Germanus . . . . 7th/8th century Patriarch of Constantinople
St. Gregory of Nazianzu . . . . 4th century . . . . Bishop

St. Gregory of Nyssa	4th century	
St. Gregory Thaumaturgus	3rd century	Bishop of Neo Caesarea
Hermas	2nd century	Author "The Shepherd"
St. Hippolytus	4th century	Confessor/Martyr
St. Ignatius	1st century	Bishop of Antioch
St. Isidore of Pelusium	4th/5th century	Abbot
St. John Chrysostom	4th/5th century	Patriarch of Constantinople/Theologian
St. John Climacus	6th/7th century	Monk
St. John of Damascus	7th/8th century	Theologian
St. Justin Martyr	2nd century	Apologist
St. Leontius (Byzantium)	6th century	Theologian
St. Marcarius the Great	4th century	Monk
St. Maximus	6th/7th century	Abbot/Confessor
St. Melito	2nd century	Bishop of Sardis
St. Methodius	4th century	Bishop
St. Nilus the Elder	5th century	Priest/Monk
Origen	2nd/3rd century	Theologian
St. Photius the Greek	9th century	Patriarch
St. Polycarp	1st/2nd century	Bishop of Smyrna
St. Proclus	5th century	Patriarch of Constantinople
St. Serapion	4th century	Bishop of Thmuis
St. Sophronius	6th/7th century	Patriarch of Jerusalem
Tatian the Assyrian	2nd century	Apologist/Theologian
Theodore	4th/5th century	Bishop of Mopsuestia
Theodoret	4th/5th century	Bishop of Cyrrhus
St. Theophilus	2nd century	Bishop of Antioch

Latin Fathers of the Church

St. Ambrose	4th century	Bishop of Milan
St. Augustine	4th/5th century	Bishop of Hippo
St. Benedict	5th/6th century	Abbot/Monastic
St. Caesarius	5th/6th century	Archbishop of Arles
St. John Cassian	4th/5th century	Abbot
St. Cyprian	3rd century	Bishop of Carthage
St. Fulgentius	5th/6th century	Bishop
St. Gregory of Elvira	4th century	Theologian
St. Gregory I	6th/7th century	Bishop of Rome
St. Hilary	4th century	Bishop of Poitiers
St. Irenaeus	2nd century	Bishop of Lyons
St. Isidore	6th/7th century	Bishop of Seville
St. Jerome	4th/5th century	Priest/Theologian
Lactantius Firmianus	3rd/4th century	Apologist
St. Leo	4th/5th century	Bishop of Rome
Minucius Felix	2nd/3rd century	Apologist
St. Pamphilus	3rd/4th century	Theologian
St. Paulinus	4th/5th century	Bishop of Nola
St. Peter Chrysologus	5th century	Bishop of Ravenna

St. Prosper of Aquitane . . . . 4th/5th century . . . . Theologian
Rufinius . . . . 4th/5th century . . Translator-Theological
Works
Tertullian . . . . 2nd/3rd century . . . . Apologist
St. Vincent of Lerins . . . . 5th century . . . . Priest/Monk

12. SAINTS: SPECIAL FRIENDS OF GOD

SAINTS IN THE ORTHODOX CHURCH

Saints are those who have been "deified." They are,"Jesus Christ's, within Jesus Christ," in the words of St. Maximos the Confessor.

In the Orthodox Church saints are men and women who have followed the teachings of Christ in a most exemplary way and have truly acquired the gifts of the Holy Spirit. Almighty God has filled saints with the light of Divine Truth. The Fathers of the Church compare the saints to links in a golden chain united in faith, works, and love with those still physically on this earth. St. John Chrysostom said we should seek the intercession of the saints because they have a "special boldness before God's throne." Saints are also the "common friends of the human race, strong ambassadors in fervent prayer" (St. Basil, "Letter 360").

Saints are special friends of God. We petition their help in our prayers and ask their intercession before the throne of Almighty God. They are also our special friends and teachers. We should become familiar with the lives of the saints, particularly one's patron saint, and follow their example of holiness and dedication to the Faith.

Scriptural references: Psalm 16:3, Ephesians 2:19, 2 Thessalonians 1:10

BAPTISMAL NAMES – PATRON SAINTS

We are given the name of a saint at our Baptism as a symbol of entering into the Church of Christ. We are both an earthly Church, those struggling here and now, and a heavenly Church, living with the Lord for all eternity. Patron saints are our intercessors, helpers and guides who understand our earthly sorrows. They are real members of the Church. Icons of the saints show that they have already been glorified by God and are praying with us, and for us, at all times.

We keep icons of patron saints in our home and invoke their assistance. One's name day is the feast of our patron saint and in some traditions the name day is more important, and celebrated with more devotion, than a birthday. Saints, and their icons, represent the place where the living members of the

Church meet those who have gone on to be with the Lord.

Icons of the saints should bring to mind that these men and women-who struggled and endured the pain of earthly life as we do–are not distant and dusty figures from the past, but real , caring personal friends. As Orthodox Christians we should be filled with loving care for each other. This love should not end in death and therefore we should continually invoke the prayers of the saints who are prepared to help us on our earthly pilgrimage.

All prayer is directed solely to Almighty God. But saints can pray with us. There are saints whom we call upon for particular needs when seeking their intercession before the throne of Almighty God. We ask them to join us in our prayers, for they too once endured, and know our needs and personal struggles. The saints are truly concerned about us on earth, even as they gloriously live in God's Heavenly Kingdom.

PRAYER TO ONE'S PATRON SAINT

Glory to Thee, O God, glory to Thee. Heavenly King, Comforter, Spirit of Truth, Who is everywhere present and fills all things, Treasury of Blessings, and Giver of Life, come and abide in us, cleanse us of all impurity, and save our souls, O Good One.

Pray to God for me, O Saint _____, who is well pleasing to God; for I fervently entreat thee, sure helper and intercessor for my soul.

Glory to the Father, and to the Son, and to the Holy Spirit. Amen

SAINTS CALLED UPON IN PARTICULAR NEEDS

For Spiritual Help
St. Ephraim the Syrian
St. Alexis
St. Seraphim of Sarov

For a Good End to One's Life
St. Joseph, Spouse of the Virgin Mary
St. Barbara
Archangel Michael

For Brides and Happy Marriages
St. Nicholas of Myra
St. Joseph

For Eye Disorders
St. Lucy
Archangel Raphael

For Those Who Are Chronically Ill
St. Achatius

For Those with Stomach/Abdominal Illness
St. Erasmus (St. Elmo)

For Those with Tuberculosis, Respiratory Ilnness, Patron of Physicians
St. Panteleimon

For Those with Lethargy, Nervous Disorders (ADHD), Bites of Venomous or Rabid Animals
St. Vitus

For Those Possessed by Evil Spirits
St. Cyriacus
St. Dennis of France

For Protection Against Fire
St. Eustis
St. Barbara

For Protection Against Epilepsy, Panic Attacks and Nocturnal Terrors
St. Giles

For Those with Pain in Loins and Legs
St. Marina – (Margaret)

For Those with Alzheimer's Disease
St. Catherine of Alexandria

For Travelers
St. Nicholas

For Those in Prison and Court Cases
St. George the Great Martyr
St. Simeon the God-receiver
St. Onuphrios and St. Peter of Athos
St. Nicholas of Myra
St. Dismas the Good Thief
St. Barbara

For Help in Distress and Poverty
St. Nicholas of Myra
St. Martin of Tours
St. Laurence of Rome
St. John the Almsgiver
St. John of Kronstadt

Against Sickness and Plagues in Underdeveloped Countries
St. Marina the Great Martyr
St. Haralampos

For Good Health of Animals
St. Ambrose of Milan

For Bakers
St. Nicholas of Myra

For Those with Rheumatism and Arthritis
Apostle, St. James the Greater

Against Demonic Worship and Witchcraft
Ss. Cyprian and Justina
St. Theodore

For Finding Lost Objects
St. Phanourios the Great Martyr
St. Menas the Great Martyr of Egypt

From Poisoning
St. Anatstasia

For Deliverance from the Scourge of Anger
St. Tikhon of Zadonsk

For Women in Childbirth
St. Anne, Mother of the Virgin Mary
St. Eleutherius

For Mothers/Grandmothers
St. Anne, Mother of the Virgin Mary and Grandmother of Christ

For Fathers/Grandfathers
St. Joseph, Spouse of the Virgin Mary
St. Joachim, Father of the Holy Virgin and Grandfather of Christ

For Finding Employment
St. Xenia of Petersburg

For Builders
St. Barbara

For Help in Studies
St. Basic the Great
St. John Chrysostom
St. Gregory the Great Theologian
St. Sergius of Radonezh
St. Ambrose of Milan
St. John of Kronstadt - especially in reading

For Penitents
St. Mary Magdalene

For Artist and Iconographers
St. Luke the Evangelist
St. John of Damascus

For Protection Against Thievery
St. Gregory the Wonderworker of the Kiev Caves
St. Dismas the Good Thief

For Good Marriages
Martyrs Adrian and Natalia
Ss. Joachim and Anne, Parents of the Holy Virgin
St. Joseph, Spouse of the Virgin Mary

For Children
St. Nicholas of Myra
St. Scholastica, Sister of St. Benedict

For Chastity and Fighting Lust
St. John the Baptist
St. Demetrius the Great Martyr
St. Moses the Hungarian
St. Mary of Egypt
St. Susanna of the Old Testament

For Desperate Situations
St. Gregory of Neo-Caesarea
St. Jude Thaddeus

For Mental Disorders
St. Naum of Ochrid
St. Anastasia
St. Gerasimos (for the possessed)
St. John of Kronstadt

For Church Musicians
St. Romanos the Melodist
St. Theodore of Chernigov

For Miners and Those who Work in Underground Construction
St. Barbara

For Patient Endurance of Suffering
St. Job, of the Old Testament
The Holy 40 Martyrs of Sebaste
St. Pimen of the Kiev Caves

For Meeting Difficult Situations/People
St. David the Psalmist

For Merchants/Salespeople
St. Nicholas of Myra

For Teachers
St. Catherine of Alexandria

For Priests and Teachers of the Gospel
St. John Chrysostom

"For the saints offer repentance not only on their own behalf, but also on behalf of their neighbors;

For without active love they cannot be made perfect.

So the whole universe is held together, and we are helped."

ANGELS

The Orthodox Church invokes angels in many of her official prayers. The honor which we grant the angels is the same as that reserved for the saints. Of particular importance to believers is one's Guardian Angel who helps us to honor Almighty God in this life, and aids us in our earthly struggles.

Scriptural references: Job 4:18-21, Psalm 91:11, Psalm 148:2

SHORT NOTES ABOUT ORTHODOXY

- The "Bearer of God" is the title given to the Mother of God. The term "God-Bearer," mistakenly used in reference to the Holy Virgin, is a title employed when naming certain saints who were models of piety. "Bearer of God" is reserved for the Theotokos alone!

- In addition to Icon Corners, it is a commendable custom to use incense before family prayers and then sprinkle one's home with Holy Water blessed by the priest at various times throughout the Church Year.

- It is also an ancient and recommended custom to consume, each day, a small piece of the prosphoron from the Divine Liturgy along with a small amount of blessed water.

- Some uninformed people use the "ad hominem" argument that Orthodox Christians worship icons. This is untrue. Orthodox faithful venerate icons and other Holy objects, however we never worship them, since worship is reserved for God alone.

The Theotokos: "The Bearer of God"

We, as Orthodox Christians, give great honor to the Mother of God. Why is this so? First, the Virgin Mary, "The Theotokos," is the greatest of saints and thus is worthy of all honor and respect. She is the most revered of the saints because she was chosen by Almighty God to be the mother of His Son, Jesus Christ. Obviously God approved of the Virgin's holiness and her wondrous ability to love, so she was granted this distinct honor. Therefore, we too, must grant her this same great respect.

Secondly, the Virgin Theotokos was the first Christian because she said "yes" to God's request and became the "Bearer" or "Birth-giver" of His Son. Even the Theotokos had the ability to say no to God, yet her example of faithfulness stands as the ultimate example of our free human will responding to God's love. The Virgin Mary became the greatest of all women because of her simple response, "Let it be done to me according to Thy word" (St. Luke 1:38).

The Virgin Theotokos is the symbol of the Church because she bore Christ in her womb, just as we, members of the Faith, are called to have Christ dwell within us on our journey through life.

The Virgin Mary is also the instrument of the Incarnation of Christ , whereby God came to us in the flesh, in the person of Jesus, our Lord. To Christians, God is not some elusive spirit but one who truly emptied Himself and took on the nature of man in order that we might be saved. The Holy Virgin, as the Mother of God, maintained her virginity even after the birth of Christ. This is an important dogma of the Church. As such, it sets the Virgin apart and underscores her freedom and cooperation with the will of Almighty God. Also, we venerate Mary as "Ever-Virgin" and "All-holy" thereby giving honor to her Son and His Divine majesty.

"Bearer of God" is a most correct title since it was Christ whom the Virgin Mary bore, and Christ is truly the Second Person of the Holy Trinity. The Virgin Mary was not the source of Christ's Divinity. He was God before time began, and Mary was the instrument through which He assumed His humanity. The Virgin Theotokos was not the cause of Christ, but the holy instrument of God's will, whereby He gained our salvation. For this reason, the Church honors the Virgin Mary above all of the saints.

Scriptural reference: St. Luke 1:45

> "Our God, Jesus Christ, was in the womb of the Virgin Mary. God took flesh of the Virgin Mary and became man."
>
> St. Ignatius of Antioch and St. Irenaeus

13. THE GIFT OF TIME IN THE KINGDOM

THE CALENDAR OF THE CHURCH

CIVIL CALENDAR DATES OF PASCHA (Easter)
Paschal dates for the next few years in the Orthodox Church are as follows:

Year	Great Lent Begins	Pascha	Pentecost
2002	March 18th	May 5th	June 23rd
2003	March 10th	April 27th	June 15th
2004	February 23rd	April 11th	May 30th
2005	March 14th	May 1st	June 19th
2006	March 6th	April 23rd	June 11th
2007	February 19th	April 8th	May 27th
2008	March 10th	April 27th	June 15th
2009	March 2nd	April 19th	June 7th
2010	February 15th	April 4th	May 23rd

Pascha – which means "Passover," represents Christ's victory over sin and death. The feast is also called the Resurrection of Our Lord, God and Savior Jesus Christ . It is named Easter in the West, although this is an incorrect term of pagan derivation. ("Easter" comes from "Oestre" a goddess of the North.) Pascha is called the "Feast of Feasts" in the Orthodox Church. In fact, every Sunday is referred to as a "Little Pascha," commemorating the resurrection of Christ from the grave, destroying forever the chains of death, bondage to sin, and the very real power of evil in our lives.

Pascha, according to the regulations of the Council of Nicaea in 325 A.D., must be celebrated on the first Sunday after the full moon following March 21st, provided the Jewish Passover has concluded. If not, Pascha will be celebrated on the first Sunday following the Passover.

Note: Western non-Orthodox Christians usually have a different date for celebrating Pascha because they no longer follow this ancient formula of the early Church.

THE SEASONS OF THE CHURCH

The Orthodox Church Year begins on September 1. This is called the Feast of the Indiction. However, the liturgical year is based on the Feast of Pascha, the Resurrection of Our Lord, and some important Church feasts revolve around it. There are basically three distinct periods in the Church year:

The TRIODION – the ten week period before Pascha;

The PENTECOSTARION – which begins with Pascha and ends after Pentecost;

The OCTOECHOS – which covers the remainder of the year.

Pascha The Greatest Feast of the Orthodox Church
Pascha or the Resurrection of Jesus Christ is the greatest feast of the Church Year and called the "Feast of Feasts."

This greatest of feasts is celebrated each year. He who gave His Son for our salvation gives us, from the same motive, this feast allowing us to pray together and to offer our thanksgiving for the gift of redemption. During the time of Pascha, Our God gathers those who are far apart and brings them together in celebrating their common redemption as a family, and a Church.

Also, the Twelve Great Feasts of Orthodoxy which celebrate our redemption, and bring to mind the riches of our Faith, are celebrated each year. They tell us the story of God's great love for us in events which changed human history forever.

THE TWELVE GREAT FEASTS

The Nativity of the Theotokos – Sept. 8th
The Feast of the birth of the Theotokos who would become the mother of Our Redeemer.

The Elevation of the Holy Cross – Sept. 14th
On this feast we celebrate the finding of the true Cross by St. Helena. During the festal service we venerate the Cross upon which Christ gained our redemption (St. Luke 23:26-49).

The Presentation of the Theotokos – November 21st
The commemoration of the Theotokos' presentation in the Temple by her parents, Ss. Joachim and Anna.

The Nativity of Our Lord Jesus Christ – December 25th
The birth of Jesus Christ in the cave at Bethlehem (St. Luke 2:1-20).

The Baptism of Our Lord – January 6th
Also called the Epiphany or Theophany (which means to "make known") Jesus is made known to St. John the Baptist as the Son of God. The Holy Spirit reveals Christ to the world (St. Matthew 3:13).

The Presentation of Our Lord – February 2nd
Jesus is presented to Simeon in the Temple at Jerusalem (St Luke 2:22-38).

The Annunciation to Mary – March 25th
The Archangel Gabriel announces to the Virgin Mary that she is to be the Mother of God (St. Luke 1:26-38).

The Lord's Entrance into Jerusalem – Palm Sunday
This is the Sunday before Pascha. Jesus enters the Holy City before His passion and death (St. Matthew 21:1-11).

The Ascension of Our Lord into Heaven
Forty days after Pascha. This commemorates the ascent of Christ into heaven following His Resurrection (Acts 1:9-11).

The Feast of Pentecost
Fifty days after Pascha. The descent of the Holy Spirit upon the apostles, fifty days after the Resurrection of Christ.

The Transfiguration of our Lord – August 6th
Jesus shows He is God in the flesh when He is transfigured on Mount Tabor (St. Matthew 17:1-13).

The Dormition – Falling Asleep of the Theotokos – August 15th
The Mother of God enters heaven after she falls asleep in the Lord.

In addition to the Twelve Great Feasts there are other feasts on the Church Calendar:

Major Feasts

Circumcision of Christ	January 1st
Nativity of the Forerunner – St. John the Baptist	June 24th
Ss. Peter and Paul	June 29th
Beheading of St. John the Baptist	August 29th
Holy Patronage (Protection) of the Mother of God	October 1st

Secondary Feasts

St. Anthony the Great	January 17th
St. Euthemius the Great	January 20th
The Three Holy Hierarchs	January 30th
St. George the Great Martyr	April 23th
St. John the Theologian	May 8th
Ss. Cyril and Methodius	May 11th
St. Vladimir	July 15th
Repose of St. John the Theologian	September 26th
St. John Chrysostom	November 13th
St. Sabbas the Blessed	December 5th
St. Nicholas the Wonderworker	December 6th

Minor Feasts

St. Seraphim of Sarov	January 2nd
Ss. Constantine and Helen	May 21st
St. Elias the Prophet	July 20th
St. Sergius of Radonezh	September 25th
St. Demetrius	October 26th

Dedication of Weekdays
Each day of the week is also dedicated to a particular saint, the Holy Angels, apostle, etc.

Monday	The Holy Angels
Tuesday	St. John the Baptist
Wednesday	The Mother of God and the Holy Cross
Thursday	The Holy Apostles and St. Nicholas
Friday	The Holy Cross
Saturday	All Saints and those members of the Church who have reposed
Sunday	The Resurrection of Jesus Christ

Days On Which We Remember the Departed

Along with prayers for the departed throughout the year, there are certain times suggested by the Church when Orthodox Christians should keep the memory of reposed members of their family, and dear friends, alive in their thoughts and prayers. They should also remember the reposed members of the Church throughout the ages.

On the 40th day after death
The half-year anniversary of one's death
The annual anniversary of one's death
On weekends designated as "Soul Saturdays"
The second Saturday of the Great Fast
The third Saturday of the Great Fast
The fourth Saturday of the Great Fast
Tuesday of the second week of Pascha
The Saturday before the feast of St. Demetrius – October 26th
The Saturday before Pentecost

Memorial services for the departed are forbidden:

During the first week of the Great Fast
From the Saturday of Lazarus to the Sunday of St. Thomas – the Sunday after Pascha
From the Feast of the Nativity of Christ (December 25th) to the Feast of St. John the Baptist on January 7th.

SUNDAY EPISTLES AND GOSPELS

Epistle with Gospel Readings following:
(Order of Sundays varies according to date of Holy Pascha)

Circumcision of Our Lord	Colossians 2: 8-12	Luke 2: 20-21, 40-52
Sunday before Epiphany	2 Timothy 4:5-8	Mark 1:1-8
Sunday after Theophany	Ephesians 4:7-13	Matt. 4:12-17
Zacchaeus Sunday	1 Tim. 4:9-15	Luke 19:1-10
Publican and Pharisee	2 Tim. 3:10-15	Luke 18:10-14
Prodigal Son	1 Corinthians 6:12-20	Luke 15: 11-32
Meatfare Sunday	1 Corinthians 8:8-9:2	Matt. 25:31-46
Cheesefare Sunday	Romans 13: 11-14:4	Matt. 6:14-21
Orthodoxy Sunday	Hebrews 11:24-26, 32-40	John 1:43-51
St. Gregory Palamas	Hebrews 1:10-2:3	Mark 2:1-12
Holy Cross Sunday	Hebrews 4:14-5:6	Mark 8: 34-9:1
St. John Climacus	Hebrews 6: 13-20	Mark 9:17-31
St. Mary of Egypt	Hebrews 9:11-14	Mark 10:32-45

Palm Sunday	Philippians 4:4-9	John 12:1-18
Pascha	Acts 1:1-8	John 1:1-17
Thomas Sunday	Acts 5:12-20	John 20:19-31
The Myrrh-Bearing Women	Acts 6:1-7	Mark 15:43-16: 8
The Paralytic	Acts 9:32-40	John 5:1-15
The Samaritan Woman	Acts 11:19-30	John 4:5-42
The Blind Man	Acts 16: 16-34	John 9:1-38
Holy Fathers	Acts 20:16-18, 28-36	John 17:1-13

First Sunday of St. Matthew   *Hebrews 11:33-12:2   Matt. 10:32-33,
(*Sundays of St. Matthew are   37-38, 19:27-30
also referred to as Sundays After Pentecost)

Second Sunday of St. Matthew	Romans 2:10-16	Matt. 4:18-23
Third Sunday of St. Matthew	Romans 5:1-10	Matt. 6:22-33
Fourth Sunday of St. Matthew	Romans 6:18-23	Matt. 8: 5-13

"Daily communion and participation in the Holy Body and Blood of Christ is a good and helpful practice. Christ clearly says, 'He who eats my Body and drinks my Blood has eternal life.' Who doubts that to partake of life continually is really to have life in abundance? For myself, I communicate four times a week, on the Lord's Day, on Wednesday, on Friday, and on Saturday, along with other days if there is a commemoration of a martyr."

St. Basil the Great

Fifth Sunday of St. Matthew	Romans 10:1-10	Matt. 8:28-9:1
Sixth Sunday of St. Matthew	Romans 12:6-14	Matt. 9:1-8
Seventh Sunday of St. Matthew	Romans 15:1-7	Matt. 9:27-35
Eighth Sunday of St. Matthew	Corinthians 1;10-18	Matt.14:14-22
Ninth Sunday of St. Matthew	1 Corinthians 3:9-17	Matt. 14:22-34
Tenth Sunday of St. Matthew	1 Corinthians 4 : 9-16	Matt. 17:14-23
Eleven Sunday of St. Matthew	1 Corinthians 9: 2-12	Matt. 18:23-35
Twelfth Sunday of St. Matthew	1 Corinthians 15:1-11	Matt. 19:16-26
Thirteenth Sunday of St. Matthew	1 Corinthians 16:13-24	Matt. 21:33-42
Fourteenth Sunday of St. Matthew	2 Corinthians 1:21-2: 4	Matt. 22:2-14
Fifteenth Sunday of St. Matthew	2 Corinthians 4:6-15	Matt. 22:35-46
Sixteenth Sunday of St. Matthew	2 Corinthians 6:1-10	Matt. 25:14-30
Seventeenth Sunday of St. Matthew	2 Corinthians 6:16-17:1	Matt. 15:21-28
Sunday Before Exaltation of the Holy Cross	Galatians 6:11-18	John 3:13-17

(Exaltation of the Holy Cross–September 14th)

Sunday After Exaltation of the Holy Cross	Galatians 2:16-20	Mark 8: 34-9:1

(Sundays After Pentecost are also known as Sundays of St. Luke)

First Sunday of Saint Luke*	1 Corinthians 9:6-11	Luke 5:1-11

(*The lessons for each Sunday, before and after Epiphany, are based on the date of Pascha.)

Second Sunday of Saint Luke	2 Corinthians 11:31-12:9	Luke 6:31-36
Third Sunday of Saint Luke	Galatians 1:11-19	Luke 7:11-16
Fourth Sunday of Saint Luke	Galatians 2:16-20	Luke 8:5-15

Fifth Sunday of Saint Luke	Galatians 6:11-18	Luke 16:19-31
Sixth Sunday of Saint Luke	Galatians 5:22-6:2	Luke 8:27-39
Seventh Sunday of Saint Luke	Ephesians 2:4-10	Luke 8:41-56
Eighth Sunday of Saint Luke	Ephesians 4:1-7	Luke 10:25-37

Ninth Sunday of Saint Luke	Ephesians 5:8-19	Luke 12:16-21
Tenth Sunday of Saint Luke	Ephesians 6:10-17	Luke 13:10-17
Eleventh Sunday of Saint Luke	Colossians 1:12-18	Luke 14:16-24
Twelfth Sunday of Saint Luke	Colossians 3:4-11	Luke 17: 12-19

Thirteenth Sunday of Saint Luke	Colossians 3:12-16	Luke 18:18-27
Fourteenth Sunday of St. Luke	1 Timothy 1: 15-17	Luke 18:35-end
Fifteenth Sunday of St. Luke	1 Timothy 4: 9-15	Luke 19:1-10
Sixteenth Sunday of St. Luke	2 Timothy 3:10-15	Luke 18:9-14

Seventeenth Sunday of St. Luke	1 Corinthians 6:12-20	Luke 15:11-25
Eighteenth Sunday of Saint Luke	1 Corinthians 8:8-9:2	Matt. 25:31-46

The following rules apply. If Pascha occurs on:

April 4th, 5th or 6th there is no lesson for the Sunday after Epiphany. The Sunday of the Publican and the Pharisee is used instead. On January 7th use the lessons for the Sunday after Epiphany.

April 7th through the 13th: readings for the Sunday after Epiphany are used.

April 14th through 21st: the Sunday after Epiphany is used, plus the 15th Sunday of St. Luke – a.k.a. Sunday of Zacchaeus.

April 21st through 27th: the Sunday after Epiphany is used, plus two additional Sundays – 12th of St. Luke and 15th of St. Luke.

April 28th through May 4th : the Sunday after Epiphany is used plus three additional Sundays – 12th of St. Luke, the 15th of St. Luke, and the 17th of St. Luke.

May 5th through 8th: the Sunday after Epiphany is used plus four additional Sundays: 12th of St. Luke, 14th of St. Luke, 15th of St. Luke, 17th of St. Luke.

Wonderful Promises to Christians

"The Lord is near to those who have a broken heart, and saves such as have a contrite spirit."

Ps. 34:18

Jesus said to him: "If you can believe, all things are possible to him who believes."

St. Mark 9:23

"But seek first the Kingdom of God and His righteousness, and all these things shall be added to you."

St. Matthew 6:33

THE READINGS FOR THE MAJOR FEASTS OF THE ORTHODOX CHURCH YEAR

The (Presentation) Entrance of the Theotokos into the Temple – November 21st
Epistle: Hebrews 9:1-7
Gospel: Luke 10:38-42, 11:27-28

The Annunciation – March 25th
Epistle: Hebrews 2:11-18
Gospel: Luke 1:24-38

Nativity of the Theotokos – September 8th
Epistle: Philippians 2:5-11
Gospel: Luke 10:38-42, 11:27-28

The (Elevation) Exaltation of the Holy Cross – September 14th
Epistle: 1 Corinthians 1:18-24
Gospel: John 19:6-11, 13-20, 25-28, 30-35

The Nativity of Our Lord – December 25th
Epistle : Galatians 4:4-7
Gospel: Matthew 2:1-12

Holy Theophany (Baptism of Our Lord) – January 6th
Epistle: Titus 2:11-14, 3:4-7
Gospel: Matthew 3:13-17

Meeting (Presentation) of Our Lord in the Temple – February 2nd
Epistle: Hebrews 7:7-17
Gospel: Luke 2:22-40
Our Lord's Entrance Into Jerusalem – (Palm Sunday)
Epistle: Philippians 4:4-9
Gospel: John 12:1-18

The Ascension of Our Lord – 40 days after Pascha
Epistle: Acts 1:1-12
Gospel: Luke 24:36-53

Pentecost – 50 days after Pascha
Epistle: Acts 2:1-11
Gospel: John 7:37-52, 8-12

The Transfiguration of Our Lord – August 6th
Epistle: 2 Peter 1:10-19
Gospel: Matthew 17:1-9

The Dormition of the Theotokos – August 15th
Epistle: Philippians 2:5-11
Gospel: Luke 10:38-42, 11:27-28

> *St. John of Damascus teaches: "We firmly believe that the Church will never fall, never will waver, and will not be destroyed. For this is what Christ taught, by whom the heavens were established, and the earth was founded, and stands firmly as the Holy Spirit says in Psalm 32:6. The Antichrist will lure to himself those who have a weak and feeble mind, and will seduce and tear them away from the living God."*

ON OBSERVING THE NATIVITY OF CHRIST

Orthodox Christians must return to a spirit of holiness in regard to celebration of the Feast of the Nativity of Christ–or Christmas. Obviously, in this country, we have now reduced (some would say "returned") the Christmas holidays to a pagan feast of lavish gift giving, overeating, drinking, gaudy decorations and a sorrowful time of self-indulgent excess. It goes without saying that the Holy Day has lost almost every vestige of its original intent of celebrating the coming of Our Redeemer. Those who wish to return to the true spirit of the Nativity will need to expend great effort and sacrifice.

To help regain the authentic spiritual meaning of the Nativity Feast – we should:

1. Prepare ourselves by observing the Nativity Fast. Instead of increasing what we normally eat – we should curtail the amount of food and drink we consume during the Christmas season.

2. Read the daily assigned Scriptural passages of the feast and attend as many of the religious services as possible – leading up to the feast – day itself.

3. Keep observation of the holiday simple, giving home-made items as gifts as often as possible. When buying gifts keep them practical and sensibly-priced. Avoid any expensive toys or faddish clothing.

4. Reduce your dependence on TV, radio and other media. Avoid lavish entertainment during the season. Use money ordinarily spent on parties to support charities maintaining the poor.

5. Celebrate the feast with all seriousness of purpose and thanksgiving for the gift of God's own Son.

OTHER FEASTS AND HOLIDAYS

Beginning of the Church Year – September 1st
1 Timothy 2:1-7, St. Luke 4:16-22

Thanksgiving Day – Last Thursday of the Month (USA)
Romans 13:1-8, St. Matthew 22:15-22

GREAT AND HOLY WEEK IN THE ORTHODOX CHURCH

The most stirring and meaningful ceremonies of the Orthodox Church Year are the services of Holy Week. The services, well known by even non-Ortho-dox, are at the same time solemn, joyful, Biblically-sound, and a reflection of the Church's role in the sanctification and education of all mankind.

The days of this eventful week retell the prophecies of Christ's work to secure our redemption and relate how these splendid events were played-out, culminating in the suffering, death and glorious resurrection of Our Lord.

During Great and Holy Week we relive Christ's powerful gift of love for our sake. It is the Church's way of reminding our often frail and forgetful memories that we are truly loved by Almighty God, and are so precious in His sight that He sent His only Son to live and die for our sake. If we are to be genuinely thankful for the gift of our salvation we will seek to understand and appreciate the retelling of those things which comprise the greatest story ever told!

As Christians, we are called not only to discuss the events of Our Lord's life, and listen to homilies about their significance, but are also commanded to relive these events that bring the past into the present. To do so, we must enter into the very spirit of the Paschal events and experience the things our Christian ancestors felt, while bringing to life the exact words, in rituals, of what the first believers lived. Since our Jewish brothers and sisters eat the same unleavened bread and herbs at Passover that their ancestors ate, how can we as Christians of the New Covenant do any less? The past is meant to be lived in the present, and we, as Orthodox Christians must re-live our sacred heritage through the events of Holy Week.

Great and Holy Week begins with the commemoration of Christ raising his friend Lazarus from the dead. It is significant because each of us is a friend of Christ and the events of Holy Week remind us that Jesus lived and died for our personal resurrection. On Saturday, death begins to tremble, and we see a classic duel between good and evil. On this day we are reminded that Christ is the Life-giver, who was promised to mankind at the time of our first parent's disobedience in the Garden of Eden.

Palm Sunday: *The Lord's Entrance into Jerusalem:* St. Matthew 21:18-43, Philippians 4:4-9, St. John 12:1-18.

On this day we acknowledge that Jesus Christ is King and Redeemer. In church we, as did the people of Jerusalem, hold palms or pussy willows to signify that Christ is Our King for all time. On Palm Sunday we renew our baptismal vows to make Christ the Lord of our lives. The hymns of the day refer to the fig tree that failed to bear fruit, as we often fail in our own lives. The prayers of the day remind us of the Patriarch Joseph who suffered much in Egypt before being glorified. This is the same scenario Jesus encounters in the solemn, yet joyful, pilgrimage of Holy Week.

Holy and Great Monday: Isaiah 50: 5-10, St. Matthew 24:3-35

The theme of this day is watchfulness and preparation. Holy Monday gives us hope in our own redemption from sin and evil. The services in the first three evenings of Holy Week – i.e. Palm Sunday, Holy and Great Monday, and Holy Tuesday are sometimes known as the "Bridegroom Services."

The services show the need for true repentance and mirror the reality of God's pardon for those who will admit their sin and turn to Him in earnest prayer and deed. At this time, we follow Christ day-by-day as He cleanses the Temple and confronts His enemies, while giving final instructions to His beloved apostles.

During the first services on Sunday evening an icon of Christ the Bridegroom is carried throughout the church where it will remain until Holy Thursday. This symbolizes our journey with Christ on His way to Golgotha to be cruci-fied. Again, we relive this event through ritual, and in doing so are reminded of the reality of Christ's sufferings that have become vivid and personalized in our own lives.

The readings for **Holy and Great Tuesday** –"Bridegroom Services" – relate the up-coming events of Holy Week, as found in Ephesians 1:1-12,

St. Matthew 24:36-26:2. Those for Holy Wednesday are in 1 Corinthians 2:6-9, St. Matthew 26:6-16.

On **Holy and Great Wednesday** the Church celebrates the moving services whereby we become anointed with Christ in the Mystery of Holy Unction. (See a full description of this Sacrament in section on Holy Mysteries.) This is the preparation for the next two days that commemorate the brutal passion and sufferings of Our Lord.

Holy and Great Thursday: 1 Corinthians 11:23-32, St. Matthew 26:1-20; 21-39, 40-75, St. John 13:3, 18:25-38, St. Luke 22:43-45.

On Thursday morning the Church remembers the institution of the Holy Eucharist at the Last Mystical Supper of Our Lord with His disciples. This is in preparation for the solemn events of the evening that initiate the passion of Jesus Christ.

At this morning Eucharist, which is Christ's gift of life to us, many Orthodox Christians receive Holy Communion with the words: "Receive me today, O Son of God, as a partaker of Thy Mystic Feast... I will not kiss Thee as did Judas, but like the thief I will confess Thee... Remember me, Lord, when Thou comes into Thy Kingdom."

The theme of Holy Thursday evening is the profound suffering of Our Lord. Twelve Gospel readings relate the last moments of Christ on earth, His sufferings, crucifixion, death on the Cross, the anguish of His dear mother the Holy Virgin Mary, and His burial by Joseph of Arimathea. After the fifth Gospel reading the "Procession of the Cross" takes place while the congregation chants, "Today is hung upon the tree He who suspended the land in the midst of the waters."

Holy and Great Friday: 1 Corinthians 1:18-31; 2:1-2, St. Matthew 27:1-38, St. Luke 23:32-49, St. Matthew 27:39-54, St. John 19:31-37, St. Matthew 27:55-61.

Holy and Great Friday is the most solemn day of the Church Year. It is a day of mourning, fasting and prayer calling to mind the sufferings and death of Our Lord so that we too, might have life everlasting.

There is no Divine Liturgy on Holy and Great Friday, popularly called "Good Friday." However the Royal Hours are sung in the afternoon, or early evening, during which the procession with the Shroud (Epitaphios/Plaschanitsa) occurs. The Shroud is placed in a flowered bier that represents the tomb where Christ's body was laid to rest after being removed from the Cross.

The morning service on Holy and Great Friday consists of the Old Testament's prophecies relating to Our Lord's death. During the afternoon hours the procession with Christ's body takes place. After being removed from the

Cross it is wrapped in a white Shroud and placed on the Holy Table. The Epitaphios/Plaschanitsa is buried in the tomb. During the evening service we chant Lamentations expressing our sorrow that Jesus has died-along with our belief that He descended to Hades to abolish the power of Satan-while trampling upon death itself. Yet our sorrow is tinged with hope in Christ's Life-giving resurrection and we sing: "By Thy death Thou has abolished death, bringing forth joy for the world." On Holy and Great Friday our hymns reflect the reality of our lives–as we meditate upon Jesus' last words from the Cross, "Do not weep for me, but weep for yourselves."

Holy and Great Saturday: Romans 6:3-11, 1 Corinthians 5:6-8, Galatians 3:13-14, St. Matthew 27:62-66, Ezekiel 37:1-14.

On this day we mourn with the Church as Christ lies in the grave. We lament our gentle Lord's death, one He surely did not deserve, but which He endured for our redemption. The Liturgy of St. Basil is served on Holy Saturday morning to await the sublime resurrection of Christ from the dead.

The day's theme is Christ's descent into Hades. The Epistles and Gospels echo the theme of the impending resurrection of Christ and during the service the priest strews flower petals or basil leaves throughout the church as a harbinger of what will be Christ's victory over the powers of death. The final reading of Holy Saturday promises the resurrection of Our Lord; "After three days I will rise again" and notes the sealing of Our Lord's tomb (St. Matthew 27: 62-66).

Finally on Holy Saturday evening we come to the climax of this sad, expectant, yet profoundly glorious week.

As the congregation gathers in the darkened church it is still Holy Saturday. The tomb is sealed and silent. The service begins as a traditional funeral dirge. Suddenly, at the stroke of midnight the old day passes into a new day of everlasting life with Almighty God. Divine light and life now permeate the world! The priest arrives at the Holy Table and announces, in excited and triumphant tones, that "Christ is risen from the dead. By His death He has trampled upon death, and to those in the tomb He has bestowed life eternal." As the priest passes the flame of life from the Paschal Candle to those assembled in the church, we rejoice that there is now hope for us! Each of us, once steeped in sin and death, is now given the opportunity for everlasting life with Our Lord in His Heavenly Kingdom.

PASCHA – THE RESURRECTION OF OUR LORD

On the afternoon of Pascha we chant the Service of Vespers when the Gospel of Christ's Resurrection is read in various languages to indicate the universality of the Good News. It is an Agape Service of Love, and we proclaim this reality of the resurrection for forty days after – with the words, "Christ is risen from the dead, truly He is risen!"

As we enter the day of life, or Pascha , the Resurrection of Our Lord, we know that our lives have been changed forever. The readings in Acts 1:1-8 and St. John 1:1-17, underscore the fact that Pascha is not just an event which happened in the past. Pascha is a real, living, and actual experience of hope for Orthodox Christians who now know that their lives are precious, so precious in fact, that the very Son of God suffered and died so that we might live forever in His sacred presence. We too, rise from the darkened, forbidding tomb of slavery to freedom, from sinful weakness to power, from utter despair to hope, from doubt to faith because Christ's Resurrection breaks forever the crushing chains of despair and death. Because of Pascha, everlasting life now awaits all those who remain faithful to God's immense love for His creation.

THE PASCHAL SERMON OF ST JOHN CHRYSOSTOM
from the 4th century

If any man be devout and love God, let him enjoy this fair and radiant
 triumphal feast.
If any man be a wise servant, let him enter rejoicing into the joy of his Lord.
If any have labored long in fasting, let him now receive his recompense.
If any have wrought from the first hour, let him today receive his just reward.
If any have come at the third hour, let him with thankfulness keep the feast.
If any have arrived at the sixth hour, let him have no misgivings, because he
 shall in no wise be deprived.
If any have delayed until the ninth hour, let him draw near, fearing nothing.
If any have tarried even until the eleventh hour, let him not be alarmed at his
 tardiness; for the Lord, who is jealous of His honor, will accept the last
 even as the first; He gives rest unto him who comes at the eleventh hour;
 even as unto him who has worked from the first hour.
He shows mercy upon the last, and cares for the first, and to the one He gives
 and upon the other He bestows gifts.
He both accepts the deeds, welcomes the intention, honors the acts and
 praises the offering.

Wherefore, enter all into the joy of your Lord.
Receive your reward, both the first and likewise the second.
You rich and poor together, hold high festival. You sober and you heedless,
 honor the day.
Rejoice today, both you who have fasted and you who have disregarded the
 Fast.
The table is fully laden; feast sumptuously. The calf is fatted; let no one go
 away hungry.
Enjoy the feast of faith, receive all the riches of loving-kindness.
Let no one bewail his poverty, for the universal Kingdom has been revealed.
Let no one weep for his iniquities, for pardon has shown forth from the grave.
Let no one fear death, for the Savior's death has set us free; He who was held
 prisoner of it has now annihilated it!

By descending into hell, He made hell captive. He embittered it when it tasted of His flesh. And Isaiah, foretelling this, cried out , "Hell was embittered when it encountered Thee in the lower regions."

It was embittered, for it was abolished.
It was embittered for it was mocked.
It was embittered, for it was slain.
It was embittered for it was overthrown.
It was embittered, for it was fettered in chains.
It took a body, and met God face-to-face.
It took earth, and encountered heaven.
It took what was seen, and fell upon the unseen.

O death where is your sting? O hell, where is your victory?
Christ is risen, and you are overthrown. Christ is risen, and the demons have fallen.
Christ is risen, and the angels rejoice.
Christ is risen and life reigns.
Christ is risen, and not one dead man remains in the grave.
For Christ, being risen from the dead, has become the first fruits of those who have fallen asleep.
To Him be glory and dominion – unto ages of ages.
Amen.

YEARLY MIRACLE AT CHRIST'S TOMB

Every year on Holy Saturday – according to the Orthodox calendar-there is a wondrous miracle at the tomb of Christ, the Holy Sepulcher, in Jerusalem. At about 1:00 in the afternoon of this day the Greek Orthodox Patriarch of Jerusalem is searched thoroughly by both Israeli and Muslim authorities. After it is discerned that there are no hidden items on his person, the patriarch is permitted to enter the tomb of Christ in which all candles and oil lamps have been extinguished. The tomb has also been certified by the civil authorities to be free of any incendiary devices.

The patriarch enters the barren tomb, and after a time of silent prayer, and anticipation, one of the oil lamps inside is miraculously set ablaze with "the fire from heaven." From this flame the patriarch lights a candle-torch of 33 candles symbolizing the years of Our Lord's life on earth and emerges from the tomb to offer this Holy Fire to the thousands of faithful gathered inside the Basilica of the Holy Resurrection.

This event happens every year on Holy Saturday, and has been occurring for the many centuries of the life of the Orthodox Church. Yet it is seldom mentioned by the world press nor is it well-known among Orthodox believers outside the Holy City. This ancient miracle of faith occurs only after the entrance of the Orthodox patriarch. It is, in the Holy Land, an annual event anticipated by the faithful, to show God's favor upon the Church – while being an answer to her fervent prayers for protection. It is a unique and continual sign of the Orthodox Church's preeminence among the world's religions.

An Eyewitness Account of the Great Miracle
Given By God Only To The Orthodox Church

THE CEREMONY OF THE HOLY FIRE IN JERUSALEM

This ceremony takes place in the Orthodox Church of the Resurrection in Jerusalem in such a way that bewilders the soul of Christians.

On Easter Saturday, at noon, the Orthodox patriarch enters the Holy Sepulcher, recites special prayers and remains waiting. Sometimes the waiting is long, sometimes short. The crowd, in the darkened church, repeats continually with a loud voice: "Lord have mercy." At a certain moment the Holy Fire flashes from the depth of the Holy Sepulcher in a supernatural way, miraculously, and lights up the little lamp of olive oil put on the edge of it. The patriarch , after having read some prayers, lights up the two clusters of 33 candles he is holding, and begins to distribute the Holy Fire to the multitude of pilgrims, who receive it with great emotion, accompanied with pealing of bells, acclamations, and an unbridled enthusiasm.

The Holy Fire is not only distributed by the patriarch, but operates also by itself. It emits from the Holy Sepulcher having a gleam of a hue completely different from that of natural light. It sparkles, it flashes like lightning, it flies like a dove around the Tabernacle of the Holy Sepulcher, and lights up the unlit lamps of oil hanging in front of it. It whirls from one side of the church to the other. It enters some of the chapels inside the church, as for instance the Chapel of Calvary, and lights up the little lamps. It lights up also the candles of certain pilgrims. In fact there are some very pious pilgrims who, every time they attended this ceremony, noticed that their candles lit up on their own accord!

This Divine Fire also presents some peculiarities: as soon as it appears it has a bluish hue and does not burn. At the first moments of its appearance, if it touches the face, or the mouth, or the hands, it does not burn. This is proof of its Divine and supernatural origin. We must also take into consideration that the Holy Light appears only by the invocation of an Orthodox (patriarch) or archbishop. Each time the heterodox (non-Orthodox) bishops tried to obtain it, they failed!

Once the Armenians paid the Turks , who then occupied the Holy Land, in order to obtain permission for their patriarch to enter the Holy Sepulcher. The Orthodox patriarch was standing sorrowfully with his flock at the exit of the church, near the left column, when the Holy Light split this column vertically and flashed near the Orthodox patriarch.

A Moslem Muezin called Tounom, who saw the miraculous event from an adjacent mosque, abandoned immediately the Moslem religion and became an Orthodox Christian. This event took place in 1549 under Sultan Mourad IV, when the Patriarch of Jerusalem was Sophrony II. (The mentioned column still exists. It goes back to the 12th century. Orthodox pilgrims embrace it as "the place of the split" when they enter the church.)

The appearance of the Holy Fire is an event that occurs every year in front of thousands of visual witnesses. Nobody can deny it. On the contrary this miracle can reinforce those who have a lack of faith

There are also some very touching recent cases of Jewish folk, who believed in Christ after having seen the Holy Fire, and who said to their compatriots, "Why are you still waiting for the Messiah?" "The Messiah has come indeed!"

From Irene Economides' book, "The Differences Between Orthodox and Roman Catholicism"

The following account is from an interview with His Beatitude, Diodorus, Patriarch of Jerusalem (who reposed on December 19, 2000) the modern link to a tradition which stretches back more than 2,000 years. Here are some excerpts from that account:

"The Miracle of the Holy Fire is known as the 'greatest of all Christian miracles.' It takes place every year, at the same time, in the same manner and at the same spot. No other miracle is known to occur so regularly and over such an extensive period of time. The miracle happens at the 'Edicule' in the Church of the Holy Sepulcher in Jerusalem, on the eve of Pascha" (Holy Saturday).

The same miracle was detailed by the Russian Abbot Daniel in 1106. The very same miracle occurs today in the Holy Tomb of Christ.

In the exact words of Diodorus, who experienced the miracle over the years as Patriarch of Jerusalem:

"I enter the tomb and kneel in holy fear in front of the place where Christ lay after His death and where He rose again from the dead. Praying in the Holy Sepulcher in itself, is for me always a very holy mo- ment in a very holy place… I find my way in darkness toward the inner chamber and say, kneeling, certain prayers that have been handed down to us through the centuries… normally the miracle happens immedi- ately after I say the prayers. From the core of the very stone on which Jesus lay an indefinable light pours forth. It usually has a blue tint, but the color may change and take on different hues. It cannot be described in human terms. The light rises from the tomb as mist rises from a lake

– it almost looks like the stone is covered with a moist cloud – but it is light. The light from the stone behaves differently each year. Sometimes it covers just the stone, and sometimes it gives light to the whole tomb, so that the people who stand outside will look into it and see the light. The light does not burn – I have never had my beard burnt in sixteen years – during which I have been the Patriarch of Jerusalem. Then one hears a rather loud mumbling from inside the tomb. I am able to light my candles from the flame. When I receive the flame on my candles I go out and give it first to the Armenian Patriarch and then to the Coptic. Hereafter I give the flame to all the people who are present in the church. Then the sound is like a roar comparable to that when a goal is scored in a soccer match.

Then a blue flame is reported to appear and is very active outside the tomb. Every year, thousands of believers report that the flame ignites the candles in their hands, of its own initiative. Often closed oil lamps are ignited with flames before the eyes of the pilgrims. The blue flame is then seen to move about the church igniting the candles and lamps of the faithful."

Note: The miracle occurs only at Orthodox Pascha (Easter) and only when there are authorities from the Orthodox Church officiating. In fact, over the centuries hierarchs from other denominations have attempted to ignite the flame on their own, to no avail.

The Resurrection of Christ

"Now when He rose early on the first day of the week, He appeared first to Mary Magdalene, out of whom He cast seven demons."

St. Mark 16:9

"And we are witnesses of all things which He did both in the land of the Jews and in Jerusalem, whom they killed by hanging on a tree. It was He whom God raised up on the third day, and showed Him openly, not to all the people, but to witnesses chosen by God, even to us who ate and drank with Him after He rose from the dead."

Acts 10:39-41

True God and True Man

He was born, but He was already begotten.
He came forth from a woman, but she was a virgin.

He was wrapped in swaddling bands, but He removed the swaddling
*   clothes of the grave when He rose from the dead.*
He was laid in a manger, but He was glorified by the angels, and
*   proclaimed by a star, and worshiped by the wise Magi.*

He had no form of beauty in the eyes of the Jews, but to David He
   was fairer than all of the children of men.

On the mountain, He was bright as the lightening and became
   more luminous than the Sun illuminating us into the mysteries of
   the future.

He was baptized as man, yet He remitted sins as God.

He was tempted as man, but He conquered as God.

He suffered hunger, but fed thousands. He knew what it was like to
   thirst, but He cried: "If any man thirst let him come to me and
   drink."

He experienced weariness, but He is the peace of all those who are
   sorrowful and heavy-laden.

He prayed, yet He also hears prayer.
He weeps, but He also put an end to tears.

He asks, "Where is the lifeless Lazarus laid?" For He was a man,
   and He raises Lazarus from the dead, for He is God!

As a sheep He is led to be slaughtered but He is the Shepherd of Israel,
   and also of the entire world.

He is bruised and wounded, but heals every disease and infirmity.
He is lifted up and nailed to the tree, but by the Tree of Life – He restores
   us.

He lays down His life but He has the power to take it up again,
   and the veil is split in two, for the mysterious doors of heaven are
   opened, and the rocks are cut in half, the dead arise!

He dies, but He gives life, and by His death effectively destroys death.

   St Gregory Nazianzus (Oration 29)

APPENDICES
Appendix 1

READINGS – for days of the Church Year
Readings for the Church Year vary from tradition to tradition. This calendar
of readings is useful as **a general guide** but may be changed if there is a
particular saint or feast celebrated according to the Typicon used within a
jurisdiction.

Day	Epistle	Gospel
Saturday before the Publican and the Pharisee	2 Timothy 2:11-19	Luke 18:2-8
Publican and Pharisee	2 Tim. 3:10-15	Luke 18:9-14
Monday	2 Peter 1:20-2:9	Mark 13:9-13
Tuesday	2 Peter 2:9-22	Mark 13:14-23
Wednesday	2 Peter 3:1-18	Mark 13:24-31
Thursday	1 John 1:8-2:6	Mark 13:31-14:2
Friday	1 John 2:7-17	Mark 14:3-9
Saturday	2 Tim. 3:1-9	Luke 20:46-21:4
Prodigal Son	1 Cor. 6:12-20	Luke 15:11-32
Monday	1 John 2:18-3: 8	Mark 11:1-11
Tuesday	1 John 3:9-22	Mark 14:10-42
Wednesday	1 John 3:21-4:11	Mark 14:43-15:1
Thursday	1 John 4:20-5:21	Mark 15:1-15
Friday	2 John 1:1-13	Mark 15:20, 22, 25, 33-41
Saturday	1 Cor. 10:23-26	Luke 21:8-9, 25-7, 33-36
Meatfast Sunday	1 Cor. 8:8-9:2	Matt. 25:31-46
Monday	3 John 1:1-14	Luke 19:29-40, 22:7-39
Tuesday	Jude 1:1-10	Luke 22:39-23:1
Wednesday	Joel 2:12-26	Joel 3:12-21
Thursday	Jude 11-25	Matt. 23:1-31, 32, 44-56
Friday	Zech. 8:7-14	Zech. 8:19-23
Saturday	Rom. 14:19-23, 16:25-7	Matt. 6:1-13
Cheesefare Sunday	Romans 13:11-14:4	Matt. 6:14-21
Monday	Isaiah 1:1-20	Proverbs 1:1-20
Tuesday	Isaiah 1:19-2:3	Proverbs 1:21-33
Wednesday	Genesis 1:24-2:3	Proverbs 2:1-22
Thursday	Isaiah 2:11-22	Proverbs 3:1-18
Friday	Genesis 2:20-3:20	Proverbs 3:19-34
Saturday	Hebrews 1:1-12	Mark 2:23-3:5

Day	Epistle	Gospel
Sunday of Orthodoxy	Hebr. 11:24-26, 32-40	John 1:43-51
Monday	Isaiah 4:2-6	Proverbs 3:34-4:22
Tuesday	Isaiah 5:7-16	Proverbs 5:1-15
Wednesday	Isaiah 5:16-26	Proverbs 5:15-6:3
Thursday	Isaiah 6: 1-12	Proverbs 6:3-20
Friday	Isaiah 7:1-14	Proverbs 6:20-7:1
Saturday	Hebrews 3:12-16	Mark 1:35-44
St. Gregory Palamas	Hebrews 1:10-2:3	Mark 2:1-12
Monday	Isaiah 8:13-9:7	Proverbs 8:1-21
Tuesday	Isaiah 9:9-10:4	Proverbs 8:32-9:11
Wednesday	Genesis 7:6-9	Proverbs 9:1-18
Thursday	Isaiah 11:10-12:2	Proverbs 10: 1-22
Friday	Genesis 8:4-21	Proverbs 10:31-11:2
Saturday	Hebrews 10:32-38	Mark 2:14-17
Veneration of the Cross	Hebrews 4:14-5:6	Mark 8:34-9:1
Monday	Genesis 8:21-9:7	Proverbs 11:19-12:6
Tuesday	Genesis 9:8-17	Proverbs 12:8-22
Wednesday	Genesis 9:18-10:1	Proverbs 12:23-13:10
Thursday	Genesis 10:32-11:9	Proverbs 13:20-14:6
Friday	Genesis 12:1-7	Proverbs 14:15-26
Saturday	Hebrews 6:9-12	Mark 7:31-37
St. John of the Ladder	Hebrews 6:13-20	Mark 9:17-31
Monday	Genesis 13:12-18	Proverbs 14:27-15:4
Tuesday	Genesis 15:1-15	Proverbs 15: 7-19
Wednesday	Genesis 17:1-9	Proverbs 15:20-16:9
Thursday	Genesis 18:20-end	Proverbs 16:17-17:17
Friday	Genesis 22:1-18	Proverbs 17:17-18:5
Saturday	Hebrews 9:24-28	Mark 8:27-31
St. Mary of Egypt	Hebrews 9:11-14	Mark 10:32-45
Monday	Genesis 27:1-41	Proverbs 19:16-25
Tuesday	Genesis 31:3-16	Proverbs 21:3-21
Wednesday	Genesis 43:26-31, 45:1-16	Proverbs 21:23- 22:4
Thursday	Genesis 46:1-7	Proverbs 23:15-24:5
Friday	Genesis 49:33-50:1-end	Proverbs 31:8-end
Lazarus Saturday	Hebrews 12:28-13:8	John 11:1-45

Day	Epistle	Gospel
Palm Sunday	Philippians 4:4-9	John 12:1-18
Monday	Isaiah 50:5-10	Matt. 21:18-43
Tuesday	Job 1:13-end	Matt. 24:36-26:2
	Jeremiah 11:18-20	
Wednesday	Isaiah 52:11-end, 53:1-7	Matt. 26:6-16
Thursday	1 Cor. 11:23-32	Matt. 26:1-27:2
Friday	No Divine Liturgy	
Saturday	Romans 6:3-11	Matt. 28: 1-20
Pascha	Acts 1:1-8	John 1:1-17
Monday	Acts 1:12-17:21-26	John 1:18-28
Tuesday	Acts 2:14-21	Luke 24:12-35
Wednesday	Acts 2:22-38	John 1:35-52
Thursday	Acts 2:38-43	John 3:1-15
Friday	Acts 3:1-8	John 2:12-22
Saturday	Acts 3:11-16	John 3:22-33
Thomas Sunday	Acts 5:12-20	John 20:19-31
Monday	Acts 3:19-26	John 2:1-11
Tuesday	Acts 4:1-10	John 3:16-21
Wednesday	Acts 4:13-22	John 5:17-24
Thursday	Acts 4:23-31	John 5:24-30
Friday	Acts 5:1-11	John 5:30-6:2
Saturday	Acts 5:21-32	John 6:14-27
Myrrh-Bearers	Acts 6:1-7	Mark 15:43-16:8
Monday	Acts 6:8-7:5a, 47-60	John 4:46-54
Tuesday	Acts 8: 5-17	John 6:27-33
Wednesday	Acts 8:18-25	John 6:35-39
Thursday	Acts 8:26-39	John 6:40-44
Friday	Acts 8:40-9:18	John 6:48-54
Saturday	Acts 9:19-31	John 15:17-16:2
The Paralytic	Acts 9:32-42	John 5:1-15
Monday	Acts 10:1-16	John 6:56-69
Tuesday	Acts 10:21-33	John 7:1-13
Wednesday	Acts 14:6-18	John 7:14-30
(Mid Pentecost)		
Thursday	Acts 10:34-43	John 8:12-20
Friday	Acts 10:44-11:10	John 8:21-30
Saturday	Acts 12:1-11	John 8:31-42

Day	Epistle	Gospel
Samaritan Woman	Acts 11:19-30	John 4:5-42
Monday	Acts 12:12-17	John 8:42-51
Tuesday	Acts 12:25-13:12	John 8:51-59
Wednesday	Acts 13:13-24	John 6:5-14
Thursday	Acts 14:20-15:4	John 9:39-10:9
Friday	Acts 15:5-34	John 10:17-28
Saturday	Acts 15:35-41	John 10:27-38
Blind Man	Acts 16:16-34	John 9:1-38
Monday	Acts 17: 1-15	John 11:47-54
Tuesday	Acts 17: 19-28	John 12:19-36
Wednesday	Acts 18:22-28	John 12:36-47
Thursday (Ascension)	Acts 1:1-12	Luke 24:36-53
Friday	Acts 19:1-8	John 14:1-11
Saturday	Acts 20:7-12	John 14:10-21
Fathers of Nicaea	Acts 20:16-18, 28-36	John 17:1-13
Monday	Acts 21:8-14	John 14:27-15:7
Tuesday	Acts 21:26-32	John 16: 2-13
Wednesday	Acts 23:1-11	John 16:15-23
Thursday	Acts 25:13-19	John 16:15-33
Friday	Acts 27:1-28:1	John 17:18-26
Saturday	Acts 28:4-31	John 21:14-25
Pentecost	Acts 2:1-11	John 7:37-52, 8:12
Monday	Ephesians 5:8-19	Matt. 18:10-20
Tuesday	Romans 1:1-7, 13-17	Matt.4:23-5:13
Wednesday	Romans 1:18-27	Matt. 5:20-26
Thursday	Romans 1:28-2:9	Matt. 5:27-32
Friday	Romans 2:14-28	Matt. 5:33-41
Saturday	Romans 1:7-12	Matt. 5:42-48
All Saints Day	Hebrews 11:33-12:2	Matt. 10:32-3, 37-8, 19:27-30
Monday	Romans 2:28-3:18	Matt. 6:31-33, 7:9-14
Tuesday	Romans 4:4-9	Matt. 7:15-21
Wednesday	Romans 4:13-25	Matt. 7:21-23
Thursday	Romans 5:10-16	Matt. 8:23-27
Friday	Romans 5:17-6:1	Matt. 9:14-17
Saturday	Romans 3:19-26	Matt. 7:1-8

Day	Epistle	Gospel
Second Sunday of Pentecost	Romans 2:10-16	Matt.4:18-23
Monday	Romans 7:1-13	Matt. 9:36-10:8
Tuesday	Romans 7:14-8:2	Matt. 10:9-15
Wednesday	Romans 8:2-13	Matt. 10:16-22
Thursday	Romans 8:22-27	Matt. 10:23-31
Friday	Romans 9:6-19	Matt. 10:32-35, 11:1
Saturday	Romans 3:28-31, 4:1-3	Matt. 7:24-8:4
Third Sunday of Pentecost	Romans 5:1-10	Matt. 6:22-33
Monday	Romans 9:18-33	Matt. 11:2-14
Tuesday	Romans 10:11-21,1:1	Matt. 11:16-20
Wednesday	Romans 11:2-12	Matt. 11:20-26
Thursday	Romans 11:13-24	Matt. 11:27-30
Friday	Romans 11:25-36	Matt. 12:1-8
Saturday	Romans 6:11-17	Matt. 8:14-23
Fourth Sunday of Pentecost	Romans 6:18-23	Matt. 8:5-13
Monday	Romans 12:4-21	Matt. 12:9-13
Tuesday	Romans 14: 9-18	Matt. 12:14-16, 22-30
Wednesday	Romans 15:7-16	Matt. 12:38-45
Thursday	Romans 15:17-29	Matt. 12:46-13:3
Friday	Romans 16:1-16	Matt. 13:3-12
Saturday	Romans 8:14-21	Matt. 9:9-13
Fifth Sunday of Pentecost	Romans 10:1-10	Matt. 8:28-9:1
Monday	Romans 16:17-27	Matt. 13:10-23
Tuesday	1 Cor. 1:1-9	Matt. 13:24-30
Wednesday	1 Cor. 2:9-16, 3:1-8	Matt. 13:31-36
Thursday	1 Cor. 3:18-23	Matt. 13:36-43
Friday	1 Cor. 4:5-8	Matt. 13:44-54
Saturday	Romans 9:1-5	Matt. 9:18-26
Sixth Sunday of Pentecost	Romans 12:6-14	Matt. 9:1-8
Monday	1 Cor. 5:9-13, 6:1-11	Matt. 13:54-58
Tuesday	1 Cor. 6:20,7:12	Matt. 14:1-13
Wednesday	1 Cor. 7:12-24	Matt. 14:35-15:11
Thursday	1 Cor. 7:21-35	Matt. 15:12-20
Friday	1 Cor. 7:35-40, 8:7	Matt. 15:29-31
Saturday	Romans 12:1-3	Matt.10:37-11:1

Day	Epistle	Gospel
Seventh Sunday of Pentecost	Romans 15:1-7	Matt. 9:27-35
Monday	1 Cor. 9:13-18	Matt. 16:1-6
Tuesday	1 Cor. 10:1-12	Matt. 16:6-12
Wednesday	1 Cor. 10:12-22	Matt. 16:20-24
Thursday	1 Cor. 10:28-11:1-7	Matt. 16:24-28
Friday	1 Cor. 11:8-23	Matt. 17:10-18
Saturday	Romans 13:1-10	Matt. 12:30-37
Eighth Sunday of Pentecost	1 Cor. 1:10-18	Matt. 14:14-22
Monday	1 Cor. 11:31-34, 12:1-6	Matt. 18:1-11
Tuesday	1 Cor. 12:12-26	Matt. 18:18-22, 19:1-2, 13-15
Wednesday	1 Cor. 13:4-13, 14:1-5	Matt. 20:1-16
Thursday	1 Cor. 14:6-13	Matt. 20:17-28
Friday	1 Cor. 14:26-40	Matt. 21:12-14, 17-20
Saturday	Romans 14:6-9	Matt. 15:32-39
Ninth Sunday of Pentecost	1 Cor. 3:9-17	Matt. 14:22-34
Monday	1 Cor. 15:12-19	Matt. 21:18-22
Tuesday	1 Cor. 15:29-38	Matt. 21:23-27
Wednesday	1 Cor. 16:4-12	Matt. 21:28-32
Thursday	1 Cor. 1:1-7	Matt. 21:43-46
Friday	2 Cor. 1:12-20	Matt. 22:23-33
Saturday	Romans 15:30-33	Matt. 17:24-18:4
Tenth Sunday of Pentecost	1 Cor. 4:9-16	Matt. 17:14-23
Monday	2 Cor. 2:3-15	Matt. 23:13-22
Tuesday	2 Cor. 2:14-17, 3:1-3	Matt. 23:23-28
Wednesday	2 Cor. 3:4-9	Matt. 23:29-39
Thursday	2 Cor. 4:1-12	Matt. 24:13-28
Friday	2 Cor. 4:13-18	Matt. 24:27-33, 42-51
Saturday	1 Cor. 1:3-9	Matt. 19:3-12
Eleventh Sunday of Pentecost	1 Cor. 9:2-12	Matt. 18:23-35
Monday	2 Cor. 5:10-15	Mark 1:9-15
Tuesday	2 Cor. 5:15-21	Mark 1:16-22
Wednesday	2 Cor. 6:11-16	Mark 1:23-28
Thursday	2 Cor. 7:1-10	Mark 1:29-35
Friday	2 Cor. 7:10-16	Mark 2:18-22
Saturday	1 Cor. 1:26-31, 2:1-5	Matt. 20:29-34

Day	Epistle	Gospel
Twelfth Sunday of Pentecost	1 Cor. 15:1-11	Matt. 19:16-26
Monday	2 Cor. 8:7-15	Mark 3:6-12
Tuesday	2 Cor. 8:16-24,9:1-5	Mark 3:13-21
Wednesday	2 Cor. 9:12-15, 10:1-7	Mark 3:20-27
Thursday	2 Cor. 10:7-18	Mark 3:28-35
Friday	2 Cor. 11:5-21	Mark 4:1-9
Saturday	1 Cor. 2:6-9	Matt. 22:15-22
Thirteenth Sunday of Pentecost	1 Cor. 16:13-24	Matt. 21:33-42
Monday	2 Cor. 12:10-19	Mark 4:10-23
Tuesday	2 Cor. 12:20-21, 13:1-2	Mark 4:24-34
Wednesday	2 Cor. 13:3-14	Mark 4:35-41
Thursday	Gal. 1:1-10, 20-24, 2:5	Matt. 5:1-20
Friday	Galatians 2:6-10	Mark 5:22-4, 35-6:1
Saturday	1 Cor. 4:1-5	Matt. 23:1-12
Fourteenth Sunday of Pentecost	2 Cor. 1:21-2:4	Matt. 22:1-14
Monday**	Galatians 2:11-16	Mark 5:24-34
Tuesday	Galatians 2:21-3:7	Mark 6:1-7
Wednesday	Galatians 3:15-22	Mark 6:7-13
Thursday	Galatians 3:23-29, 4:5	Mark 6:30-45
Friday	Galatians 4:8-21	Mark 6:45-53
Saturday	1 Cor. 4:17-21,5:5	Matt. 24:1-13

**Note: If The Exaltation of the Holy Cross falls before this week occurs, then the lessons from Saint Luke appear where St. Mark is listed here.

Day	Epistle	Gospel
Fifteenth Sunday of Pentecost	2 Cor. 4:6-15	Matt.22:35-end
Monday	Galatians 4:28-31,5:10	Mark 6:54-7:8
Tuesday	Galatians 5:11-21	Mark 7:5-16
Wednesday	Galatians 6:2-10	Mark 7:14-24
Thursday	Ephesians 1:1-9	Mark 7:24-30
Friday	Ephesians 1:7-17	Mark 8:1-10
Saturday	1 Cor. 10:23-26	Matt. 24:34-44
Sixteenth Sunday of Pentecost	2 Cor. 6:1-10	Matt. 25:14-30
Monday	Ephesians 1:22-2:3	Mark 10:46-52
Tuesday	Ephesians 2:19-3:7	Mark 11:11-23
Wednesday	Ephesians 3:8-21	Mark 11:23-26
Thursday	Ephesians 4:14-19	Mark 11:27-33
Friday	Ephesians 4:14-25	Mark 12:1-12
Saturday	1 Cor. 14 :20-25	Matt. 25:1-13

Day	Epistle	Gospel
Seventeenth Sunday of Pentecost	2 Cor. 6:16-7:1	Matt. 15:21-28
Monday	Ephesians 4:25-32	Luke 3:19-22
Tuesday	Ephesians 5:20-25	Luke 3:23-4:1
Wednesday	Ephesians 5:25-33	Luke 4:1-15
Thursday	Ephesians 5:33-6:9	Luke 4:16-22
Friday	Ephesians 6:18-24	Luke 4:22-30
Saturday	1 Cor. 15:39-45	Luke 4:31-36
Eighteenth Sunday of Pentecost	1 Cor. 9:6-11	Luke 5:1-11
Monday	Philip. 1:1-7	Luke 4:38-44
Tuesday	Philip. 1:8-14	Luke 5:12-16
Wednesday	Philip. 1:12-20	Luke 5:33-39
Thursday	Philip. 1:20-27	Luke 6:12-19
Friday	Philip. 1:27-2:4	Luke 6:17-23
Saturday	1 Cor. 15:58-16:3	Luke 5:17-26
Nineteenth Sunday of Pentecost	2 Cor. 11:31-12:9	Luke 6:31-36
Monday	Philip. 2:12-16	Luke 6:24-30
Tuesday	Philip. 2:16-23	Luke 6:37-45
Wednesday	Philip. 2:24-30	Luke 6:46-7:1
Thursday	Philip. 3:4-8	Luke 7:17-30
Friday	Philip. 3:8-19	Luke 7:31-35
Saturday	2 Cor. 1:8-11	Luke 5:27-32

Note: The Advent Cycle is celebrated from 20th Sunday of Pentecost – 26th Sunday After Pentecost

Day	Epistle	Gospel
Twentieth Sunday of Pentecost	Galatians 1:11-19	Luke 7:11-16
Monday	Philip. 4:10-23	Luke 7:36-50
Tuesday	Colossians 1:1-11	Luke 8:1-3
Wednesday	Colossians 1:18-23	Luke 8:22-25
Thursday	Colossians 1:24-29,2:1a	Luke 9:7-11
Friday	Colossians 2: 1-7	Luke 9:12-18
Saturday	2 Cor. 3:12-18	Luke 6:1-10
Twenty-First Sunday of Pentecost	Galatians 2:16-20	Luke 8:5-15
Monday	Colossians 2:13-20	Luke 9:18-22
Tuesday	Colossians 2:20-23,3:3	Luke 9:23-27
Wednesday	Colossians 3:17-25,4:1	Luke 9:44-50
Thursday	Colossians 4:2-9	Luke 9:49-56
Friday	Colossians 4:10-18	Luke 10:1-15
Saturday	2 Cor. 5:1-10	Luke 7:1-10

Day	Epistle	Gospel
Twenty-Second Sunday of Pentecost	Galatians 6:11-18	Luke 16:19-31
Monday	1 Thess. 1:1-5	Luke 10:22-24
Tuesday	1 Thess. 1:6-10	Luke 11:1-10
Wednesday	1 Thess. 2:1-8	Luke 11:9-13
Thursday	1 Thess. 2:9-14	Luke 11:14-23
Friday	1 Thess. 2:14-20	Luke 11:23-26
Saturday	2 Cor. 8:1-5	Luke 8:16-21
Twenty-Third Sunday of Pentecost	Ephesians 2:4-10	Luke 8:26-39
Monday	1 Thess. 2:20-3:8	Luke 11:29-33
Tuesday	1 Thess. 3:8-13	Luke 11:34-41
Wednesday	1 Thess. 4:1-12	Luke 11:42-46
Thursday	1 Thess. 4:18,5:1-10	Luke 11:47, 12:1
Friday	1 Thess. 5:9-13, 24-28	Luke 12:2-12
Saturday	2 Cor. 11:1-6	Luke 9:1-6
Twenty-Fourth Sunday of Pentecost	Ephesians 2:14-20	Luke 8:41-end
Monday	2 Thess. 1:1-10	Luke 12:13-15, 22-31
Tuesday	2 Thess. 1:10-12, 2:1-2	Luke 12:42-48
Wednesday	2 Thess. 2:1-12	Luke 12:48-59
Thursday	2 Thess. 2:13-17, 3:1-5	Luke 13:1-9
Friday	2 Thess. 3:6-18	Luke 13:31-35
Saturday	Galatians 1:3-10	Luke 9:37-43
Twenty-Fifth Sunday of Pentecost	Ephesians 4:1-7	Luke 10:25-37
Monday	1 Tim. 1:1-7	Luke 14:1, 12-15
Tuesday	1 Tim. 1:8-14	Luke 14:25-35
Wednesday	1 Tim. 1:18-20, 2:8-15	Luke 15:1-10
Thursday	1 Tim. 3:1-13	Luke 16:1-9
Friday	1 Tim. 4:4-16	Luke 16:15-18, 17:1-4
Saturday	Galatians 3:8-12	Luke 9:57-62
Twenty-Sixth Sunday of Pentecost	Ephesians 5:8-19	Luke 12:16-21
Monday	1 Tim. 5:1-10	Luke 17:20-25
Tuesday	1 Tim. 5:11-21	Luke 17:26-36
Wednesday	1 Tim. 5:22-25, 6:11	Luke 18:15-17:26-30
Thursday	1 Tim. 6:17-21	Luke 18:31-34
Friday	2 Tim. 1:1-2,8-18	Luke 19:12-28
Saturday	Galatians 5:22-26, 6:1-2	Luke 10:19-21

Day	Epistle	Gospel
Twenty-Seventh Sunday of Pentecost	Ephesians 6:10-17	Luke 13:10-17
Monday	2 Tim. 2:20-26	Luke 19:37-44
Tuesday	2 Tim. 3:16-4:4	Luke 19:45-48
Wednesday	2 Tim. 4:9-22	Luke 20:1-8
Thursday	Titus 1:5-14	Luke 20:9-18
Friday	Titus 1:15- 2:10	Luke 20:19-26
Saturday	Ephesians 1:16-23	Luke 12:32-40
Twenty-Eighth Sunday of Pentecost	Colossians 1:12-18	Luke 18:35-43
Monday	Hebrews 3:5-10, 17-19	Luke 20:27-44
Tuesday	Hebrews 4:1-13	Luke 21:12-19
Wednesday	Hebrews 5:11- 6:8	Luke 21:5-8; 20-24
Thursday	Hebrews 7:1-6	Luke 21:28-33
Friday	Hebrews 7:18-25	Luke 21:37-22-28
Saturday	Ephesians 2:11-13	Luke 13:19-29
Twenty-Ninth Sunday of Pentecost	Colossians 3:12-16	Luke 17:12-19
Monday	Hebrews 8:7-13	Mark 8:11-21
Tuesday	Hebrews 9:8-23	Mark 8:22-26
Wednesday	Hebrews 10:1-18	Mark 8:30-34
Thursday	Hebrews 10:35-11:7	Mark 9:10-16
Friday	Hebrews 11:8-16	Mark 9:33-41
Saturday	Ephesians 5:1-8	Luke 14:1-11
Thirtieth Sunday of Pentecost	Colossians 3:12-16	Luke 18:18-27
Monday	Hebrews 11:17-31	Mark 9:42-10:1
Tuesday	Hebr. 12:25-7, 13:22-4	Mark 10:2-12
Wednesday	James 1:1-18	Mark 10:11-16
Thursday	James 1:19-27	Mark 10:17-27
Friday	James 2:1-13	Mark 10:24-32
Saturday	Colossians 1:1-6	Luke 16:10-15
Thirty-First Sunday of Pentecost	1 Tim. 1:15-17	Luke 18:35-end
Monday	James 2:14-26	Luke 10:46-52
Tuesday	James 3:1-10	Mark 11:11-23
Wednesday	James 3:11-4:6	Mark 11:23-26
Thursday	James 4:7-17, 5:1-9	Mark 11:27-33
Friday	1 Peter 1:1-25, 2:1-10	Mark 12:1-12
Saturday	1 Thess. 5:14-23	Luke 17:3-10

Day	Epistle	Gospel
Thirty-Second Sunday of Pentecost	1 Tim. 4:9-15	Luke 19:1-10
Monday	1 Peter 2:21-25,3:1-9	Mark 12:13-17
Tuesday	1 Peter 3:10-22	Mark 18:13-27
Wednesday	1 Peter 4:1-11	Mark 12:28-37
Thursday	1 Peter 4-12-19,5:1-5	Mark 12:38-44
Friday	2 Peter 1:1-10	Mark 13:1-8
Saturday	2 Tim. 2:11-19	Luke 18:1-8

(Readings for 32nd Pentecost are for Week of Publican and Pharisee)

Day	Epistle	Gospel
Thirty Third Sunday of Pentecost	2 Tim. 3:10-15	Luke 18:9-14
Monday	2 Peter 1:20-21, 2:1-9	Mark 13:9-13
Tuesday	2 Peter 2:9-22	Mark 13:14-23
Wednesday	2 Peter 3:1-18	Mark 13:24-31
Thursday	1 John 1:8-10, 2:1-6	Mark 13:31-14:2
Friday	1 John 2:7-17	Mark 14:3-9
Saturday	2 Tim. 3:1-9	Luke 20:46-21:4

(Readings for 33rd Pentecost are for Week of Prodigal Son)

Day	Epistle	Gospel
Thirty-Fourth Sunday of Pentecost	1 Cor. 6:12-20	Luke 15:11-32
Monday	1 John 2:18-29, 3:1-8	Mark 11:1-11
Tuesday	1 John 3:9-22	Mark 14:10-42
Wednesday	1 John 3:31-4, 4:1-11	Mark 14:43-15:1
Thursday	1 John 4:20-21, 5:1-21	Mark 15:1-15
Friday	2 John 1:1-13	Mark 15:20, 22, 25, 33-41
Saturday	1 Cor. 10:23-26	Luke 21:8-9, 25-7, 33-6

(Readings for 34th Pentecost are for Meat Fare Week)

Day	Epistle	Gospel
Thirty- Fifth Sunday of Pentecost	1 Cor. 8:8-9:2	Matt. 25:31-46
Monday	3 John 1:1-15	Luke 19:29-40, 22:7-39
Tuesday	Jude 1:1-10	Luke 22:39-23:1
Wednesday	Joel 2:12-26	Joel 3:12-21
Thursday	Jude 1:11-25	Luke 23:2-34, 44-5
Friday	Zech. 8:7-14	Zech. 8:19-23
Saturday	Rom. 14:19-15:25-26	Matt. 6:1-13

(Readings for 35th Pentecost are for Cheese Fare Week)

Meanwhile ...

*We have new heavens and a new
earth to look forward to –*

*The dwelling place of holiness;
that is what He has promised.*

Beloved, since these expectations are yours

*Do everything to make sure that He
will find you innocent and undefiled,*

At Peace...

2nd Peter 3:13,14

Appendix 2

SYNAXARION – Commemorations of Saints for each day of the Ecclesiastical Year. Beginning with September 1st – "The Feast of the Indiction" – the first day of the Ecclesiastical Year.

Note: Although each day of the Ecclesiastical Calendar contains many commemorations only the major remembrances are listed here. Consult a Church Calendar for a complete listing.

SEPTEMBER

1.	Church New Year – Venerable Symeon Stylites
2.	Martyr Mamas
3.	Hieromartyr Anthimos of Nicomedia
4.	Hieromartyr Babylas, Prophet Moses
5.	Prophet Zacharias and Righteous Elizabeth
6.	Miracle of Archangel Michael at Colossae
7.	Martyr Sozon of Cilicia
8.	The Nativity of the Most Holy Theotokos
9.	Righteous Joachim and Anna, St Theodosios of Chernigov
10.	Martyrs Menodora, Metrodora and Nymphodora
11.	Venerable Theodora of Alexandria, Trans. of Relics of Ss. Sergius and Herman of Valaam
12.	Hieromartyr Autonomous of Italy
13.	Centurion Cornelius
14.	Exaltation of the Holy and Life-Giving Cross
15.	Great Martyr Nicetas the Goth
16.	Great Martyr Euphemia
17.	Martyrs Sophia and her three daughters
18.	St. Eumenes of Gortyna
19.	Martyrs Trophimus, Dorymedon, Savvatios and Susannah
20.	Great Martyr Eustathius and his family
21.	Apostle Quadratus of the Seventy
22.	Hieromartyr Phocus; Prophet Jonah
23.	Conception of St. John the Baptist, the Forerunner
24.	First Martyr Thecla. Equal to the Apostles
25.	St. Sergius of Radonezh, Venerable Euphrosyne of Alexandria
26.	Repose of St. John the Apostle and Evangelist
27.	Martyr Callistratus and his company of martyrs
28.	Confessor Chariton of Palestine
29.	Venerable Cyriacus the Hermit of Palestine
30.	Hieromartyr Gregory of Armenia

OCTOBER

1. Protection of the Theotokos
2. Martyrs Cyprian and Justine
3. Hieromartyr Dionysius the Aeropagite
4. Hieromartyr Hierotheus of Athens
5. Ss Peter (1326), Alexis (1378), Jonah (1461), Marcarius (1563), Philip (1569), Hermogenes (1612), Philaret (1867), Innocent (1879) and Tikhon (1925) Metropolitans of Moscow, Martyr Charitina
6. Apostle St. Thomas
7. Martyrs Sergius and Bacchus in Syria
8. Venerable Pelagia the Penitent
9. Apostle St. James son of Alphaeus
10. Martyrs Eulampius and Eulampia at Nicomedia, Synaxis of St. Ambrose and all the Saints of Optina
11. Apostle Philip of the Seventy, one of the seven deacons
12. Martyrs Probus and Tarachus
13. Hieromartyr Carpus, Papylus, Agathodorus, Agathonica, et al.
14. Martyr Nazarius, Gervase, Protase and Kelsos
15. Venerable Euthymius the New, Martyr Lucian of Antioch
16. Martyr Longinus the Centurion at the Cross
17. Prophet Hosea, Venerable Andrew of Crete
18. Apostle and Evangelist St Luke
19. Prophet Joel, St. John of Rila, Wonderworker St. John of Kronstadt
20. Great Martyr Artemius of Antioch
21. Venerable Hilarion the Great of Palestine
22. St. Abericius; Kazan Icon of the Theotokos
23. Apostle St. James – Brother of the Lord
24. Martyr Arethas
25. Martyr Marcian and Martyrius
26. Great Martyr Demetrius
27. Martyr Nestor
28. Martyr Terence and Neonilla
29. Venerable Martyr Anastasia
30. Hiermartyr Zenobius and sister Zenobia
31. Apostle Stachys and others of the Seventy

NOVEMBER

1. Unmercenaries Cosmas and Damian
2. Martyr Acindyrus and others of Persia
3. Martyr Acepcimus and Martyr Aeithalas
4. Venerable Joanicius the Great
5. Martyr Galacteo and Epistima
6. St. Paul the Confessor
7. Thirty Three Martyrs of Melitene

8.	Synaxis of Archangel Michael and All Angels
9.	Martyr Onesiphorus and Porphyrius
10.	Apostles Erastus, Olympas, and Herodian
11.	Martyr Menas of Egypt, St. Theodore of the Studion
12.	Venerable John the Merciful, St. Nilus of Sinai
13.	St. John Chrysostom
14.	Apostle St. Philip, St. Gregory Palamas
15.	Martyrs Gurias, Samonas and Habib, Repose of St. Herman of Alaska
16.	Apostle and Evangelist St. Matthew
17.	Wonderworker Gregory of Neo-Caesrea
18.	Martyrs Platon and Romanus
19.	Prophet Obediah
20.	Venerable Gregory of Decapolites, Proclus of Constantinople
21.	The Entrance of the Holy Theotokos into the Temple
22.	Apostle Philemon of the Seventy, St. Clement of Ochrid
23.	Gregory of Agrigentum, Repose of Alexander Nevsky
24.	Great Martyr Catherine of Alexandria
25.	Hieromartyr Clement of Rome
26.	Venerable Alypius the Stylite, Repose of St. Innocent of Irkutsk
27.	Great Martyr James the Persian
28.	Martyr Stephen the New
29.	Martyr Paramon and his 370 companions
30.	St. Andrew the Apostle, First-Called

DECEMBER

1.	Prophet Nahum
2.	Prophet Habakkuk
3.	Prophet Sophonias (Zephaniah)
4.	Great Martyr Barbara, Martyr Juliana
5.	Venerable Sabbas the Sanctified
6.	St. Nichoas of Myra, Wonderworker
7.	St. Ambrose of Milan
8.	Venerable Patapius of Thebes
9.	Conception of the Theotokos by St. Anne
10.	Martyr Menas
11.	Venerable Daniel the Stylite
12.	St. Herman of Alaska, Wonderworker and Wonderworker Spyridon
13.	Martyr Eustratius and others at Sebaste
14.	Martyrs Thrysus, Leucius and Callinicus
15.	Hieromartyr Eleutherius
16.	Prophet Haggai
17.	Prophet Daniel

18.	Martyr Sebastian and Companions
19.	Martyr Boniface
20.	St. Ignatius the God-bearer of Antioch, Repose of St. John of Kronstadt
21.	Virgin Martyr Juliana and companions
22.	Great Martyr Anastasia
23.	Holy Martyrs of Crete, St. Naum of Bulgaria
24.	Eve of the Nativity of Christ
25.	The Nativity of Our Lord and Savior Jesus Christ
26.	The Synaxis of the Theotokos
27.	Holy Protomartyr Stephen
28.	Twenty-thousand Martyrs of Nicomedia
29.	Holy Innocents slain by Herod
30.	Virgin Martyr Anysia at Thessalonica
31.	St. Melania of Rome

JANUARY

1.	Circumcision of Our Lord
2.	St. Seraphim of Sarov, St. Sylvester of Rome
3.	Prophet Malachi
4.	Synaxis of the Seventy Apostles
5.	Eve of the Theophany (Epiphany)
6.	The Theophany of Our Lord – His Manifestation to the world
7.	Synaxis of St. John the Baptist; The Forerunner
8.	St. George the Chozebite
9.	Martyr Polyeuctus
10.	St. Gregory of Nyssa
11.	St. Theodosius the Great
12.	Tatiane, Euthasia and Mertios the Martyrs
13.	Martyr Hermylos and St.ratonikos at Belgrade
14.	St. Nina Equal-to-the-Apostles, Enlightener of Georgia
15.	St. Paul of Thebes in Egypt
16.	Veneration of the Chains of St. Peter, Martyr Peusippos, Neonilla and Companions
17.	St. Anthony the Great
18.	Ss. Athanasius the Great and Cyril of Alexandria
19.	St. Marcarius the Great, St. Mark of Ephesus
20.	St. Euthymius the Great
21.	St. Maximus the Confessor
22.	Apostle, St. Timothy of the Seventy
23.	Hieromartyr Clement
24.	Venerable Xenia of Rome
25.	Gregory the Theologian, Auxentios the Neomartyr
26.	Venerable Xenophon

27.	Translation of the Relics of St. John Chrysostom, Marciana the Empress
28.	St. Ephraim the Syrian
29.	Translation of the Relics of St. Ignatius of Antioch
30.	Synaxis of the Three Hierarchs: Ss Basil the Great, Gregory the Theologian and St. John Chrysostom
31.	Ss. Cyril and John the Wonderworkers

FEBRUARY

1.	Martyr Tryphon of Syria
2.	The Meeting of Our Lord in the Temple
3.	Synaxis of Righteous Simeon and Anna, St. Nicholas of Japan
4.	St. Isidore of Pelusium
5.	Holy Martyr Agatha
6.	Ss. Photius and Bucolus
7.	St. Parthenius
8.	St. Theodore Stratelates, Prophet Zachariah
9.	Martyr Nicephorous of Antioch
10.	Martyr Haralampos
11.	Hieromartyr Blaise of Sebaste
12.	St. Melitus of Antioch
13.	Venerable Martinian of Palestine
14.	St. Cyril, Apostle to the Slavs
15.	Onesimus of the Seventy
16.	Martyr Pamphilia
17.	Great Martyr Theodore
18.	St. Leo the Great of Rome
19.	Archippus of the Seventy
20.	St. Leo of Catania
21.	St. Timothy of Symbola
22.	Finding of the Relics of the Martyrs at Gate of Eugenius
23.	Hieromartyr Polycarp of Smyrna
24.	Finding of the Head of the Forerunner, St. John the Baptist
25.	St. Tarasius of Constantinople
26.	St. Porphyrius
27.	St. Procopius
28.	St. Basil the Confessor
29.	St. John Cassian (Comm. on 2/28 in Non-Leap Years)

MARCH

1.	St. Eudoxia
2.	St. Theodotus of Cyrenia
3.	St. Eutropius of Amasea
4.	St. Gerasimus
5.	Martyr Conon of Isauria

6.	Forty-two Martyrs of Sebaste
7.	Hieromartyr Basil and companions at Cherson (4th century)
8.	St. Theophylactus
9.	Forty Martyrs of Sebaste (4th century)
10.	Martyr Quadratus
11.	St. Sophronius of Jerusalem
12.	St. Theophanes the Confessor
13.	Translation of the Relics of St. Nicephorus
14.	Venerable St. Benedict of Nursia, Abbot – Founder of Western Monasticism
15.	Martyr Agapius
16.	Martyr Sabinas of Egypt
17.	St. Alexis, St. Patrick, Apostle of Ireland
18.	St. Cyril of Jerusalem
19.	Martyrs Chrysanthus and Daria
20.	Holy Fathers slain at Sabbas
21.	St. James the Confessor
22.	Hieromartyr Basil of Ancyra
23.	Martyr Nicon, Martyrs of Illyria
24.	St. Zacharius the Recluse
25.	Annunciation of the Theotokos
26.	Synaxis of the Archangel Gabriel
27.	Martyr Matrona of Salonica
28.	Venerable Hilarion the New
29.	Martyr Mark, Bishop of Arethusa
30.	St. John Climacus of Sinai
31.	St. Hypatius the Wonderworker

APRIL

1.	St. Mary of Egypt
2.	St. Titus the Wonderworker
3.	St. Nicetas the Confessor
4.	Venerable Joseph the Hymnodist
5.	Martyr Agathopodes
6.	St. Eutychius of Constantinople
7.	Venerable George of Mytilene
8.	Holy Apostles of the Seventy
9.	Martyr Eupsychius
10.	Martyr Terence
11.	Hieromartyr Antipas
12.	Venerable Basil the Confessor
13.	Hieromartyr Artemon
14.	St. Martin the Confessor
15.	Apostles Aristarchus, Pudens and Trophimus
16.	Martyrs Agape, Irene and Chionia

17.	Hieromartyr Simeon of Persia
18.	Venerable John of Decapolis
19.	Venerable John of the Old Caves
20.	Venerable Theodore the Hermit
21.	Hieromartyr Januarius
22.	St. Theodore the Sykeote
23.	Great Martyr St. George
24.	Martyr Sabbas Stratelates
25.	Apostle and Evangelist, St. Mark
26.	Hieromartyr Basil of Amasea
27.	Hieromartyr Simeon
28.	Apostles of the Seventy, Jason and Sosipater
29.	Nine Martyrs at Cyzicus, St. Nectarius of Optina
30.	Apostle, St. James

MAY

1.	Prophet Jeremiah
2.	St. Athanasius the Great
3.	St. Theodosius of the Kiev Caves
4.	Virgin Martyr Pelagia of Tarsus
5.	Great Martyr Irene of Thessalonica
6.	Righteous Job the Long Suffering
7.	Sign of the Precious Cross over Jerusalem
8.	Apostle and Evangelist St. John the Theologian
9.	Translation of the Relics of St. Nicholas of Myra; Prophet Isaiah
10.	Simon Zelotes, Venerable Laurence of Egypt
11.	Ss. Cyril and Methodius, Enlighteners of the Slavs
12.	St. Epiphanius of Cyprus
13.	Virgin Martyr Glyceria
14.	Martyr Isidore of Chios
15.	Venerable Pachomius the Great
16.	Venerable Theodore the Sanctified
17.	Apostle Andronicus and Julia of the Seventy
18.	Martyr Theodotus of Ancyra
19.	Hieromartyr Patrick of Prusa
20.	Martyr Thalelaeus of Cilicia
21.	Ss. Constantine and Helen
22.	Martyr Basiliscus
23.	Venerable Michael the Confessor
24.	Venerable Symeon the St.ylites
25.	3rd Finding of the Head of St. John the Baptist
26.	Apostle Carpus of the Seventy
27.	Hieromartyr Therapon
28.	Venerable Nicetas
29.	Virgin-Martyr Theodosia of Tyre

30.	Venerable Isaac of Constantinople
31.	Apostle Hermes

JUNE

1.	Martyr Justin the Philosopher
2.	St. Nicephorous the Confessor
3.	Martyr Lucillian
4.	St. Metrophanes, Ss. Mary and Martha, sisters of Lazarus
5.	Hieromartyr Dorotheus
6.	Wonderworker Bessarion of Egypt
7.	Hieromartyr Theodotus of Ancyra
8.	Translation of the Relics of Theodore St.ratelates
9.	St. Cyril of Alexandria
10.	Martyr Timothy, Martyr Alexander
11.	Apostles Ss. Barnabus and Bartholomew
12.	Venerable Onuphrius the Great
13.	Martyr Aquilina
14.	Prophet Elisha
15.	Prophet Amos
16.	St. Tikhon of Amathus
17.	Martyrs Manuel, Sabel, and Ismael
18.	Martyr Leontius
19.	Apostle, St. Jude
20.	Hieromartyr Methodius
21.	Martyr Julian of Tarsus
22.	Hieromartyr Eusebius
23.	Martyr Agrippina of Rome
24.	Nativity of St. John the Baptist
25.	Virgin Martyr Febronia
26.	Venerable David of Salonica
27.	Venerable Sampson the Hospitable
28.	Translation of the Relics of Cyrus and John
29.	Ss. Peter and Paul
30.	Synaxis of the Twelve Apostles

JULY

1.	Unmercenaries Cosmas and Damian
2.	Placing of the Robe of the Theotokos at Blachnerae
3.	Martyr Hyacinth
4.	Venerable Andrew of Crete
5.	Venerable Athanasius of Mt Athos
6.	Venerable Sisoes the Great
7.	Venerable Thomas of Maleon
8.	Great Martyr Procopius of Caesarea
9.	Hieromartyr Pancratius

10.	Venerable Anthony of the Kiev Caves
11.	Blessed Olga, Equal to the Apostles, Great Martyr Euphemia
12.	Martyrs Procius and Hilary
13.	Synaxis of the Archangel Gabriel
14.	Apostle Aquila of the Seventy, Joseph the Confessor
15.	Martyr Kyrikos, St. Vladimir
16.	Hieromartyr Athenogenes
17.	Martyr Marina
18.	Martry Emilian
19.	St. Macrina Sister of St. Basil the Great
20.	Holy Prophet Elias
21.	Venerable Symeon and John
22.	St. Mary Magdalene
23.	Prophet Ezekiel
24.	Great Martyr Christina of Tyre
25.	Dormition of St. Anne
26.	Hieromartyr Hermolaus
27.	Great Martyr and Healer Panteleimon
28.	Prochororus, Nikanor, Timon, and Parmenas – Deacons and Apostles of the Seventy
29.	Martyr Callinicius
30.	Apostle Silas and Silvanus of the Seventy
31.	Righteous Eudocimus, Righteous Joseph of Arimathea

AUGUST

1.	Procession of the Holy and Life-Giving Cross
2.	Translation of the Relics of St. Stephen, Protomartyr
3.	Venerable Isaac and Dalmatius
4.	The Seven Holy Youths of Ephesus
5.	Martyr Eusignius of Antioch
6.	Transfiguration of Our Lord
7.	Venerable Martyr Dometius of Persia
8.	St. Emilian the Confessor
9.	Apostle, St. Matthias
10.	Great Martyr Laurence
11.	Martyr Eupius of Catania
12.	Martyr Photius of Nicomedia
13.	Venerable Maximus the Confessor
14.	Prophet Micah
15.	Dormition of the Theotokos
16.	Translation of the Image of Our Lord
17.	Martyr Myron
18.	Martyrs Florus and Laurus
19.	Martyr Andrew Stratelates
20.	Prophet Samuel

JESUS, Name above all names. His Name is higher than any other. His name is Wonderful. His Name is Counselor. His Name is Prince of Peace, Redeemer, Son of God become flesh. He suffered and died for us. He rose for us and is living today. He loves us. He patiently waits for us to receive Him. He tells us He stands at the door of our heart and knocks. He sends His spirit to us. He gives us the power to become the Children of God when we receive Him. He gives us the free gift of salvation. He plants within us the seed of faith when we receive Him as Our Lord. He plants within us the seeds of love, joy and peace, patience, kindness, goodness, faithfulness, gentleness, and self-control. He makes these seeds grow. He transforms us when we take Him out of our intellect and receive Him into our heart. He is the Good Shepherd, Love and the Root of Jesse. He is the Great Creator, the Way the Truth and the Life. He is the Way to the Father's presence. He is our Brother, the Lamb of God, Emmanuel (God with us). He is the Man of Sorrows the Prophet, Our Spiritual King, the Vine, the Dayspring, All-Mighty, God, Savior of the World. He is Healer, the One Who Baptizes in the Spirit, Teacher, Messiah, Servant, King of Kings and Lord of Lords. Author and Finisher of Our Faith. Rock of Ages, Light of Life. The Alpha, the Omega, the Beginning and the End.

Lay Ministry in the Church

"God created us in His image and likeness, and every Christian is obligated to be sanctified by good works."

St. John Chrysostom

Lay ministry is that work which every member of the parish holds in common with the universal Church and her mission of worship, teaching, and service to all mankind.

Each of us is called to ministry, men and women, young and old. However, this ministry can seem bewildering , unattainable or challenging to the extreme.

From the earliest days of the Church the faithful have cooperated in the work given to them by Our Lord, so much so, that St. John Chrysostom, in the fifth century, spoke the words, "Every Christian is obligated to be sanctified by good works."

Good Works: A Ministry of Love

"Nothing is more frigid than a Christian who does not care or for the salvation of others. You cannot plead poverty here , for she that cast in her two mites will be your accuser (Luke 21:1). And Peter said," Silver and gold I have not" (Acts 3:6). And Paul was so poor that he was often hungry and lacked the necessary food. You cannot plead lowness of birth, for they too were ignoble man, and of ignoble parents. You cannot allege want of education, for they too were unlearned men (Acts 4:13). Even if you are a slave, therefore, and a runaway slave, you can still do your part, for such was Onesimus – you cannot plead infirmity for such was Timothy who often had infirmities. Everyone can profit his neighbor, if he will fulfill his part."

by St. John Chrysostom

"As a wrestler constantly engages in bodily exercises, so also the pious struggler ought to exercise himself in every good work."

St. Ephraim the Syrian

Some Suggestions for Lay Ministry in Parishes:

SERVING THE SICK, AGED AND INFIRM

Send notes on special days such as birthdays, anniversaries, or holidays. Names and addresses may be obtained from the rectory, or a parish list could be developed if one does not exist.

Establish special ministerial teams to regularly visit those who are ill, shut-in, or elderly. One or two parishioners visiting on a regular basis is the best witness a parish could offer.

Form a parish reassurance-caller group. A regular phone call is an excellent way to let people who live alone know that they are cared for and that help is there when needed.

A "one-to-one visitors team" could help with simple household chores or daily routine when the elderly or sick are unable to do these things themselves.

Develop a hospital visitors group. Two people could be assigned to each hospital in a specific area. When a parish member is admitted a card or small gift, along with a visit, if possible, could be made in the name of the members of the parish. This will help the priest immensely in his hospital ministry. This may also be done in conjunction with local nursing homes.

Sponsor a social gathering in the parish for senior citizens. Provide refreshments, entertainment, and most importantly, transportation to and from the function.

Establish a mechanism for transportation of those unable to drive to Church services.

Encourage an "Adopt a Grandparent" program among the youth of your parish.

Invite those alone, or in need, to your home for an afternoon or evening of fellowship.

SERVING THE YOUTH AND YOUNG ADULTS OF A PARISH

Let youth and young adults of a parish know that they are needed and vital to the life of the local Church.

Maintain a registry and keep contact with all high school graduates away from home through regular mailings of bulletins.

Plan get-togethers during school breaks, summertime, and holidays. Let youth request certain activities – since a visit "home" should always include time spent in the parish family.

Encourage young adults to be active members of the Church by offering them a voice in parish affairs.

Sponsor relevant activities that address issues important in their lives – contrast our Faith with others, discuss fighting materialism and consumerism in our lives, combating evil in society, terrorism, moral issues, etc.

Offer a welcome when friends visit with young adult parishioners. Be specific about Church teachings, tolerant of variant views and non-judgmental.

Plan regular retreats and youth days with scheduled speakers from outside the parish, entertainment and prayer.

Specify that at least one young member of the parish serve on the parish committee to represent the views and concerns of young people/young adults.

SERVING THE PARISH FAMILY

Work on developing a warm first impression to visitors. Establish a hospitality committee to maintain the guest registry, follow-up on visitations, and invite first timers to come again. Send bulletins to guests and visitors from time to time.

Develop a parish media center with books, tapes, etc. oriented to a variety of ages and interests.

Support, or operate, a food pantry to provide non-perishable items to those in need.

Establish an adult education program, especially during the major feasts of the Church Year.

Plan annual retreats to discuss the future of the parish and visions for the coming years.

Seek the "lost sheep" of the parish who have left the local Church for one reason or another. Do this via parish publications and visitations.

Provide a publication rack with brochures and pamphlets on various topics. Avoid full-length books – unless it is a parish lending library – since they are seldom, if ever, borrowed.

Establish a missionary committee to develop ways to reach out to others in the neighborhood or community.

Avoid publicity for self-aggrandizement. Neither the pastor, nor the same individuals, should be seen in publications over and over. This creates internal resentments and leads to a "pharisaism" in the parish family

SERVING THE COMMUNITY

Establish educational programs for parish visitation groups.

Open the parish facilities for special community events.

Sponsor a visitation committee to prisons and detention facilities. Bring simple reading materials, for example Bibles, pamphlets, small brochures about the Church/Christianity, and keep contact once a visitation is made.

Visit, care for, and welcome those who are disabled-or unable to get to worship services.

Purchase books about the Church and donate them to local libraries.

Invite a local home for the physically or mentally-handicapped to share liturgy and fellowship at your parish on a Sunday morning.

Aware that many of these programs are already in place in parish communities, it is useful to remind ourselves of the many, and varied opportunities for serving others – while not drawing attention to our good works.

To do any of these things simply to gain publicity, or to show the community how "active" your parish may be – is wrong!

Compiled (with help) from the booklet "Lay Ministry" published by The Ukrainian Orthodox League, Chicago IL

"The bodies of our fellow human beings must be treated with more care than our own. At the Last Judgment, I shall not be asked if I was successful in my ascetic exercises, or how many prostrations I made in the course of my prayers. I shall be asked, 'Did I feed the hungry, clothe the naked, visit the sick and prisoners?' That is what I shall be asked."
Mother Maria of Paris 1977

A GLOSSARY

- A -

Abba – means "father", it was an endearing term used by Christ in referring to His Father in heaven.

Abbot – the head of a monastery. His office includes maintaining the authentic spiritual life of the monastery, instructing in the traditions of the Church, and property management. His rank is usually an archimandrite or hegumen.

Absolution – the formal declaration of God's forgiveness of sins confessed in the Mystery of Penance.

Acacian Schism – occurred between 482-519 AD. It was a temporary break of relations between Rome and the Eastern Church.

"Acts of the Apostles" – the fifth book of the New Testament which recounts the growth of the early Church. Authorship is generally attributed to St. Luke.

"Acts of the Martyrs"– earliest account of Christian martyrs, some of which is based on eyewitness testimony. The book has various levels of reliability.

Addai – in tradition he was a founder of the Church at Edessa, a center of Syriac-speaking Christianity.

Adoptionism – an early heresy of the 8th century that claimed Christ was only the "adopted Son of God".

Aer – in Slavonic "Vozdukh" – the largest of the veils used in the Divine Liturgy.

Agape – The Greek term for love which was used by the writers of the New Testament. It means the love of God for mankind and the love of Christians for one another. Agape also refers to the common religious feast that was celebrated in the early Church. Agape has connections with the Holy Eucharist.

"Agios O Theos" – Greek term for "Holy God ", an early hymn of the Church.

Agnets – the Slavonic word for "Lamb" which is taken from the prosphoron and consecrated into the Body of Christ at the Divine Liturgy.

Agnosticism – belief that a knowledge of God as Divine Being is impossible, since only material things can be the subject of knowledge.

Akathist – a Greek word for "not sitting". It is a liturgical hymn to the Theotokos prayed while standing.

Alb – the white linen or silk garment worn under the priestly vestments. In the Eastern Church it is called a sticharion.

Albania, Church in – Christianity reached Albania in the early days of the Faith. When the Turks conquered Albania in 1521 there was much falling away from Orthodox Christianity.

Alban and Sergius, Ss – a fellowship founded in 1928 to encourage good relations between Orthodox and Anglicans.

Alexandria – a center of Christianity in Egypt. The Church here was believed to be founded by Saint Mark. Others, such as St. Clement, St. Athanasius, St. Cyril and Origen were important personages connected with the Church in Alexandria.

Allelujah – Hebrew for "Praise Yahweh".

All Saints Day – first Sunday after Pentecost that celebrates all the saints of the Church both those proclaimed and those unknown.

Alpha and Omega – the first and last letters of the Greek alphabet used to show that God is the first of all things and is also infinite, with no end.

Altar – usually referred to in Orthodoxy as the "Holy Table". It was used for the celebration of the Eucharist from the first days of the Church.

Altar cloths – used on the Holy Table:
1 – *Katasaskion* – (Gk.) and Sratchitsa (Sl.) – the white cloth covering the entire Holy Table. It represents the winding sheet used to wrap our Lord for burial.

2 – *Inditia* (Sl.) – a richly embroidered cloth representing Christ's "Robe of Glory". It is placed over the Katasakion.

3 – *Iliton* (Sl.) – the cloth in which the Antimens is wrapped.

Ambo – a raised platform from which the Holy Scriptures are read, and where some parts of the liturgy were once celebrated. In the 14th century ambos were replaced by a raised pulpit.

Amen – a Hebrew word which means "So be it" or "Verily". It is an expression of assent.

Anabaptists – those who refuse to have children baptized and who believe strongly in the "Priesthood and Baptism of All Believers". The major Anabaptist groups are: Zwickau Prophets, the Swiss Brethren, Hutterites, Melchorites and the Mennonites.

Analogian – Analoy (Sl.) – a high desk-like piece of furniture usually with the sloping top on which icons or the Gospel Book are placed.

Anamnesis – the commemoration of the passion, death, resurrection and ascension of Christ in the Divine Liturgy.

Anaphora – the central prayer of the Divine Liturgy containing the Consecration, the Anamnesis, and the Communion.

Anastasis – Greek term for the Resurrection of Christ and of mankind in general, i.e. the resurrection of the dead to eternal life.

Anastasius, St – c. 700 A.D. Abbot of the Greek monastery of St. Catherine on Mount Sinai. He wrote and taught against heresy of Monophysitism, or that Christ had only a Divine nature.

Anathema – a word that means "accursed or cut off". It is used in Holy Scripture by St. Paul. It was a way to insulate heretics from teaching within the Church. The term can also mean what one offers to God in fulfillment of a vow.

Anchorite – a monastic who withdraws from the world in order to live of life of solitude in prayer, silence and fasting.

Andrew, St – an apostle of Christ. He was the brother of St. Peter and later evangelized the areas around present-day Russia.

Andrew of Crete, St – a seventh-century theologian. He wrote many hymns and canons, several of which are still in use.

Angel – a host of heavenly beings who act as intermediaries between God and mankind. They form the heavenly court that continually praises Almighty God.

Anne, St – mother of the Theotokos. Her name is not found in Holy Scripture, although she has been popular in religious traditions since the first days of the Church.

Anointing – an act which separates the holy from the mundane. Through the act of anointing a person, or thing, is set apart by an infusion of Divine grace.

Anthropomorphism – giving human characteristics to God.

Anti–Christ – usually identified with those who deny the incarnation of Christ. Anti-Christ is named the prince of Christ's enemies.

Antidoron – the pieces from the prosphora (the Eucharistic bread) – distributed to the faithful at the conclusion of the Divine Liturgy.

Antimens (Antimension) – a silk or linen cloth on which the deposition of Christ is portrayed. It contains a relic that must be used to celebrate the Divine Liturgy. It was originally utilized when there was no consecrated altar available.

Antioch – sometimes called the "third city of the Roman Empire". It was in Antioch that believers in Christ were first called Christians, (Acts 11:26). Antioch was the third Patriarchal See in Christendom, after Rome and Alexandria. Later Constantinople would replace Antioch in importance.

Antiochian Theology – a belief system that underscored the oneness of Almighty God. It lost importance after the early heresies that questioned the humanity/Divinity of Christ.

Antiphon – a way of chanting where the words are sung first by one choir and then responded to by another. Various hymns of the Church are sung in this manner.

Anthony of Egypt, St – a desert hermit. He is considered the father of monasticism because he gathered disciples to live a common life of solitude and penance.

Apocrypha – certain books of the Bible such as: 1 Esdras, Tobit, Judith, 1, 2 and 3 Maccabees, The Wisdom of Solomon, Ecclesiasticus (Sirach), Baruch, The Letter of Jerimias. (4 Maccabees is sometimes added to this list.) They are thought to be on a lower footing than the rest of Holy Scripture, and may not be used to define doctrine. Also called the Deutero-Canonical Books.

Apodeipnon – the liturgical service held late in the evening which corresponds to Western Compline.

Apologetics – defending the truth of Christianity using logical or scientific thought in concert with the demands of human reason.

Apolysis – the blessing given at the end of liturgical rites in the Eastern Church.

Apolytikion – this is the major Troparion (verse) of the day, usually dedicated to a saint, or the feast being celebrated.

Apostasy – the total abandonment of the Christian Faith.

Aposticha – liturgical chants that complete the verses of the psalms.

Apostles – the "Twelve" who followed Christ. They are Ss. Peter, Andrew, James, John, Philip, Bartholomew, Thomas, Matthew, James the Less, Thaddaeus , Simon the Zealot and Judas Iscariot. After the suicide of Judas, Matthias took his place among "The Twelve". The term "apostle" is sometimes given to the Epistle read at the Divine Liturgy.

"Apostle's Creed" – a Western statement of faith referred to by Saint Ambrose in the fourth century. It is not used in the Eastern Church except in the Western Rite.

"Apostolic Church Order" – an early document that noted Church order and practice. It was composed in Egypt in the early fourth century.

"Apostolic Constitutions" – a compilation of Church laws that was composed in the late fourth century, probably in Syria.

Archangel – in Holy Scripture , Michael and Gabriel are mentioned as having specific roles in Salvation History.

Archimandrite – a monastic who is the head of a monastery or group of monastic houses. This term can also be used as a title of distinction for a monk.

Archpriest – is a title of honor given to clergy who have specific functions in the diocese, or for a long and distinguished life as a priest.

Arianism – sometimes referred to as the major heresy in the early Church that denied the Divinity of Christ. It taught that Christ was not co-eternal with the Father but created by Him as an instrument for the salvation of the world. This heresy was condemned at Nicaea in 325 A. D.

Armenia, Christianity in – Armenians were brought to Christianity by St. Gregory the Illuminator in the third century. Armenians are Monophysites in that they believe there is a single Divine nature in Christ rather than espousing the Orthodox teaching of a dual nature, fully Divine and fully human.

Artophorion – the place where the consecrated Eucharist is kept for emergencies, or later use. It is equivalent to the Tabernacle used in the Western Church.

Artos – a loaf of specially-made bread with a representation of Christ's resurrection imprinted on top. This represents Our Lord as the "Bread of Eternal Life". Prayers are recited over the Artos on St. Thomas Sunday after Pascha, and it is distributed to the faithful.

Ascension of Christ – the occasion of Christ's return to His Father in heaven. It is related in Luke 24:50 –52 and Acts 1:9-11. The Ascension was witnessed by the apostles as the post-resurrection appearances of Christ came to an end. The Ascension marks Christ's enthronement in glory next to His Father.

Ascetical Theology – Christian teaching which is more practical than Mystical Theology. The Ascetical Way teaches a practical approach to holiness and sees Christian perfection as possible through human means, aided by Divine grace.

Aspasmos – ("Tselovaniye" Sl.) – meaning "salutation". In giving honor to an object or person with a kiss, i.e reverencing an icon, Gospel Book, or the hand of a clergyman.

Aspersion – one of three ways of Baptism used in the Christian tradition. Aspersion consists of sprinkling rather than immersion, or pouring. Immersion is the ordinary method of Baptism in the Orthodox Church.

Assumption or "Dormition of The Mother of God" – the belief that Mary, the Mother of God, was raised into heaven-body and soul. The belief was dogmatized by the Roman church in 1950 but the Eastern Church views the teaching in a more general manner – less precise than the Roman Church. It is not considered an essential belief for salvation, as in the Roman Church.

Assyrian Christians – a group of believers who follow Nestorian teachings, i.e. there are two separate persons in the incarnate Christ, which is contrary to Orthodox teaching that in Christ, there is one person, who is at once both God and man.

Asterisk – ("Zvezditsa" Sl.) – is the star which is made of two metal pieces, bent to form a cover, placed on the diskos.

Athanasius St – late third and early 4th century Bishop of Alexandria in Egypt. He was a staunch opponent of Arianism. Athanasius was exiled from his position at Alexandria on several occasions by powerful Arian enemies. St. Athanasius wrote the book "De Incarnatione" which spoke of God restoring mankind to His Divine image.

Atheism – refusal to believe in the existence of God.

Athos, Mount – the center of Orthodox monasticism. Located at the tip of a peninsula in Greece, the first monastery was established in 961 A.D. by St. Athanasius the Athonite. Today there are 20 independent monasteries on Mt. Athos.

Aureole – in iconography, the background of gold that surrounds the figure. An aureole is distinguished from the nimbus – a halo-like background around the head.

Autocephalous – national Churches in Orthodoxy that are governed by local synods.

Autonomous – self-ruled Church which is still in communion with the Mother Church.

Axios – the exclamation made by the faithful and clergy at the ordination of a priest, or consecration of a bishop. It is repeated three times. Axios means "He is worthy."

- B -

Baptism – the Mystery (Sacrament) that unites us to Christ. It is a rite of passage, an entrance into the Kingdom of God and eternal life. Through Baptism we become members of Christ's Church.

Christ gave the command to his disciples to baptize in His name. (Matt. 28:19) Baptism was practiced from the first days of the Faith. It was administered by total immersion and was closely bound with the Mysteries of Chrismation and the Eucharist.

Baptism was usually administered at either Pascha, or Pentecost, but was later done at other times during the year. Up to the fifth century, Baptism was postponed until death seemed imminent – because of the difficulties and serious responsibilities attached to it. Later, with the Baptism of infants and the general acceptance of the penitential system, the practice of delaying the Mystery was gradually abandoned.

Baptism in the Holy Spirit – an experience of the Holy Spirit which is thought to set one apart for special service. It is a spiritual type of Baptism, as opposed to "Water Baptism", and is very popular among Pentecostal believers. Many serious scholars question the teaching and its Scriptural basis.

Barbara, St – was the daughter of a pagan official in Nicomedia. Upon her conversion to Christianity, St. Barbara's father denounced her to the authorities. She was martyred for her Orthodox Faith and her intercession is now sought as protectress against fires and lightning. St. Barbara is the patron saint of miners and firefighters.

Barnabas, St – an early Christian disciple at Jerusalem. He was responsible for introducing St. Paul to the apostles and accompanied him on his first missionary journey. Later, in a dispute, he departed from Paul and went into Cyprus. St. Barnabas is considered the founder of the Cypriot church.

Bartholomew, St – one of "The Twelve", he is sometimes called Nathaniel. Bartholomew was a missionary in India. He suffered martyrdom by being flayed alive, in Armenia. (John 1:43-51).

Basil, St – a.k.a "The Great" – is one of the "Cappadocian Fathers". His brother was St. Gregory of Nyssa. Basil became a hermit in 358 A.D. but was called to be bishop at Caesarea to defend the Church against the heresy of Arianism. He had a profound influence on Eastern monasticism because of his great skills at organization.

Basil, Liturgy of St – used in the Orthodox Church on ten occasions during the ecclesiastical year. The liturgy's original form was probably influenced by St. Basil, however it has been greatly modified through the centuries. The present form is similar in structure with the Divine Liturgy of St. John Chrysostom although some prayers are much longer.

Basilica – an early form of church edifice modeled after the Roman style of building with the same name.

Beatitudes – Christ's promises and blessings given in the Sermon on the Mount, (Mt. 5:3-11) and the Sermon on the Plain (Luke 6:20-26). They are a discourse on human perfection.

Bede, St – called "The Father of English Church History". He was also a Biblical scholar whose historical commentaries are greatly valued by his successors and contemporaries.

Beelzebub – a name for Satan, the Prince of Devils, found in Holy Scripture, (Mark 3:22-26).

Benedict, St – a monk at Nursia, Italy who in the fifth century withdrew from the world to live as a hermit. A group of monks gathered around him and he eventually established 12 monasteries. He left for Monte Cassino around 525 A.D. and composed the famous "Rule of St Benedict".

Berakah – the Jewish prayer of blessing and thanksgiving to God. Parts of the Christian Eucharist are thought to have been based on the Berakah.

Betrothal – a promise of marriage to come. In many countries the Betrothal is the first step in the marriage ceremony, and must be proclaimed in front of witnesses.

Bishop – the highest order of ministry in the church. The bishop is the overseer of the congregation and clergy in a geographical region. Often the terms "bishop and elder" are used interchangeably in Holy Scripture, with the bishop being the recognized leader of the elders, (Acts 20:17, 28).

Blasphemy – any words, thoughts, or actions which show contempt for God. This contempt may be against God, the Church or the saints.

Blessing – the pronouncement of God's favor upon people, places or things. Blessings are used throughout the Church's liturgy.

Bowing – from the first days, Christians have bowed at the name of Christ, or in the presence of sacred things, (Philippians 2:10).

Bread – the Orthodox Church uses leavened bread for the Divine Liturgy unlike the Western Church which employs an unleavened kind. Bread which has risen – (i.e. leavened) is used by the Orthodox Church to commemorate the resurrection of Christ from the dead.

Bulgaria, Christianity in – the Christian Faith was introduced into Bulgaria in 864-5 A.D. In 870 Prince Boris decided in favor of establishing the Eastern Church, (with its traditions and liturgies) in his realm.

Byzantine Text, of the New Testament – the form of the Greek New Testament which has become the official text in the Greek-speaking church. It is known as the Lucianic Text.

- C -

Cabasilas, Nicholas – a 14th century writer. He wrote on union with Christ through the Holy Mysteries (Sacraments) and an interpretation of the Divine Liturgy.

Caesaropapalism – the system in which the secular ruler, as monarch, has complete control over the Church.

Candles – used from the earliest days of the Church. One interpretation for their use is that as the wax becomes soft and pliable by warming, so our heart should become sympathetic and compassionate through participation in the Divine Liturgy.

Canon – in the Orthodox Church a Canon (or stanza), is inserted between the verses of Scriptural Canticles sung at Matins.

Canon Law – there is no such thing as "Canon Law" in the Orthodox Church comparable to that of the Western Churches, i.e. Roman Catholic Canon Law. The Western form of Canon Law is highly legalistic. Orthodox Canons are recommendations for spiritual growth and life in the Holy Spirit. They are milestones over the course of one's life by which we measure our spiritual direction and life in Christ.

Canon of Scripture – the term "Canon" refers to the listing of books which were officially received by the Church as inspired by God. St. Athanasius compiled the official Canon in 367 A.D. that corresponds with our listing today.

Cantor – (Lector), a person who has been blessed for service as a singer of the Divine services. A Cantor may also chant the Epistle.

Capital Punishment – officially sanctioned death, inflicted for a major crime, which as such, is the judicial sentence of the State. St. Paul seems to recognize its practice in Romans 13:1-5.

Cassock – is the Western term for the Orthodox ryassa, the robe worn by priests, bishops, monastics, etc. It is usually black, has wide sleeves and is worn over another robe with narrow sleeves called a podryasnik, a Russian term.

Catacombs – underground burial places of early Christians where the Eucharist was celebrated on the anniversaries of martyr's deaths.

Catechism – is an instructional book of the Faith in the form of questions and answers.

Catechumens – those who are undergoing training and instruction in preparation for Baptism and reception into the Church. In the early days of the Faith, catechumens were received at the Paschal Vigil Liturgy.

Cathedra – the chair of the bishop which is placed in his official church, known as the cathedral.

Cathedral – the church which contains the cathedra, or chair, of the bishop. It is usually a large ornate building in which major ceremonies of the ecclesiastical year are held.

Catholic – is a Greek word which means universal or "general". It is used to describe Christians who are in historical and continuous tradition of faith and practice with the early Church.

Catholic Epistles – used to denote the Epistles of James, 1 and 2 Peter, 1 John and Jude. It is also customary to include 2 and 3 John in this listing. They are called "General" because they are directed to the universal Church and not to specific individuals.

Celibacy of the Clergy – in the Orthodox Church the position has always been that priests and deacons may marry before their ordination to the priesthood, but not after. Bishops and monastics must be celibate. Celibacy of the clergy was first demanded in the Western Church by a local Council in the fourth century, yet it was not enforced in the West until after about 1200 A.D. However, it was only after 1563 that the Roman Church's Council of Trent ruled definitively on the matter, and then the discipline extended only to the Church of Rome and its clergy.

Cell – the private room of a monastic. It contains the barest of necessities. The word can also be used to denote a monastic house dependent upon its mother house, although this term is seldom used today.

Celtic Church – the Church that existed in the British Isles before the arrival of St. Augustine in 597 A.D.

Cemetery – a place which is consecrated solely for the burial of the faithful. It comes from the Greek word which means "a place for sleeping".

Censer – in Slavonic called the "kadillo". It is a vessel with a cover, hung on chains, and used for burning incense during liturgical services.

Censure – a penalty imposed by the Church for the correction of an offense.

Chalice – (Gk "poterion") – the cup used to hold the wine that is consecrated into the Blood of Christ at the Divine Liturgy.

Chalice Veils – in Slavonic they are called "Vozduh Aer". The veils are square pieces of material, the same color as the priest's vestments, used to cover the sacred vessels on the Prothesis Table. The largest veil, the Aer, covers the vessels after they are transferred to the Holy Table at the Great Entrance.

Chants – (Sl. "Glas") – are the eight chants or Tones, for the singing of the Troparions, the versicles at Vespers and the Canon at Matins. The chants (or Tones) change every week, following in progressive order, keeping various cycles throughout the year.

Chapel – sacred building used for religious services which is usually smaller than parish churches. A chapel can also be a small room within a larger church building dedicated to a particular saint or feast.

Chasuble (phelonion) – the Western term for the outer garment, usually with elaborate decoration, worn by bishops and priests for the celebration of the Divine Liturgy. It derived from the outer cloak worn during the days of the early Church. In the Eastern Church this large bell-shaped garment is worn over the sticharion and epitrachelion and is called the "phelonion".

Cherubicon – a.k.a. "The Cherubic Hymn", sung during the Great Entrance of the Divine Liturgy.

Cherubim – the second of the nine orders of angels.

Chirotonia – Greek for "laying on of hands"– is the handing down of Apostolic Succession (ordination from the apostles) conferred on a bishop, or priest.

Chrisom – in Slavonic "Krizhma" – which is the white cloth placed upon the newly- baptized person as a sign of innocence and purity of faith.

Chrism – a mixture of olive oil and other spices, such as balsam which is used in the ritual of the Church.

Chrism is consecrated only by a patriarch or Synod of Bishops. It symbolizes the gift and action of the Holy Spirit. Chrism is used in the Mysteries of Baptism, Chrismation, and Holy Orders. The many oils used in its preparation signify the "Gifts of the Holy Spirit".

Chrismation – the practice of anointing a person immediately following Baptism. The "newly enlightened", or baptized person, receives the manifold "Gifts of the Spirit" in Chrismation which were promised by Jesus Christ, (Acts 2:38).

Christ – literally "the Anointed One". The term is the Greek translation of "Messiah" which is a Hebrew word. It was used by the early believers as a proper name for the Risen Lord.

Christian – the name was first used by the followers of Jesus Christ according to Acts 11:26. It was applied to the early believers at Antioch. It was later used by the Church to distinguish itself from other religious systems.

Chrysostom, St John – known as "The Golden Mouthed". His many works show a great talent for seeing both the literal and practical sides to Holy Scripture and the Tradition of the Church. He was made Patriarch of Constantinople in 398 A.D. His plain, bold and reasonable preaching gained him many enemies. He was exiled several times because he angered powerful people in the Church.

Chrysostom, Divine Liturgy of St John – the Eucharistic liturgy used most commonly in the Orthodox Church. It was the liturgy of the Imperial Capital although its present form dates to a much later time than that of St. John himself.

Clement of Alexandria, St – was a well-known and respected theologian. He was head of the Catechetical School at Alexandria in 190 A.D. To Clement, Christ was the "Logos" or the Second Person of the Trinity, truly God, also the source of human reason and the interpreter of God's will to mankind.

Climacus, St John – an ascetic and writer of spiritual works. He lived in the 7th century and became the Abbot of Sinai. His "Ladder of Paradise" deals with both the virtues one should emulate and the vices one should avoid. He is especially suspicious of emotions, which must be greatly tempered in order to live an ideal Christian life.

Colossians, Epistle to – composed by St. Paul when he was imprisoned either at Rome or Ephesus. The Epistle calls Christians to a realization of Christ as their Redeemer and Lord.

Commandments, Ten – laws given to Moses by God. They were revealed on Mount Sinai after the Israelites escaped from Egypt. The text was written on two stone tablets. There are two versions given in Exodus 20:1-17 and Deuteronomy 5:6-21. The Ten Commandments have had a profound influence on the moral code of the Christian Church and secular society as well.

Communion in Both Kinds – until the 12th century it was the general custom in the Western Church to receive the consecrated Body and Blood of Christ. The custom died out and only the bread was commonly given after that time. Orthodoxy has always preserved the tradition of the early Church by imparting consecrated bread and wine to the faithful.

Communion of Saints – all members of the Church living or reposed, as the one body of Christ.

Compline – (Sl. "Velikoye Povecheriye") a service of the Church read after nightfall in monasteries. In parishes it is combined with Orthros (Matins) to form the All-Night Vigil on the eves of the Nativity and Theophany.

Con–celebration – the celebration of the Eucharistic Divine Liturgy by a number of priests. The custom was universal in the early Church but was suppressed by the West in the Middle Ages. The Orthodox Church has continually observed the custom of con- celebration.

Conscience – human capacity for determining the goodness of an act. Conscience is reserved for the human species alone.

Consecration – in Christianity people and things are consecrated, i.e. in the Eucharist, the bread and wine are consecrated to become the Body and Blood of Christ. Men are consecrated bishops when the character of their office is imparted through the "laying on of hands" of other bishops. Things such as altars, chalices, and church buildings are consecrated, or set-aside, for the exclusive service of God.

Constantine, St – Roman Emperor of the fourth century. Constantine's policy was to bring together the Church under the protection of the secular state. Constantine the Great embraced Christianity just before his death in 337 A.D. During his reign Constantine lavished many gifts on the Christian Faith, especially church buildings.

Contakion – also spelled *Kontakion*, or a hymn composed for liturgical use.

Contrition – interior repentance or sorrow for sin. "Contrition" means sorrow because of love for God. "Attrition", means imperfect sorrow because of fear of punishment.

Convert – one who joins himself with the Orthodox Church through Baptism (if not already validly baptized), a Confession of Faith and Chrismation/Holy Eucharist.

Coptic Church – a Church founded by Saint Mark. After fierce persecution this Church gave birth to monasticism in the early fifth century. St. Anthony of the Egypt was a leader of the Church before it accepted Monophysitism in 451 A.D. The Coptic Church then became increasingly isolated from the Orthodox Church after the former rejected the Council of Chalcedon.

Corinthians, Epistles to the – Epistles of St. Paul written in the early '50s. 1st Corinthians deals with the Eucharist, love and resurrection. In 2 Corinthians the main topic is St. Paul's relationship with the Church as an apostle, and his comment on the failure of morality in the Church at Corinth.

Covenant – a bond or pledge entered into by two parties whereby each promises to come to the assistance of the other. There was a covenant between God and the chosen people of Israel and in the life and death of Jesus Christ we find the perfect love bond between God and man.

Creed – a short statement of belief. The Creed stresses the most important aspects of Christian doctrine and serves as a standard of orthodox teaching within the Church.

Cremation – reducing the remains of the dead by burning. Rejected by the early Church it is still resisted in Orthodoxy.

Crucifixion – death by nailing the human body to wooden supports. Crucifixion was outlawed by the Emperor Constantine as a legal form of punishment.

Crusades – a series of formal, recognized expeditions from Western Europe to the Holy Land and the Levant. The First Crusade began in 1095 and was organized by the Roman Catholic Church to recover the Holy Land from Islamic domination. The Crusades were brutal and did much damage to the Orthodox Church. They effectively ended in 1464.

Cupola – the domes found on top of Orthodox churches. The number may range from 1-13. One dome represents Christ, those around it signify either the Evangelists, apostles, etc.

Cyprian, St – was converted to Christianity into 46 A.D. St. Cyprian opposed the readmission of lapsed Christians (lapsi) who denied the Faith in the face of persecution. The Roman Church, however, admitted the lapsi after suitable penance. This caused an exchange of letters between St. Cyprian and Pope Stephen of Rome which were later used as proof that the pope's jurisdiction was limited, and that he did not possess universal oversight in the Church, as Rome was wont to claim.

Cyprus, Christianity in – the island of Cyprus was evangelized by St. Paul and St. Barnabas. The Cypriot Church was allowed independence from the patriarchates but later subjugation by the Arabs and Roman Catholics, kept the Church subservient until it received autonomy in 1571.

Cyril, Saint – there are three men who hold the name Cyril and are major figures in Christian history:

1. St. Cyril, Bishop of Jerusalem, c. 349 A.D. opposed Arianism
2. St. Cyril, Patriarch of Alexandria put into form the doctrines of the Trinity and the Person of Christ
3. St. Cyril, one of the "Apostles to the Slavs" who, with St. Methodius, left Constantinople to become a missionary in Moravia. Saints Cyril and Methodius lived in the ninth century.

Cyrillic Alphabet – used by Slavonic-speaking people in the Orthodox Church. It is named after Saint Cyril, "Apostle to the Slavs", although he technically invented the Glagolitic alphabet, not the Cyrillic.

- D -

Dalmatic – the Western term used for the vestment worn by the deacon or bishop underneath the outer garments. In Slavonic the term used is "sticharion".

Deacon – the rank of the priesthood below presbyter and bishop. The Orthodox Church has always maintained the office of permanent deacons who assist at the Divine Liturgy but do not celebrate the Eucharist, or give absolution in the Mystery of Penance.

Deaconess – the early Church allowed women a specific ministry such as caring for the sick or the poor of her own sex, and assisting in the Rite of Baptism for women. When adult Baptisms became rare, the office declined. The Office of Deaconess was officially abolished around the 6th century but survived in some places until the 11th or 12th century.

Dead Sea Scrolls – a collection of ancient Hebrew and Aramaic texts discovered in 1947. The location was near Qumran around the Dead Sea. Almost the entire canonical Old Testament was represented along with some other books not known before the find.

Decalogue – another name given to the Ten Commandments.

Deism – a form of natural religion which began in England around the late 17th-18th centuries. Deism teaches that although God created the world – He has no interest in it now because it would degrade His omnipotence and unchangeable nature.

Devil – the chief of the fallen angels, known as Lucifer. His great sin was that of pride-in wanting to be like God. Christ teaches that the Devil can be defeated by resisting his lures and temptations, through prayer and fasting.

Diaconicon – the sanctuary area where vessels, vestments and service books are stored.

Didache – Greek for "teaching". This is the teaching ministry of the Church as opposed to her "kerygma", or preaching apostolate.

"Didache" – an early Christian manual on morals and Church practice. The author, date and place of origin are unknown – however scholars seem to think it was the first in a compilation of early Church texts dealing with discipline and practice.

Dionysius the Aeropagite – his conversion by St. Paul is recorded in Acts 17:34.

Dionysius the Pseudo Aeropagite – was a fifth-century theologian. He is believed to have authored a series of writings which attempted to contrast and synthesize Christian doctrine and Neo-Platonist teaching.

Diptychs – a list of the living and dead for whom Orthodox Christians pray.

Docetism – an early heresy which taught that Christ's humanity and suffering were apparent, rather than real. Docetists considered flesh and matter to be evil.

Dogma –religious truth established by the revelation of God, and defined by the Church.

"Donation of Constantine" – a spurious document of the eighth-ninth century distributed by the Roman See, which claimed that the pope was given universal jurisdiction by the Emperor Constantine. This fictitious document gave the pope authority to judge the clergy, while insisting that he was the rightful claimant to the Imperial Throne. The document was proved, in the 15th century, to be a forgery composed by the papacy to gain absolute power over all Christians.

Donatism – opposed the so-called "traditores", or those who surrendered the Holy Scriptures to secular authorities during persecutions. The Donatists believed that they alone composed the authentic Christian Church

Doukhobors – a Russian sect which teaches that Jesus Christ is not God, but a mere man with Divine reason. They also believe that the human soul can travel from one body to another, in successive deaths and rebirths, until it gains perfection through purification.

Dulia – veneration which is paid to the saints. It differs from "hyperdulia" which is veneration of the Mother of God, and "latria", (worship) which is reserved for God alone.

- E -

Easter – is the common term for the Feast of the Resurrection of Christ. It is derived from a pagan term. The correct term to use for the Feast of the Resurrection is Pascha. In the early Church catechumens were baptized during the Paschal Service after spending most of Holy Saturday in prayer and preparation.

Eastward position – the practice of the celebrant of the Eucharistic Liturgy to face East, the direction of our redemption.

Ebionites – a Jewish sect which flourished during the early years of the Church. They believed Jesus was only the human son of Mary and Joseph, and that the Holy Spirit gave Him authority to claim the status of a prophet. Ebionites overemphasized the Mosaic Law and its binding character on early Christians. They rejected the Pauline Epistles and used only one synthesized Gospel.

Ecphonesis – the concluding words, in an audible voice, of a prayer which has been said quietly.

Ecumenical Councils – an assembly of Church representatives legally convoked for settling controversies, formulating dogma and establishing Canons of morals and faith. The Orthodox Church recognizes seven Ecumenical Councils.

Ektenia – a prayer consisting of petitions said by the deacon, or priest, to which the choir responds.

Enarxis – in the Divine Liturgy it is the section between the Proskomedia and the Lesser or Small Entrance. It contains litanies with antiphons sung by the choir.

Encolpion – an oval medallion worn by bishops in the Orthodox Church. It usually contains an icon of the Mother of God.

Eparchy – in the Eastern Church, an eparchy is an ecclesiastical province.

Ephesians, Epistle to – generally attributed to St Paul. It deals with the riches of Jesus Christ in the Church.

Epiclesis – although the term originally meant "invocation or prayer" it is commonly used today to refer to the Eucharistic petition which asks God the Father to send the Holy Spirit upon the bread and wine, consecrating them into the Body and Blood of Christ.

Epigonation – a diamond-shaped part of priestly vesture which hangs from the right side of certain ecclesiastical dignitaries. (Slavonic: "Palitsa")

Epimanikia – cuffs made of fabric worn over the sleeves of the sticharion.

Epiphany – the Greek term for "manifestation". It is celebrated on Jan. 6th. On the Epiphany there is a special blessing of waters. The feast is also known as the "Theophany", or the manifestation of God in the Holy Trinity.

Epitaphion – in the Orthodox Church this is an elaborately decorated tomb which represents the burial place of Christ. On Holy and Great Friday the burial shroud is placed in the Epitaphion and remains there until Saturday Vespers. In Slavonic the burial shroud is referred to as the Plaschanitsa.

Epitrachelion – the part of the priestly vestment corresponding to the Western stole, which is worn around the neck of the priest. Unlike its Western counterpart (stole) the epitrachelion is joined. It hangs in front of the alb.

Eschatology – the part of theology which deals with the final destiny both of the individual and mankind in general. It also deals with the Second Coming of Christ.

Eucharist – Greek term for " thanksgiving". The Mystery (or Sacrament) under which the bread and wine become the very Body and Blood of Christ. Along with Baptism, the Eucharist it is at the core of the Christian Faith

Euchologian – the text of the three Eucharistic Rites used in the Church, non-variable parts of the Divine Office and the prayers required for the administration of the Holy Mysteries, or Sacraments. (Slavonic: "Sluzhebnik".)

Eusebius – late second, early 3rd century, historian of the Church. He is known as the "Father of Church History". Another Eusebius, Bishop of Nicomedia, was a leader of the Arian heresy and baptized the Emperor Constantine.

Euthanasia – since the late 19th century the term has come to denote the termination of human life on humanitarian grounds.

Evagrius Ponticus – 3rd century writer and preacher at Constantinople. In the late 3rd century he set out for the desert to live a monastic life. He was the first monk to write extensively about Christianity.

Evangelist – term used to denote a writer of the four Gospels, or a traveling missionary.

Exaltation of the Cross – the feast observed in honor of the Holy Cross of Christ, Sept. 14th.

Exegesis – the art of explaining a Scriptural text, to reveal what the author wished to say, or to apply a contemporary meaning to the work.

Exorcist – a Church office which confers the power to drive out evil spirits.

"Equal to the Apostles" – a title given to certain saints who were outstanding in bringing the Christian Faith to the masses. Examples are, St. Mary Magdalene, Ss. Constantine and Helen, Ss. Cyril and Methodius and the Great Prince Vladimir.

Evangeliye – a book containing the four Gospels from which the appointed lessons are read at the Divine Services.

Exaposteilarion – from the Greek word for "dispatching". It is a hymn sung at Orthros after the Canon. It refers to Christ sending out His disciples to preach the Gospel to all nations.

- F -

Faith – the power given to us by Almighty God which enables us to believe what He has revealed. St. Paul notes in Hebrews 11:1 that faith is "the substance of things hoped for , the evidence of things not seen." Faith is necessary for salvation and must be accompanied by good works, (Mark 16:16 and James 2:17-20).

Fans, Liturgical – (Greek : "Exapteryga") used from the early centuries to keep flying insects from the sacred oblations. The fans are usually metal with imprinted images of the six-winged angels known as Seraphim.

Fast – a penitential and ancient practice designed to strengthen one's spiritual life by weakening the attractions of sensible pleasures.

Father – originally the title of bishops, the word was later applied to all clergy.

"Father of Orthodoxy" – St. Athanasius is granted this title because of his strong opposition to the heresy of Arianism.

Fathers of the Church – those who explained and defended the Christian Faith in the first six centuries of her existence.

Feast – a special day set apart for the liturgical commemoration of some saint, the Mother of God, or an event in the life of Christ. Immovable feasts occur on fixed dates during the year and movable feasts are determined by the date of Holy Pascha.

Ferial Menaion – a service book which has the stichera for all feasts of the Church Year.

Filioque – the clause, "and the son" not found in the Nicene-Constantinople Creed, which denotes the double procession of the Holy Spirit , i.e. "from the Father and the Son". This phrase was not in the original Creed having been added by the Western Church in the ninth century.

Florence, Council of – met at Ferrara, Florence and Rome (all in Italy) from 1438- 1445. Its chief object was reunion with the Orthodox Church. The decrees were challenged in the East by the vast majority of the people. The Orthodox Church rejects this council.

- G -

Galatians, Epistle to – written by St. Paul for Christian converts at Galatia because they were being instructed to observe the entire Jewish Law as a prelude to salvation. To St. Paul, this endangered the new Christian's witness to Christ.

Galilee – the scene of almost all of Our Lord's earthly life and ministry.

Gentiles – the name given to non-Jews.

George, St – known as "The Great Martyr". He lived in the early 3rd century and is greatly venerated in the Orthodox Church.

Georgia, Church at – the royal house of Georgia was converted in 330 A.D., which led to the adoption of Orthodoxy as the prevailing religion of the nation. It was under the Church of Russia until 1917 when its autocephaly was again granted. .

Glossolalia – the faculty of speaking in tongues. Its abuse has been widespread in recent years among various Pentecostal groups. See: Acts 2:4 and 1 Corinthians 14:1-25.

Godparents – sponsors at Holy Baptism who undertake the sacred responsibility for the spiritual upbringing of the person baptized. This entails a Faith-based relationship and therefore the sponsors must be Orthodox. Godparents must take a permanent interest in the spiritual welfare of their Godchildren.

Gospel – the title given to the books of Holy Scripture which reveal the "Good News" of salvation and in which the Christian Faith was set forth by SS. Matthew, Mark, Luke and John.

Grace – the supernatural gift of God which is freely given to men and women to help them gain eternal life. See: Ephesians 4:7.

Great Entrance – the solemn procession before the Offertory at which the priest and deacon transfer the gifts (bread and wine) from the Prothesis, or Table of Preparation, to the Holy Table.

Great and Holy Friday – the Friday on which we commemorate the death of Jesus on the Cross. This is a very strict fast day and there is no Divine Liturgy celebrated, except when the Feast of the Annunciation falls on Holy and Great Friday.

Great Schism – separation in the 11th century of the Western (Roman) Church from the Orthodox Church. This separation came about gradually in previous centuries, but was formalized in 1054 A.D.

Greece, Christianity in – the Christian Faith was preached in Greece since the first century, principally by St. Paul. The Greek Church is in communion with the Patriarch of Constantinople.

Gregory, Dialogus St – a title sometimes given to Pope Gregory I of Rome.

Gregory – the name given to various saints of the Orthodox Church, namely:

1. Gregory the Illuminator, St. – the "Apostle of Armenia".
2. Gregory of Nazianzus, St. – one of the Cappadocian Fathers who was Bishop of Constantinople. His preaching helped restore the Faith which was being attacked on many sides.
3. Gregory of Nyssa, St. – another Cappadocian Father who was the brother of St. Basil. He was an apologist against the Arians. His sister was St. Macrina.
4. Gregory Palamas, St. – Greek theologian and exponent of Hesychasm (the tradition of inner, mystical prayer) associated with the monks of Mount Athos. Hesychasm attempted to bring about the union of the mind with the heart.
5. Gregory Thaumaturgus, St. – a Church Father of the late 2nd century who was a convert to Christianity. The title "Thaumaturgus" means "Wonder Worker". St. Gregory opposed several early heresies in the Church.
6. Gregory Dialogus, St. – Pope of Rome – introduced Gregorian Chant and initiated much-needed reforms in the Western Church.

Guardian Angels – angels appointed by Almighty God to protect and give guidance to the faithful.

- H -

Hagia Sophia – the Church of the Holy Wisdom at Constantinople. It was captured by the Turks in 1453, turned into a mosque and since 1934 has been a museum.

Hagiography – the writing and study of the lives of the saints.

Halo – (Nimbus) – a circle or disk of light portrayed around a figure in iconography. It usually surrounds the head of the figure and sometimes, the entire body.

Hands, Imposition of – a manner of blessing and handing down certain Offices and Mysteries of the Church.

Heaven – the state of perfect blessedness prepared for those who love God. Heaven is eternal.

Hebrews, Epistle to – an Epistle, believed to have been authored by St. Paul, although there are differences when compared with his other writings. The Epistle asserts the superiority of Christianity to the old covenant. It contains profound teachings about Jesus Christ.

Hedonism – a philosophy which maintains that the end of all human existence is pleasure.

Hegumenos – (Sl. "Egumen") means "leader" in Greek and is the common name given to the head of a monastery.

Helena, St – mother of Emperor Constantine. She supported the Christian Faith and established many churches and holy sites.

Hell – the state of those who have rejected the love of Almighty God. Hell is eternal.

Heresy – the complete rejection or denial of a revealed truth by one who has confessed the Christian Faith.

Hermit – a monastic who retires into solitary life to practice the works of prayer, fasting, and mortification in order to more perfectly serve God.

Hierarchy – the higher clergy, rulers in spiritual things.

Hilarion, St – c. 291-371 – a saint who was the founder of the anchorite (solitary) life in Palestine.

Holy and Great Thursday – Thursday of Holy Week. It is observed in commemoration of the Last (Mystical) Supper. The Divine Liturgy of St. Basil is celebrated and the Twelve Passion Gospels are read at the Service of Matins.

Holy Orders – the Mystery or Sacrament through which men are set aside for service to God and His Church. In this Mystery, men receive the power and grace to perform the duties of the priesthood. Holy Orders are bestowed on deacons, priests and bishops.

Holy Spirit – the third person of the Holy Trinity distinct from, but consubstantial, co-eternal, and co-equal with the Father and the Son. The Holy Spirit is, in the fullest sense, Almighty God.

Holy Water – water blessed usually on the Feast of the Theophany – Jan. 6th. It can be blessed however at any time during the year.

Honorius I, Pope of Rome from 625-638 – He was accused of heresy by the Third Ecumenical Council of Constantinople and finely anathematized.

Horologian – (Sl. "Chasoslov") a liturgical book containing the services for the different hours of the day for example Compline, All Night Vigil, Matins, Vespers and the First, Third, Sixth and Ninth hours.

Hosanna – the Greek form of the Hebrew prayer, "Save, we beseech Thee."

Hyperdulia – the special veneration paid to the Mother of God. It is distinguished from "dulia", i.e. veneration of the saints and "latria", reserved for God alone.

Hypostatic Union – the union of the Divine and human natures of Jesus Christ, formally accepted as a dogma of the Church by the Council of Chalcedon in 451 A.D.

- I -

Ichthus – the Greek word for fish. It is made up of the initial letters of the Greek words for Jesus Christ, Son of God, Savior. IXTHUS

Icon – a painting on wood or other material representing Our Lord, the All Holy Virgin, saints, or events in their lives. The veneration given to an icon is to the one represented on the icon, not the material itself.

Iconoclastic Controversy – the controversy over the veneration of icons which disturbed the Church in the 7th and 8th centuries. The First Sunday of the Great Lent ("Triumph of Orthodoxy") is observed, to this day, as commemoration of the restoration which allowed the veneration of icons.

Iconography – the art of painting icons which was originally developed in the monasteries. There are several schools of iconography each having its particular style.

Iconostasis – a term used for the screen which separates the sanctuary from the nave of the church building. Another term used is "Templon", and on it, are found icons of Christ, His mother and the saints.

Idiorrhythmic – the term applied to certain monasteries in Orthodoxy which allow considerable freedom to monks, including the right to use personal property.

Ignatius, St – first-century Bishop of Antioch. He wrote eleven letters on the reality of Christ's Divine and human natures. He taught that the reality of Christ is continued in the Eucharist and that the unity of the Church is dependent upon one's loyalty to the local bishop.

Iliton – the silk cloth used to wrap the Antimens.

Immanence, Divine – the fact of God's presence throughout the universe.

Immersion – in Baptism it is the submerging of the body to signify that as we die with Christ, we also rise with Him in the waters of Baptism.

Incarnation – the dogma of the Church that the eternal son of God, Jesus Christ, took human flesh from His human mother. The historic Christ is at once , both fully God and fully man.

Incense – a resin-like substance that usually comes from trees and is blended to produce a sweet-smelling smoke used during Divine Services. The smoke is produced by placing the incense on a burning coal within the bowl of the censer.

Inclination – the bowing of the head as a sign of deep respect. It is usually accompanied by the Sign of the Cross.

Infant Baptism – although Baptism of infants is implied in the New Testament, since it was administered to entire families, the first extant documentation of this tradition comes from the second/third century. In the Orthodox Church, Baptism is followed immediately by Chrismation and the reception of the Holy Eucharist.

Infusion – a method of Baptism by pouring water on the head instead of immersion of the entire body. Infusion may be used in the Orthodox Church but only in cases of extreme emergency.

Inquisition – the persecution of those suspected of heresy. The Inquisition began in 1232 A.D., when Pope Gregory IX claimed the Inquisition for the Roman Catholic Church. It was conducted under the auspices of the Roman Church until 1542. The Inquisition was formally suppressed in 1820.

Intone – to recite a response, or chant in a singing tone.

Irenaeus, St – first-century Bishop of Lyon. He wrote extensively against several heresies namely, Arianism and Montanism.

Isaiah – Hebrew prophet who asserted the total supremacy of the God of Israel. In his moral commands Isaiah stressed the Divine Holiness of the One God.

- J -

James – the name ascribed to:

1. James, St. – the Lord's "brother" (Mark 6:3). His position in the family is disputed. He became the chief authority of the Church at Jerusalem.
2. James the Great, St. – an apostle of Our Lord. He was the elder brother of St. John. Jesus named his brother and he, "Sons of Thunder" because of their zeal. James was beheaded in 44 A.D.
3. James the Less, St. – was the son of Alphaeus (cf. Mark 3:18). He was one of "The Twelve".

James, Epistle of St – written to the twelve tribes of the Diaspora. It stands first among the "Catholic" or Universal Epistles.

James, Liturgy of St – an ancient Liturgy traditionally ascribed to St. James, the Lord's kin. It is usually served on his feast day, October 23rd.

Jerome, St – Biblical scholar and Father of the Church. He wrote many Biblical commentaries and translated Holy Scripture into Latin (The Vulgate). He argued that the Church should accept the Hebrew Canon (or listing of New Testament books), leaving out the Apocrypha. He was involved in many controversies because of his exceptionally passionate nature.

Jerusalem – the capital of Judah and the site of the Temple. Called the "Holy City" by Christians in all ages.

Jesus Prayer – the prayer "Lord Jesus Christ, Son of God, have mercy on me a sinner." It can be traced back to the sixth century and is widely used in the Orthodox Church.

Joachim, St – the father of Mary (Theotokos) and husband of Saint Anne.

John – the name used by:

1. St. John the Beloved Apostle. He was the author of the fourth Gospel, probably influenced the Book of Revelation and of three "Catholic Epistles". Together with his brother St. James and St. Peter they formed the core of the apostolic group.

241

2. John of Antioch – leader of the moderate Nestorians, a heretical group. He was later reconciled to St. Cyril and the Orthodox Faith.
3. John Climacus, St. – 570-649 A.D. – St. John was an aesthetic and spiritual writer of the early Church. He was also a monk and Abbot of Sinai. His "Ladder of Paradise" discusses Christian virtues and vices teaching the nature of complete detachment from the world. He taught the Christian ideal.
4. John of Damascus, St. – 675-749 A.D. – Greek theologian and Father of the Church. He became a monk and defended the Church against the Iconoclasts. He wrote commentaries on Scripture, Christian doctrine, along with the moral and aesthetic life.
5. John the Faster, St. – 6th century Patriarch of Constantinople. He is credited with composing a manual for confessors.

John, Epistles of St – these are three New Testament letters ascribed to St. John the Evangelist. They oppose false doctrine rampant in the early Church, discussed hospitality and how to avoid those who teach heresy.

John , Gospel of St – the Fourth Gospel which differs from the Synoptics (Matthew, Mark, Luke) by shifting the emphasis to Christ's ministry in Jerusalem and expanding His ministry from one year to three. This Gospel is different from the others in that Our Lord speaks in long discourses rather than in short sayings or parables as in the Synoptics.

Josephat – canonized by the Roman Church, he was a persecutor of Orthodox Christians and attempted to bring about unity by force and bloodshed. Josephat, sometimes named "the malevolent", is not recognized as a saint in the Orthodox Church.

Josephus, Flavius – a first century Jewish historian. He wrote a splendid history of his people.

Judaism – the Faith and practice of the Jewish people.

Jude, St – an apostle of Christ. He is sometimes identified as the author of the New Testament Epistle of Jude. He did missionary work in Persia where he was martyred.

Jude, Epistle of St – one of the Catholic (Universal Epistles) in the New Testament. Its aim is to combat the spread of early heresies and dangerous doctrines.

Justin, Martyr St – convert and Christian apologist who attempted to reconcile faith and reason. His works defend Christianity as the only true rational belief and contain descriptions of Baptismal ceremonies, the Eucharist, and other rites. St. Justin identifies the "Logos" with the God of the Old Testament and speaks of the call of Gentiles to assume the place of Israel in God's plan.

- K -

Kamilauka – a hat worn by the clergy, it is round with a flat top, sometimes with a rim.

Kathisma – one of twenty parts into which the Psalter is divided. It is also the name of the second Canon that is sung at Matins on certain major feasts.

Kellia – the name typically given to monastic's room, or cell.

Kerygma – the Greek word for preaching the Gospel which is contrasted with the "Didache", or its instructional aspect.

Kolyva – the wheat, honey and nut mixture blessed during memorials for the departed and distributed to those present at the service.

Kontakion – a short hymn which gives the meaning of the day's celebration, used at the Divine Liturgy, and during the Hours.

Kyrie Eleison – Greek for "Lord have mercy". Sung as a response by the choir to certain petitions of the liturgy.

- L -

Laity – members of the Church who do not belong to the clergy.

Lamb – the portion of the prosphoron which is consecrated into the Body of Christ at the Divine Liturgy

Lance – a small knife used to cut the bread at the Proskimedia, or Service of Preparation.

Lapsi – those who denied the Christian Faith during the persecutions. At first they were not allowed to re-enter the Church, however, this policy was later changed.

Last Supper – the final meal of Christ with His apostles on the night before the crucifixion. More properly called "The Mystical Supper".

Latria – the fullness of worship which should be shown to God alone.

Lavra – Greek term for "street or alley". In the early Church it referred to the small huts which were assembled together in a monastic community. Members were subject to a single abbot. The oldest lavra were found in fourth-century Palestine.

Lector – another term for a reader in the Church.

Lent – a word derived from the Old English for "Springtime" is technically a Western term. It is the period of fasting or preparation for particular feasts such as Pascha, the Nativity, etc. Orthodox usually refer to these times of preparation as the Nativity Fast, the Apostle's Fast, the Great Fast, and the Theotokos' Fast.

Lesser Entrance – the procession of the priest, clergy and servers during the singing of the Beatitudes at the Divine Liturgy. The priest carries the Gospel Book whereas, if a bishop is serving, he enters the sanctuary from the cathedra.

Litiya – the blessing of the breads which is joined to Vespers on the eve of major feasts. Five small loaves of bread, along with oil and wine are blessed at the Litiya. It is the commemoration of Christ feeding the multitudes. The bread is cut and distributed to the faithful at the end of the service.

Liturgical Books used in the Orthodox Church are:
Sluzhebnik – prayers, order, ceremonies of Vespers, Matins and the Divine Liturgy.
Trebnik – (Euchologian) – book containing the services for administration of the Holy Mysteries or Sacraments, and other ceremonies.
Horologian – (Slavonic: "Chasoslov") – contains services for the different hours of the day.
Menaion – 12 books – one for each month – contains services for each day in addition to the Feasts of the Lord and Theotokos.
Typicon – liturgical calendar and instructions (rubrics) for various services.
Oktoechos – contains the Canons and hymns of the eight Tones used at Vespers and Matins.
Triodion – contains services for the ten weeks before Pascha, the ten weeks before the Great Fast and the services of Holy Week.
Pentecostarion – liturgical services for the period between Pascha and the Sunday after Pentecost, inclusive.

"Logia" – the actual sayings of Christ as recorded in Holy Scripture.

Liturgy – the work or public duty of the Church. It has several aspects such as the Divine Liturgy and the other public services of the Orthodox Church.

Logos – (Greek for "Word") – is the expression for the Word of God, the Second Person of the Holy Trinity, Who was God from all eternity and is of one essence with the Father.

Lord's Prayer – another term for "The Our Father."

Luke, Gospel of St – the third of the Synoptic Gospels. St. Luke gathered his material from eyewitnesses to the events depicted in the Gospel. It was composed from the earlier Gospel of St. Mark and the "Q" (Ger. "quelle") which was a listing of the sayings of Christ, the so-called "Logia".

Macarius , St of Egypt – also known as Macarius the Great, he was a native Egyptian who gathered monks around the desert of Scetis. It became the center of monasticism in that area.

Macarius of Moscow – Metropolitan of Moscow from 1879. His books on theology reflect the official position of Russian Orthodoxy. He also wrote a complete history of the Russian Church.

Macrina, St – sister of St. Basil the Great and St. Gregory of Nyssa.

Magi – name given to the "Wisemen" who were guided by a star to the cave where Christ was born.

Magnificat – traditionally the name given to the hymn in honor of the Mother of God, (Luke 1:46-55). It is sung at various services, especially Matins.

Mantia – the long robe worn by a bishop. It is usually purple or blue in color, open at the front and embroidered with four squares (signifying the Evangelists) which lead out in streams of red and white stripes. The stripes represent the doctrine of the Church emanating from the teachings in the Gospels.

Marcellina, St – sister of St. Ambrose.

Mark, St – one of the Evangelists who wrote the first Gospel (in dating) which was used by St. Matthew and St. Luke to compile their accounts. St. Mark later went on several missionary journeys with Ss. Barnabas, Peter and Paul.

Mark, Gospel of St – this Gospel is believed to be the first Gospel written, and used by both Matthew and Luke. It is believed that St. Mark had first-hand information from Saint Peter with whom he traveled. The Gospel was written in Koine Greek.

Marriage – the formal contract between a man and women by which they are united in Matrimony, blessed by the Church.

Martyr – one who has suffered death for the Faith.

Martyrology – the list for every day of the year and the saints who are commemorated on that date.

Mary of Egypt, St – converted from a life of infamy and lust, she is a model of penitence who spent her last forty-seven years in the desert outside of Jerusalem.

Mary Magdalene, St – a follower of Christ out of whom He cast seven devils, (Luke 8:2). She was a model of penitence and an example of how Christ can truly change lives.

Matins – (Greek: "Orthros") Morning service of prayer. It begins with six psalms, has Gospel readings, Canon with odes, and the Great Doxology. It is served before the Divine Liturgy and sometimes on the evening before a feast.

Matthew, St – an apostle of Christ and Evangelist. St. Matthew authored the Gospel of his name. He also compiled Christ's sayings, (the "Logia") in Hebrew.

Matthew, Gospel of St – this Gospel stands first in the New Testament Canon. It is concerned with the New Covenant in relation to the Jewish Law and the special commission given to the apostles to preach and teach throughout the known world.

Matthias, St – the apostle who was chosen to fill the vacancy left by the suicide of Judas.

Matins – another name given to the early morning service of Orthros.

Matushka – a Slavonic term for the wife of a priest. It means "mother". In Greek the word for a priest's spouse is "Presbytera".

Maximos, St – named "The Confessor". He was a Greek theologian and ascetical writer. His works centered on the Incarnation of Jesus Christ. He taught that the goal of all human existence is total union with God.

Melkites – Christians of Syria and Egypt who are in communion with the Roman See.

Menaia – twelve books, one for each month, containing the services for commemoration of the saints or feasts.

Menas, St – Egyptian martyr whose birth site has become a place of pilgrimage, known for miraculous cures.

Messiah – the Hebrew word for "Anointed One" referring to Jesus Christ. It is rendered in Greek as Christos , from which the word "Christ" is derived.

Metropolitan – the head archbishop of ecclesiastical province. In the Slavic tradition the Metropolitan wears a white klobuk with a Cross.

Mitre – (Mitra) – the official headdress of a bishop, archimandrite and sometimes an Arch-priest.

"Mnogaya Lyeta" – a prayerful wish for "Many years", in blessings, life, and good fortune.

Monastery – the dwelling place of monastics, both men and women.

Monk – Greek for "solitary," or one who renounces the world to lead a consecrated life of prayer, fasting and works of charity.

"Monogenes, The" – a Greek hymn "Only Begotten One" which forms part of the Divine Liturgy.

Monophysitism – the doctrine which claims that in Jesus Christ there is but a single Divine nature. This is opposed to the Orthodox doctrine that there are two natures in Christ, Divine and human.

Monotheism – belief in one, personal and transcendent God.

Monothelitism – a heresy from the 7th century which declares that there is only one will in Jesus Christ. The 3rd Council of Constantinople in 681 declared that there are two wills in Christ, one Divine and one human. This is Orthodox doctrine.

"Mother of God" – which comes from the Greek term Theotokos, a word familiar to Orthodox Christians. Mary as the "Birth Giver of God" was proclaimed by the Council of Ephesus in 431. This was her fundamental dignity and therefore great honor is bestowed on her by the Church.

Mount Athos – "The Holy Mountain" in Greece, "The Garden of the Theotokos", the center of Orthodox monasticism.

Myrrh – (Chrism) the sacred oil which is blessed to be used at the Mystery of Chrismation. It is made of oils and many herbs/ spices.

Mystery – Orthodox refer to the Sacraments (a Latin term) as "Mysteries". In Slavonic the term is "Tainstvo".

Mysticism – a knowledge of God attained through personal religious experience.

- N -

Nabedrennick – (Greek: "epigonation"), a priestly vestment. It is the diamond-shaped shield which is worn by certain clergy who have special rank in the Church. In the West it is also called the "genual".

Name Day – celebration of the feast day of one's patron saint. In some places it is more common to celebrate a Name Day than one's birth date.

Narthex – the vestibule area of the church building. Also called the portico.

Nativity – the name given to feasts such as the celebration of the birth of Christ on Dec. 25th. It also refers to the birth dates of the Theotokos, and St. John the Baptist, the Forerunner.

Nave – the central part of the church building.

Nectarius, St – a 4th century bishop who became the successor to St. Gregory of Nazianzen in the See of Constantinople.

Neophyte – a newly baptized convert to the Church, usually referred to as "newly enlightened".

Nestorianism – a heresy of the early Church which taught that there were two separate persons in the incarnate Christ, the one Divine and the other human. This is opposed to Orthodox teaching that the incarnate Christ was a single person, at the same time both God and man.

New Testament – the canonical books of Holy Scripture belonging to the Church as opposed to the Old Testament which is partially shared with Judaism. The New Testament contains the Four Gospels, Acts, the Pauline Epistles, the "Catholic" Epistles, and Revelation.

Nicholas, St – Bishop of Myra. He is the patron saint of Russia, of children and sailors. He was known for his outstanding works of charity. It was upon St. Nicholas that our secular character of Santa Claus is based – although there is now almost no sensible comparison between the two.

Nicodemus of the Holy Mountain – a saint of the 18th-19th centuries who was a monk of Mount Athos and a famed spiritual writer. His main works are the Philokalia and the Pedalion ("Rudder"), a commentary on Orthodox Church canons (regulations).

Nikon – Patriarch of Moscow from 1652-1658. He sought reforms in the Russian liturgy by bringing the service books into conformity with the Greek usage and purged the services of corruptions. He was deposed from the Church in 1667, although his reforms were seen as useful and necessary. He is now considered one of the greatest patriarchs of the Russian Church.

N I K A – initials of the Greek words meaning –"Jesus Christ, Victor" also means "By this Sign, Now Conquer."

Nil Sorsky, St – Russian monk and ascetic. He discovered his vocation in monasticism and practiced Hesychasm. He wrote a commentary on monastic life and introduced the idea of the "skete" gathered around the spiritual father.

Nilus the Ascetic, St – a writer on moral and ascetical subjects.

Nomo-canon – a compendium of Orthodox Church canons, or regulations.

Novice – a Western term which has come to mean one who is in preparation for monastic life.

Nun – a woman who has chosen the monastic life.

- O -

Oblation – an offering, sometimes used to refer to the Service of Proskimedia (Oblation) which consists of the preparation of the gifts of bread and wine before the Divine Liturgy.

Octave – an eight-day period during which a particular feast is celebrated , i.e. from the day of the feast itself, to the "leavetaking" i.e. "Apodosis of the Feast".

Ode – (Slavonic: "Irmos") – one of the nine Canticles of the Canon sung at Matins.

Oktocheos – the service book containing the canons and hymns of the Tones used at Vespers and Matins.

Old Believers – the part of the Russian Church which refused to accept the reforms of the Patriarch Nikon. They were deposed in 1667 and persecuted.

Omophorion – a part of the vestment of a bishop. It is a broad , brocaded band which goes around the neck and the left shoulder. The other part hangs down the back from the right shoulder. It signifies Christ as "The Good Shepherd" who takes the lost sheep upon his shoulders.

Orarion – a part of the deacon's vesture. It is worn over the left shoulder and under the right arm. Subdeacons wear the orarion crossed over the breast and back.

Ordination – the Mystery (Sacrament) through which the bishop lays- on hands to impart power and grace to a man to perform a sacred office.

Origin – Biblical critic, theologian and spiritual writer. Origin recognized a three-fold interpretation of Holy Scripture – 1) a literal sense, 2) a moral sense and 3) an allegorical one. He favored the last. Later he left Orthodox Christianity although his earliest works are still honored for their content. He was condemned by the Second Council of Constantinople in 553 A.D.

Orthodox – one who professes the true doctrine as taught by the Orthodox Church.

Orthodox Sunday – the first Sunday of the Great Fast which commemorates the restoration of the icons after the Iconoclastic heresy. It was first celebrated in 842 A.D.

Orthros – the morning service sometimes called "Matins". It consists of six psalms, a litany, Troparia, Kathisma, Gospel and Canon.

- P -

Pachomius, St – the founder of coenobitic monasticism, a form of monastic life which is lived in community, as opposed to a life as a hermit or anchorite.

Palitsa – another word for epigonation/nabedrennik.

Panagia – Greek term for "All Holy". A Panagia is a round or oval image of the Savior, or the Mother of God, usually enameled, which is worn by a bishop. It hangs from a gold chain.

Paneheda – a service chanted for the repose of the soul of the departed.

Parastas – a solemn service for the repose of the soul of the departed. It is longer and more elaborate than a Paneheda.

Pascha – the correct term for "Easter". It is sometimes used in place of the term "Passover".

Paschal Week – the week following Holy Pascha , the Feast of the Resurrection. It is sometimes called "Bright Week".

Paschalia – the table (calendar) used to determine the date of Pascha and the moveable feasts dependent on it.

Paten – the Western term used for the "discos" or footed-plate on which the Holy Bread (Lamb) is placed during the Divine Liturgy.

Patriarch – the highest ecclesiastical ranking in the Orthodox Church. In the early Church there were five jurisdictional patriarchates – Jerusalem, Antioch, Alexandria, Rome and Constantinople. Other patriarchates were later established in Moscow, Serbia, Romania and Bulgaria.

Patron Saint – a saint chosen to be the protector(ess) of a person, place, or organization.

Pectoral Cross – a Cross worn by priests and bishops as a reminder that they are servants of Christ and preachers of the Gospel.

Penance, Mystery of (Sacrament) – properly named "The Mystery of Penitence", whereby one's sins are forgiven by God. The penitent must acknowledge sins, confess them before a priest ,and be truly sorry, in order to receive forgiveness from Almighty God. The priest acts as a representative of the Church, (St. Matthew 16:19).

Pentecost – Greek for "50th day". The feast on which we commemorate the manifestation of the Holy Spirit upon the apostles, Acts 2:1-4. On Pentecost it is customary to decorate the church with green branches symbolizing new life and power.

Pentecostarion – the liturgical book which contains services and prayers for the time between Pascha and the Sunday after Pentecost, inclusive.

Phanar – a name for the part of Constantinople (present day Istanbul) where the residence and offices of the Patriarch of Constantinople are situated. It is the Greek- quarter of the city.

Phelonion – the large bell-shaped outer vestment of the priest. It is usually richly embroidered or decorated.

Plaschanitsa – See: Winding Sheet

Pleroma – the fullness of teaching and belief in Orthodoxy.

Polychronion – another term for the chant "Many years" or the "Mnogaya Lyeta".

Polyeileon – Greek for "Much mercy and much oil". The second part of Orthros on Sunday evening glorifies the Lord's Resurrection or the particular feast or saint whose day it is. It is the most solemn, joyful and glorious part of the service.

Pre-Sanctified Liturgy of – a liturgy at which there is no consecration. The Holy Bread (Lamb) has been consecrated at the previous Sunday's Divine Liturgy. The Liturgy of the Pre-Sanctified is usually celebrated on Wednesdays and Fridays during the Great Fast but may be done on any weekday. The first part of the liturgy is a Vespers service.

Presbyter – (Greek) another term for priest.

Prestol – (Slavonic: "throne") refers to the Holy Table, or altar which represents the Throne of God.

Priest – one who has been properly ordained to administer the Holy Mysteries and preach/teach the Word of God.

Primate – the title of a ruling archbishop.

Prokimenon – a verse which is chanted just before the reading of the Epistle.

Prosphora – the loaf, or loaves, of bread which are prepared for the Divine Liturgy.

Prostration – a posture of reverence during prayer where one kneels and bows the head to the floor.

Prothesis – (Proskimedia, Proskomidiya) technically refers to the table upon which the Proskimedia or the Service of Preparation (Oblation) is performed.

Protomartyr – the first martyr. Usually the title given to Saint Stephen, (Acts 7:60).

Protopresbyter – another term for "arch-priest", a title given for outstanding service to the Church.

Psalter – the Book of Psalms.

Psalomschix – one who chants the psalms or does the responses.

Pseudographa – writings ascribed to someone other than their true author.

- R -

Raskolniki – (Russian for " Schismatic") an alternate name for the "Old Believers".

Reader – one who is blessed to read portions of the Divine Services and offer responses.

Rector – a priest who is in charge of the parish. He is ex-officio head of all organizations.

Redemption – fallen man was in need of reconciliation with Almighty God. Unable to reconcile through his own power someone needed to pay the price of our redemption, i.e. a direct relationship with God. Jesus Christ paid the price of redemption and blotted out our sins, therefore reuniting mankind with its creator.

Relics – parts of the bodies of saints which the Church venerates. We honor relics because the person is sanctified and virtuous and because the relics may bring us to an imitation of the life of the saint. Relics are placed in the Holy Table, in Antimensia, and special reliquaries. The honor shown to relics is common because the Holy Eucharist was offered on the tombs of martyred saints in the early Church.

Reverend – from the Latin word for "worthy of respect". It is a title reserved for clergy. The higher ranks of clergy are "The Very Reverend" or "The Right Reverend".

Ripidion – (Greek for "fan") – a flat metal disk with representations of the six- winged Seraphim. There are two fans behind the Holy Table. Ripidia are carried in procession at certain times during the Divine Services.

Rite – the rubrics with words and gestures performed at religious services.

Romans, Epistle to the – the longest of St. Paul's letters and the most theologically profound. St. Paul points to the universality of sin and concludes that mankind cannot be justified by any human effort. Justification for sin is imparted by the All-holy goodness of God that is revealed in Jesus Christ, whom our Creator sent forth to be a propitiation for sin.

Romania, Christianity in – the Orthodox Faith was introduced into Romania in the 4th century. Its ecclesiastical jurisdiction was later placed under Constantinople. The Church in Romania became independent in 1885.

Rule – the order and regulations which determine the life of monastics.

Russia, Christianity in – Christianity first came to Russia in the 9th and 10th centuries. The Emperor Vladimir was baptized in 988 A.D. and Christianity became the official religion of the land. During the schism of 1054 the Russian Church remained within Orthodoxy. The story of the Church in Russia becomes unified with the establishment of the Moscow Patriarchate in 1589. The history of the Church parallels the fortunes of the monarchy and secular state from that time forward.

Ryasa – the black robe worn by a priest or bishop. There are two types of ryasa, the inner and outer. The inner ryasa has narrow sleeves while the outer robe, the exo-ryasa, has wide flowing sleeves.

- S -

Sabaoth – as in "The Lord of Sabaoth". The word comes from the Hebrew meaning "hosts".

Sabas, St – a Cappodocian monk who founded a large "lavra" (monastic community) in Palestine.

Sabbath – the day set aside to be kept holy.

Sacramental Fans – (Slavonic: "Ripidion") See: Ripidion

Sacrifice – (Slavonic: "Zhertva") is the Holy Gift to God which Orthodox offer at the Divine Liturgy.

Sacrilege – violation or contempt of a sacred person, place or thing.

Sacristy – (Slavonic: "Riznitsa") a space set apart from the sacristy where vestments, vessels and service books are kept.

Saint – a person who has merited the glorification of the Church because of a holy and pure life, exemplifying dedication to Almighty God.

Sakkos – the outer vestment bishop which corresponds to the phelonion of the priest.

Santa Sophia – the famous Church at Constantinople (Istanbul) dedicated to Holy Wisdom. It is now a Moslem museum.

Satan – the Devil.

Sava, St – patron saint of Serbia who became a monk on Mount Athos and returned to Serbia as archimandrite of the monastery at Studenica.

Scete – the Northern part of the Nitrian desert which was the center of monasticism in the 4th and 5th centuries.

Schism – formal separation from the unity of the True Church.

Scufia – the Slavonic term for the head covering worn by monastics or clergy.

Sebaste, Forty Martyrs of – the 40 Roman soldiers who accepted Christianity and were martyred at Sebaste in Armenia during the very early years of the Faith.

Septuagint – The LXX – the most influential edition of the Greek versions of the Old Testament. The LXX differs from the Hebrew Bible both in order of books and the inclusion of the so-called "Apocrypha". In the early Church the LXX was regarded as the standard form of the Old Testament.

Seraphim of Sarov, St – Russian monk and starets who became known for his great holiness, receiving visitors from all parts of Russia. He had the gift of great spiritual insight.

Serbia, the Church in – Byzantine missionaries first came to Serbia in the 9th century. Christianity became the official religion although the Serbs did not accept Eastern Orthodox Christianity until the 13th century. The Church became autocephalous in 1219 and received a patriarch in 1375. The Patriarchate was lost during the Ottoman period but restored in 1920.

Sergius, St – Russian monastic reformer, having the gift of spiritual insight. He co-founded the monastery of the Holy Trinity near Moscow. He exerted great influence over Russian monasticism by establishing over forty monasteries. (1314-1392 A.D.)

Sexton – layman whose duty it is to keep the church building in proper order.

Sign of the Cross – used to sanctify actions of everyday life. It comes to us from the early Church.

Simeon, the New Theologian, St – Byzantine spiritual writer, gifted with insight, he was influential in the rise of Hesychasm.

Simony – the sale or purchase of spiritual things. See: Acts 8:18-24.

Sin – literally, "missing the mark ". A transgression of the law of God in thought, word or deed.

Sobornost – a word not able to be translated into English. Generally, it means the unity of many people within the fellowship of the Church. It is a spiritual entity and is noted as a characteristic of the Orthodox Church and its nature as opposed to the severe, juridical nature of the Roman Church.

Sluzhebik – a Slavonic term for the Service Book which contains the prayers, rubrics and order for Vespers, Orthros and the Divine Liturgy.

Solea – the raised section of the floor in front of the Iconostasis. The portion directly in front of the Royal Doors is called the amvon or ambo.

"Son of Man" – a title applied to Jesus Christ. Its origin is disputed but often applied as a paraphrase for "I" or "human being".

Soul – spiritual part of man as distinct from his body. Man is composed of body and soul, the soul being immortal which will never die.

Staretz – in the Russian church, a religious leader who was sought out as a spiritual guide. A staretz is known for his personal holiness.

Stauropigion – a monastery directly subject to a hierarch.

Sticharion – corresponding to the Western alb, it is worn by the priest, deacon and subdeacon.

Subdeacon – (Slavonic: " Ipodiakon") a man blessed to assist at liturgy, especially serving the bishop at various times during the Divine Liturgy and other services.

Synaxarion – a brief account of a saint or a priest.

Synaxis – an assembly for liturgical worship. It is also used as a term for the teaching (i.e. Scriptural readings) portion of the Divine Liturgy.

Synaxis – day(s) set aside to honor persons connected with a feast previously celebrated, i.e. "Synaxis of the Mother of God" on the day after the Feast of the Holy Nativity.

Synod – an ecclesiastical council for consulting, advising, or deciding upon matters relevant to the Church.

Synod, Holy - the governing body of each autocephalous Orthodox Church, usually all bishops under the presidency of the patriarch.

Syrian Orthodox – Christians who trace their lineage from those refused to accept the decisions of the Council of Chalcedon re: the person of Jesus Christ. They are sometimes referred to as Jacobites or Monophysites.

- T -

Tabernacle – See: Artophorion

Tertullian – African Church teacher. He eventually joined the Montanists, a heretical sect in the early Church.

Tetrapod – a square table placed before the solea on which an icon of the feast or particular saint is venerated.

Thaddeus, St – sometimes identified as the Apostle Jude. He is mentioned in St. Matthew 10:3 and St. Mark 3:18.

Thaumaturgus – literally "worker of wonders". A title given to saints such as St. Nicholas, or St. Panteleimon.

Thebaid – the upper part of the Nile River. From the third century it was the cradle of Egyptian monasticism.

Theology – the sacred science dealing with Almighty God and things of God.

Theophany – referring to the Baptism of Our Lord or God revealing Himself in the Holy Trinity.

Theotokion – (Slavonic: "Bogorodichen") a hymn chanted in honor of the Mother of God.

Thessalonians, Epistles to the – two New Testament Epistles written by St. Paul are probably the earliest of his letters. Paul assures new converts of the Second Coming and that those who died in the Lord will rise again. The Second Epistle deals with the Parousia, or things regarding the last days.

Thomas, St – apostle, one of "The Twelve". At first Thomas doubts the Lord's Resurrection then proclaims his belief in Christ as Lord, and God. He later did missionary work among the Parthians, and possibly in India.

Three Holy Hierarchs – referring to the Holy Fathers and universal teachers such as St. Basil the Great, St. Gregory the Theologian and St. John Chrysostom. Their memory, and work, is commemorated on January 30th.

Tikhon – first patriarch of the Russian Church since 1700. In 1917 he became Metropolitan of Moscow and resisted the State takeover of the Church. He was placed under arrest after which he professed "loyalty" to State control of the Church. He spent the remainder of his life in a monastery in Moscow. His support of the Soviets and their methods are almost certainly due to coercion and torture.

Tikhon of Zadonsk, St – Russian spiritual writer who spent most of his later years as a great force in the monastic life of central Russia (1724-1783).

Timothy, St – St. Paul's companion on his Second Missionary Journey and one of his closest friends.

Timothy and Titus, Epistles to – these are part of the Pastoral Epistles which dealt with the organization of the early Church, the duties of Church ministers, and certain doctrinal difficulties. They give us valuable insight into the structure of the early Christian Church.

Titus, St – a disciple of St. Paul. He is believed to have organized the Church in Crete and to have been its first bishop.

Tone – the standard melody for verses, Troparions, and Prokimenons as arranged into eight types. They are sung in continuous cycles during the Church Year.

Tradition – handing down the doctrines, truths and customs of the Church as determined by Holy Scripture, the teachings of the Fathers, the formal written Canons of the Church and things which have been transmitted orally pertaining to revelation or faith. Also refers to the standards of belief determined by Creedal statements.

Transfiguration – the appearance of Jesus Christ in the glory of His Divinity. This took place in the presence of Ss. Peter, James and John, (St. Luke 9:28-36).

Trikerion – a triple candlestick representing the three persons of the Holy Trinity. It is used by bishops during Divine Services to bless the congregation.

Trinity, Holy – the three persons in One God. It is a Divine ministry revealed by Our Lord.

Triodion – a liturgical book containing the services of the feasts for the ten weeks before Pascha, the services of the four weeks before the Great Fast, and the services of Holy Week.

Trisagion – The "Thrice Holy Hymn" which is sung at the Divine Liturgy.

Troparion – a short hymn sung after the Small Entrance at the Divine Liturgy. Every Tone and feast has its own Troparion.

Typikon – the liturgical book containing a perpetual calendar and the rubrics for celebrating the Divine Services.

- U -

Unction – the rite anointing with oil. The Mystery of Holy Unction is for healing the ailments of the body and the soul.

Uniate – the Churches which use the Eastern ritual, have some parallels in belief and tradition with Orthodoxy, yet are in union with the Pope of Rome. The term Uniate was first used by the opponents of the so-called "Union of Brest-Litovsk" in 1595 to characterize those who abandoned the Orthodox Faith for political alliances.

- V -

Veil – (Slavonic: "Vozduh") coverings for the chalice and discos which are used during the Divine Liturgy.

Veneration – respect and honor given to the saints and certain items such as icons used in the Church's liturgical services.

Vespers – the evening service of the Church. On the eve of certain Holydays, Vespers includes the Service of the Blessing of the Loaves, (Litiya) and Orthros (Matins).

Vessels, Sacred – the chalice, discos, spoon and lance used at the Divine Liturgy.

Vestments – the garments worn by bishops, priests, deacons and others during the liturgy of the Church.

Vigil – the day before a major feast, observed with special services and fasts.

Vow – a solemn promise made to God, with freedom and deliberation, to maintain a way of life such as monasticism or marriage, or to perform some good work.

- W -

Warden – (Slavonic: "Starosta") – a lay official presiding over a local church council.

Winding Sheet – (Slavonic: "Plaschanitsa") – a large embroidered velvet cloth with the image of the deposition of Christ upon it. It is used on Great and Holy Friday and placed in the "tomb", or Epitaphion.

Worship – reserved for God alone.

- Z -

Zanavess – (Sl.) – the name for the curtain which is hung before the Royal Doors. It is opened and closed at certain times during the Divine Liturgy.

Zhertvennik – (Sl.) – another name for the Prothesis or Table of Oblation.

Zone – the vestment worn about the waist which is made of the same material as the phelonion, sticharion and epitrakhil.

FORMS OF ADDRESS
OF THE ORTHODOX CLERGY

BISHOPS

Ecumenical Patriarch (Patriarch of Constantinople) – Your Holiness,
        His Holiness (n)
Other Eastern Patriarchs – Your Beatitude, His Beatitude (n)
Metropolitans and Archbishops – Your Eminence
        His Eminence (n), The Most Rev (n)
Bishops – Your Grace, His Grace, The Rt. Rev. (n)

PRIESTS

a. Archimandrite – Your Reverence, His Reverence, The Rt. (Very) Rev. (n)
b. Mitred Archpriest – Your Reverence, Father or Mitrate, The Rt. Rev. (n)
c. Archpries Protoierey – Your Reverence, Father, Protoierey,
        The Very Rev. (n)
d. Priest – Your Reverence, Father, The Reverend (n)

DEACONS

Archdeacon or Deacon – Your Reverence, Father, Archdeacon
        or Father Deacon, The Reverend (n)

MONASTICS

a. Monks – Father (n)
b. Monk (n)
c. The Reverend Father, Monk (n)

Nun (n)
Sister (n) – The Rev. Sister, Nun (n)
Mother (n) – The Rev. Mother (n)
The Very Rev. Abbess (n)